Global Management, Local Resistances

This book originates from a research project involving extensive collection and analysis of primary and secondary materials (scholarly literature, statistical data, and interviews with key actors) on global management and local resistances in all major world regions during the last years. It seeks to assess the overall management situation in the world, looking at the world as a social system where some countries act as winners of socioeconomic globalization, others as losers, and some as both. Offering analytical and comparative insights at the global level, this book will be useful for scholars, students, NGOs, and policy makers.

Ulrike Schuerkens is Senior Lecturer at the École des Hautes Études en Sciences Sociales (EHESS), France.

Routledge Advances in Sociology

For a full list of titles in this series, please visit www.routledge.com

Global Management, Local Resistances

Theoretical Discussion and Empirical Case Studies

Edited by Ulrike Schuerkens

Routledge
Taylor & Francis Group

NEW YORK AND LONDON

First published 2015
by Routledge
711 Third Avenue, New York, NY 10017

and by Routledge
2 Park Square, Milton Park, Abingdon, Oxfordshire OX14 4RN

First issued in paperback 2016

Routledge is an imprint of the Taylor & Francis Group,
an informa business

Library of Congress Cataloging-in-Publication Data

Global management, local resistances : theoretical discussion and
    empirical case studies / edited by Ulrike Schuerkens.
        pages cm. — (Routledge advances in sociology)
    Includes bibliographical references and index.
    1. Anti-globalization movement.   2. Globalization.   I. Schuerkens,
Ulrike.
    HN17.5.G566 2014
    303.48′4—dc23
    2014010047

ISBN 13: 978-1-138-70076-5 (pbk)
ISBN 13: 978-0-415-73220-8 (hbk)

Typeset in Sabon
by Apex CoVantage, LLC

Contents

PART II
Resistance Movements to the Globalized Management Discourse

Figures

Tables

Preface

This book originates from a comparative research project entitled "Globalized Management Practices: Implementation Efforts and Resistance Movements" that started in 2011 and was materialized by academic sessions organized by Ulrike Schuerkens, president (2010–2014) of the Research Committee 09 *Social Transformations and Sociology of Development* of the International Sociological Association, during the 2nd Forum of the International Sociological Association in Buenos Aires (Argentina) in August 2012 and the presentation of some of the reunited articles at this conference. Other articles have been added after a separate call for papers.

The book derives from extensive collections and analyses of primary and secondary materials (scholarly literature, statistical data, Internet sources, and all other relevant documentations, including interviews with key actors) on various management practices of Anglo-European origin in globalized regions all over the world during the last 20 years. In other words, this book discusses the kind of management that puts market principles above and beyond other considerations in globalized regions (cf. Somers and Block 2005, Davis 2009). An expert in the field of management practices has written each chapter. The material reviewed covers both English-language sources and studies or other documentation that only exists in national languages. I consider this last point a particular asset of this volume as it enables a wide English-speaking readership to have access to resources that have, up to now, been available only to national scholars and students.

A second important asset of the book is the coverage of all actual major world regions, geographically speaking. The book is thus proposed as a reader on aspects of management practices in globalized regions that will be useful for scholars, students, and policy makers in the field, including international organizations such as the EU and different UN organizations (World Bank, UNDP, ILO). The book benefits from a clear focus and a high level of coherence in terms of the methods used, the data collected, and the literature reviewed, as well as the research questions addressed in each regional case study.

This volume offers analytical and comparative insights at world level, with regard to globalized management practices as well as an assessment of the overall globalization phenomenon in the world. The introductory chapter discusses the notion of management practices and its implications under globalization conditions that prove important in the contemporary context, where management practices have become an international phenomenon and are no longer limited to the nation-state. This first chapter reviews from a critical comparative perspective how different regions have dealt with globalized management practices, so that this publication seeks to assess some aspects of the overall management situation in the world, looking at the world as a social system where some countries act as winners, others as losers, and some as both winners and losers of socioeconomic globalization. I also tentatively offer some predictions for future transformations of global management practices and resistance movements in the world.

In the empirical part of this book, different chapters tackle problems that are still under-researched in the study of management practices and discuss corporate social responsibility, resistance movements in the service sector, in distribution, banks, and transnational enterprises. The case study approach used in this volume is advantageous in that the experience of each country serves as a source of policy recommendations for use in cross-country comparisons. In the overview of the volume in the first chapter, I outline the findings of this book and underline some outcomes that may ask, on the one hand, for further research and, on the other hand, for possible important measures on the future development of management practices in a global world.

It is worth noting that while this book is comprehensive in its coverage of global management practices and in its geographical coverage (all major world regions), it is also theoretically informed. Hence, further theoretical or empirical research questions may be raised by single authors for further study but are extensively discussed only in some chapters mainly for reasons of space. The volume aims thus to become a specialized monograph developing new advances in the field of globalization studies.

MANAGEMENT: THEORETICAL, HISTORICAL, AND COMPARATIVE PERSPECTIVES

The first chapter of the book asks questions that permit us to analyze the globalization of management practices in the social sciences. The general question here is: How do the social sciences respond to globalized management practices that are introduced in many social fields and all over the world in cultures rather different from the Anglo-European model of economic management? Ulrike Schuerkens presents a theoretical introduction on the topic focusing on the particularities of the understanding of management practices in global sociology and some general practices of management in different world regions.

In the second part of the book, the authors ask questions that tackle the macro- and micro-sociological level of the implementation of globalized management practices all over the world: How is Anglo-American management experienced and implemented in different countries and regions? How does it impact the global economic scene? How does it change relations between transnational enterprises and local governments? How does management impact on hegemonic structures? What new visions of global management are being formulated? This part of the book tackles social processes in different geographic settings such as the North, the South, and the East so that the social phenomenon of management practices can be analyzed according to a comparative-historical approach.

In the third part of the book, the authors present local case studies on resistance movements to globalized management practices. Some of the following questions are asked: What responses do institutions, elites, parties, unions, social movements, and other collective actors mount? Which alternative trajectories appear in the social imaginaries? Do gender differences matter? Which futures do these resistance movements let appear?

This edited book combines different perspectives: social transformations and the sociology of development, comparative sociology, and social anthropology. The different chapters are influenced by diverse theoretical and methodological approaches, including, but not limited to, comparative studies of political economics, cultural anthropology, and economic sociology.

Last, but not least, I want to thank Nina Bandelj for her critical reading of the preface of this book and her support during the preparation of the manuscript. Furthermore, I am grateful to the International Sociological Association and its Research Committee 09 *Social Transformations and Sociology of Development* that supported the edition of the different chapters with a small grant.

Ulrike Schuerkens, Paris, October 2013

REFERENCES

Davis, Gerard F. (2009) *Managed by the Market: How Finance Reshaped America.* Oxford: Oxford University Press.
Somers, Margaret R. and Fred Block (2005) "From Poverty to Perversity: Ideas, Markets, and Institutions over 200 Years of Welfare Debate," *American Sociological Review* 70 (2): 260–287.

1 Globalization

A Challenge for Management Practices in Worldwide Enterprises

Ulrike Schuerkens[1]

This edited book aims to analyze the implementation of the Anglo-American management discourse in the East and the South and the multiple forms of resistance against this hegemonic discourse of management. The authors present theoretically inspired case studies of public and private sector workers, trade unionists, activists, shareholders, and other groups. They ask the following question: How can we resist or adapt to the global discourse on management at work or outside the workplace? This book demonstrates the variety of movements against or in favor of the hegemonic discourse in the global age of management and its potential influence on the future of the world. The various chapters advance our knowledge of these different forms of new social movements and the particular characteristics of the steady growing influence of Western management practices in the South and the East. These forms of resistance that the volume presents challenge the discourse of global economic management that has shaped the current global age and will shape the future of the globalized world.

The book includes 10 case studies from different continents and all major world regions. It allows a critical assessment of the phenomenon in a globalized world that is experiencing protests in the economy in the aftermath of the global financial crisis. This publication involves scholars coming from different disciplines: economists, socioeconomists, sociologists, and anthropologists from different countries, both European and non-European (Asia, Latin America, Africa, etc.).

GENERAL PROBLEMATIC OF THE TOPIC

What is the future of "management"? What are the forces that are opposed to its search for effectiveness that may push management into the direction of a democratization of social organizations? The notion of management has increasingly been included in various societal fields. Management has evolved into a more and more important factor in society, not only in business and government but also in trade unions, universities, charities, leisure organizations, and a growing number of daily routines of human beings. The global discourse on management focuses on the principles of the market that have been introduced in all spheres of social life through university programs, training seminars, organizational strategies, government policies, and personal counseling literature.[2] This knowledge is produced, distributed, and consumed by social actors in the South, North, and East. These forms of disciplinary knowledge have contributed to the creation of a world controlled by managers and management technologies. The technologies that have been used vary as much as the places of their utilization. However, a wide range of resistance movements has been created in recent years spanning from individual misconduct in work behaviors to collective strategies channeled by social movements.

One of the most important societal influences in the last quarter of the 20th century was this growing importance of the management discourse.[3] There was a spread of the idea of management from large firms to the professions, NGOs, the public sector, and the daily lives of social actors. This management discourse consists of a given language and practices that global players of Anglo-American origins produce in the socioeconomic world (Fourcade and Khurana 2013). This discourse is so widespread today that it seems difficult to escape its grip.

This edited book tackles on the one hand, an analysis of its increasing propagation in non-Western societies and, on the other, an analysis of multiple forms of resistance against this discourse of management. After the global financial crisis of 2008, it is important to understand these resistance movements in order to accompany and guide them so that they may benefit society as a whole. Even if these resistance movements resemble in some aspects the Marxian class struggle, they are rather movements that target problematic issues of the current neoliberal economics that we can no longer ignore in a world characterized by crises and, in particular, if we want to maintain and preserve certain basic structures of the current post-neoliberal economies and their understanding of human well-being.

One aspect of this research is: How do groups cope with the global discourse of management in a globalized world? In fact, there are several major resistance movements that relate to business management: unions, movements that contest business policies, and civic movements that seek to disrupt the hegemonic discourse of management.

For the last twenty years, management practices were propagated throughout the globalized world but only few studies on its local acceptance exist even if there are studies on the problematics of market fundamentalism (Parker 2002, Albers et al. 2006).[4] Because of the challenges related to globalization and the global financial crisis, it is important to understand this discourse of management and its functioning in global companies in order to better conceive future developments of the socioeconomic world in the South and the East. Knowing that a large-scale confrontation of capital and labor seems currently rather improbable, this research will help to clarify an issue that should become increasingly important in the coming years.

It seems today as if societies should be exposed again and again to financial crises that appear to be structural rather than conjectural and that challenge our understanding of economies.

A THEORETICAL OVERVIEW OF THE GLOBALIZATION OF MANAGEMENT PRACTICES

The paradigm the authors are advocating focuses on changes taking place in the course of contacts between the local autochthonous systems, on the one hand, and the colonial and postcolonial or socialist and post-socialist societies, on the other hand. They highlight the specific situation of social actors in a process of structural transformations. This volume is thus an analysis of an objectified reality. The authors historically reconstruct concrete cases in the sense of a puzzle solving. This approach takes into account the power factor and in this sense the country with a much more differentiated knowledge structure than indigenous local societies may have. An analysis that seeks the characteristic elements of "tradition" and "modernity" or a *neutral* socio-cultural contact is no longer possible. This volume emphasizes thus the importance of a possible post-neoliberal globalization (cf. Crouch 2011) for the future of localized societies. Accepting this challenge, social anthropology and sociology will continue to analyze new areas of social reality that will have a real impact on the economies of societies in the South and the East.

Research on Social Change between Local Social Life-Worlds and Globalization

In the last years, social change has been studied in major world regions influenced by economic globalization and local socio-cultural life-worlds. During the last decades, research in this field has focused on micro-analyzes of socio-economic and cultural experiences through the continuing and intensifying localization of social processes of neoliberal globalization. In the emerging global world, two contemporary processes of social mixture are increasingly linked. On the one hand, there are universal processes of modernization and globalization often of Western origin, which have spread worldwide. On the other hand, there are tendencies to maintain traditional social systems trying to preserve the authenticity of some local cultures. The interaction of these various processes leads to different forms of implementation and adaptation to global modernity and Western cultures, different mixtures and hybrid modes between global modernity and local traditions, various forms of reactions and resistance to the imposition of a Westernized model, or various forms of social change triggered by the impact of Western globalization.

Globalization is here conceived as a process that unfolds through actions influenced by identifiable actors as opposed to a vision that emphasizes systemic forces and the market. Modern economies are currently globalized to different extents. Companies are forced to follow this trend if they want to remain competitive. It is pertinent to ask how much time cultures will need to adapt to or resist the pressure of the global economy. What is the future of local cultural particularities in economic globalization? How are globalized economies linked to local cultures? Are cultural particularities forced to disappear in an economy influenced by post-neoliberal thinking?

In fact, companies have to develop new skills if they want to relocate in places where different cultures meet. In a cultural encounter linked to the establishment of transnational enterprises at new places, the overseas staff of the company has to implement foreign socio-cultural elements according to the categories of local cultures. Therefore, stakeholders need to give sense to localized encounters. Furthermore, transnational managers have to study foreign cultures and their own cultural belonging in order to be capable to adapt the economic project of transnational companies to the local cultural micro-cosmos.

The aim of this volume is to better understand and assess some specific management practices in various cultures in the North, the South, and in the East—in parts of the world in Western and Eastern Europe, Asia, Africa, and Latin America—and their capabilities and conditions of socioeconomic change. This analysis of the confrontation of different socioeconomic cultures will permit us to understand that managers can and should become aware of the uniqueness of each culture or at least refine their own socio-economic and cultural knowledge. This will then allow a better approach of intercultural management tools and will avoid local intercultural clashes.

The objective of this volume is to explore the socioeconomic practices of some cultures. One can also ask questions on the "natural" cultural practices of socioeconomic actors. Thus, this volume will show how to analyze current socioeconomic issues such as globalized management practices in different cultures, using the concepts and principles of economic sociology and anthropology.

Indeed, in the South and the East, in order to obtain smooth operations of large business groups in local settings, management practices should be consistent with local forms of social interactions. Most of the ongoing economic processes in faraway cultures are still very hesitant. Very often, management methods that are mainly of Anglo-American origin are imported into local settings. An analysis of the mixture of local and global socioeconomic practices is rarely realized in transnational companies and business schools. The challenge of this volume is thus to focus on aspects of transnational businesses that can and should be adapted to Southern and Eastern cultural settings or, in other words, that can be translated from one cultural understanding to another.

This research asks questions on some of the characteristics of economic globalization in different parts of the world such as Western and Eastern Europe, Asia, Latin America, and Africa. We will consider, among other things, the peculiarities of local and national business cultures, the main rules governing the lives of some Southern or Eastern economic communities while comparing their socioeconomic practices to the practices known in the West, including Western Europe and the U.S. This research will be devoted to case studies from various economic regions interesting to the global business world.

Economic Globalization, Culture, and the Transformation of Management Practices

The underlying principle of the presented case studies is that Southern and Eastern enterprises can hardly withstand economic pressures of global players. Managers in these plants are forced to adapt to local socioeconomic standards if they want to be successful. The questions that should be asked are how cultures can learn and how socio-cultural rules can be integrated in business operations linked to the relocalization of plants.

Today, it is clear that economic entities need new skills if they create new businesses. They need to improve management techniques in the South and the East. In recent decades, it has become more and more questionable to transplant Euro-American management practices into non-Western cultures, as it was common practice until the 1960s and 1970s. Instead, local and transnational managers begin to question their own values and try in some plants to adapt particular management aspects to foreign local cultures insofar as synergies appear to be necessary for economic success and higher performance levels.

As our knowledge in this field of research is still quite limited, this volume will include economic conditions in factories and services. The authors discuss specific situations of gender rules and the particularities of regional or global socioeconomic discourses when transnational corporations such as European, American, or Chinese ones, to name only a few, interact with local socioeconomic cultures. This volume discusses management practices, social communication, leadership, and decision-making in different socioeconomic contexts. The theoretical approaches used are those of economic sociology and economic anthropology. They are influenced by economic and management studies to help understand the increasingly complex image of the global economy that more and more influences working practices of people around the world.

Socioeconomic Practices between Localization and Globalization

One aspect of this research concerns socioeconomic practices. Since the end of the global political and economic competition, characteristic of the era of the Cold War, the process of international competition has played a less pronounced role because democratic institutions in developing countries have often been poorly developed and elites have tended to confront along ethnic lines what has often triggered violent conflicts. However, with the increase of global modernity during the last decades, the collapse of most communist states, and the dispersion of the neoliberal creed, the discussion on the notion of competition in the field of social change started again. The question was whether economic ideology put forward by global modernity could have an impact on social and cultural systems in very different non-Western societies. Since there seems to be no real alternative to the Western ideal of economic competition based on the rule of the "strongest," economists and sociologists have asked the question whether the concept of competition could be integrated into social, legal, and economic systems in Eastern Europe, Asia, Latin America, and Africa. The response has largely depended on the socioeconomic structures of societies in different parts of the world. It now seems clear that some cultures are better situated than others to become active participants in global modernity. Perhaps such a position would be better conceptualized by the notion of cultural experiences than as a local socioeconomic and political constellation (cf. Schuerkens 2008). So if this is the case, a reflection on the cultural construction of socioeconomic experiences in today's various *glocal* (global-local) modernities seems to be a prerequisite for an analysis of globalized management practices in non-Western civilizations.

Global players put pressure on the responsiveness and effectiveness of local and regional cultures. The global market defined by competitive capitalism, the importance of private property, and the virtue of individualism has become the dominant world system, introduced by colonial and post-colonial or post-socialist processes in non-Western societies during the last centuries and more recently in the last three decades of neoliberal globalization. Civilizations have been defined by their adaptive character to global socioeconomic processes. Culture as a place for investment and capital utilization has been considered being a selection criterion. According to global players, a competition of social systems that allow greater profits has been established around cultural values worldwide. Some national companies have been able to learn better reactivity measures than other ones in order to resist changes required by the neoliberal capitalist logic of the market. However, a parenthesis should here be included: If one looks at the interventions of political elites from fall 2008 until today, we can find that the economic system has been transformed according to many regulatory factors that states and global financial institutions have implemented. In the long run, this will then require a change of the modern capitalist system oriented towards market regulation and give a much more important role to the state.

The approach outlined here includes economic and cultural preferences of institutions in one logical system and analyzes why some transnational enterprises are more able than others to confront global market conditions. Some years ago, I edited a book entitled *Transformations of Local Socio-economic*

Practices and Globalization (Routledge 2008) where I showed, with a dozen case studies from different regions of the world, how the globalization of the last 25 years has changed the local socioeconomic practices of non-Western societies. In the introduction and conclusion, I described the theoretical underpinnings of these changes. I can now go further and can analyze tendencies of globalized management practices of transnational companies in local socioeconomic settings in Eastern European, Asian, Latin American, and African globalized economies.

The Theory of Social Transformations

I wish to put an emphasis here on a last point that seems necessary to understand the approach of this book: the particularity of the transformation of a social system. The whole social system, not just a particular subsystem, is thus characterized by the simultaneous occurrence of several interdependent transformation processes. These are open processes that can lead, if successful, to the establishment of new structures. Today, as well as some decades ago, these new structures are intended to avoid situations that are no longer functional and no longer able to ensure the stability of the newly created social systems. According to this understanding, transformations are defined as a system change to another societal unity that includes a transformation of the basic structures of a societal system over time (cf. Schuerkens 2001). All subsystems are thus subject to change. A theory of transformations can not only rely (cf. Rist 1996: 75) on the transformations of the societies of the South but should also include societies of the North and the East and their experiences, such as the major structural change, for example, after 1989 of the countries of former Socialist Eastern Europe. Such an approach must be open-ended and cannot fix *a priori* a goal to societal changes. This model has to include the analysis of positive changes but also negative outcomes (e.g., violence) as Sztompka (1991) underlines in his approach of social change and cultural trauma.

A theory of transformations that focuses on the history of a society does not try to reconstruct the overall development of a society in a narration, but it describes the changes of the fundamental structures of societies focusing on their mechanism of change (cf. Schuerkens 2001). Transformation theory focuses on the one hand on individual and collective actors that transform their societies by intentional actions and on the other hand on system changes that include intentions, goals, and efforts of societal actors (Khondker and Schuerkens 2014).

The particular characteristics of a theory of transformation become thus clear: It is necessary, first, to conduct research in the globalized countries of the South, the East, and the North, which focuses on "negative" effects what Sztompka called a "cultural trauma," such as crises, increasing social conflicts, the confrontation of cultures of different origins, etc. Second, research in different world regions on transformation processes, mostly carried out without great theoretical ambitions, should then lead to a theoretical synthesis, including recent globalization processes and its particular characteristics of change. It thus becomes obvious that it is no longer possible to identify only structural transformations, but we have to analyze structural adaptations to societal challenges influenced by globalization. This volume intends to develop these aspects by focusing on socioeconomic systems and the characteristics of globalized management processes implemented by transnational enterprises. The results of these transformation processes will be demonstrated by empirical case studies that further our thinking of globalized processes of change that influence worldwide socioeconomic structures. It then becomes obvious that we can no longer speak of the developing and the developed world, the North and the South, or the East and the West as separated entities.

Managing in Different Globalized Cultures and Regions

The need to study the subject of managing in and between different cultures is not just important for those who want to work for multinational companies forming strategic alliances with companies from other countries but for everyone who is involved in managing people in different societies. In the following pages, I will provide the reader with an understanding of various national approaches to management in order to develop a better distinction between approaches of management in multiple cultural settings. This volume defines globalized management practice as the management of local employees globally and international employees locally, meaning that approaches, e.g., of transnational companies in the countries of the South influence local cultures and that even international staff is influenced by local approaches at particular places. I ask the question if national cultural differences will continue to exist and to what extent influences on employment policies are determined by globalized businesses and/or localized cultures. In this sense, my interest is in comparative research results on this topic. When we understand how management is practiced in particular societies, we are able to establish differences and similarities between countries and societies. My goal is thus to gather our knowledge on different national contexts, make comparisons between them, and learn to understand the particularities of managing in different national contexts.

In the last decades, it became obvious that expatriates had difficulties understanding the complexities of cultural differences so that business success across cultures was not guaranteed. The high growth rates of Southeast Asian economies attracted Western companies that wanted to invest in the region. But this move required knowledge on the work ethics of Asian people and an understanding of the socioeconomic context in which employees were recruited and developed. One of the main challenges for employers investing in China is the understanding of Chinese culture and its impact on work behavior. The highly skilled workforce of the Indian subcontinent has also attracted foreign firms. The move of call centers of multinational companies from the U.S. and Europe to India demonstrates this beneficial role of the international labor market that necessitates cross-cultural adaptation and learning processes from managers and employees. The end of the Cold War and the collapse of the former communist states have led to a sort of *Westernization* of Eastern Europe. Enterprises in these countries have implemented economic reforms and have used Western ideas of management. In the last 30 years, market-related skills and management knowledge have been transferred from the U.S., Canada, and Western Europe to other parts of the world. International investors need to understand local socioeconomic processes and localized employment practices. One of the first steps after the fall of the Iron Curtain and the end of socialism was thus to create management schools in the region with the help of the West (cf. chapter 2 written by N. Bandelj in this volume).

In the current global age, multinational companies need more knowledge on international staff whether they are managers, professionals, or technicians. International competition decides on successes and failures of plants and one of the most important criteria is the quality of the workforce. Innovative employees can provide a comparative advantage in markets where similar material means of production are available. To acquire a highly qualified workforce, multinational companies need efficient management knowledge across cultures. In the last decades, regional and global economic integration has led to the development of common approaches to business practices sustained by international agencies, such as the World Bank and the World Trade Organization.

Economic and political dependence of many countries of the global South on the West has triggered a transfer of Anglo-Saxon and European management theories to many countries of the world. When one looks at students of an MBA in an American or British university, one finds out that there is an increasing internationalization of Western management education, as management students have to work in countries worldwide and no longer only in their own country of origin. Students from the global South are exposed to Western management theory and practice in courses at colleges and universities worldwide. International conferences and exchange programs contribute to narrow the gaps in management knowledge between countries. In fact, management education taught in MBA programs seems to be rather similar worldwide. Textbooks rarely make reference to non-Western management theory and practice. In this sense, it has become simple to disseminate this already established knowledge so that enterprises find it easier to invest in different countries despite a large variety of cultural systems and a meager knowledge of them.

Developing countries in Africa, South America, and Asia have adopted economic and political reforms aiming at a liberalization of their economies. The socioeconomic reforms realized have attracted high multinational investments. This growth of international investments has led to an increasing need for more knowledge on managing in different cultures. Managers should thus be aware of national economic trends and organizational characteristics as societies differ in their management systems according to their organizational characteristics and their particular economic status. Managers should be able to share some managerial practices in countries of similar economic development (for instance in the Arab states or in Latin America). Organizations may differ from one society to another but there are some common patterns. For example, organizations are centralized and bureaucratic in many African, Middle Eastern, and Southeast Asian countries where authority is delegated to relatives and trusted close friends. In fact, globalization and its economic consequences mean not only that enterprises create subsidiaries in the South and in the East but also that the culture of consumerism and competition is spreading not only through Eastern societies but also through the globalized South where it touches parts of the upper classes and increasingly larger middle classes.

The reunited case studies in this volume allow us to obtain insights into how international companies cope with global activities while trying to adapt to local socioeconomic systems. These management studies allow us to share learning on the particular local work dimensions and to generate knowledge from the described case studies. They contribute to a better understanding of the local working environment and the development of improved approaches to managing in various cultural contexts.

MANAGEMENT PRACTICES IN SELECTED COUNTRIES

The Popular Republic of China

China's economy has seen important changes in the last decades with an increasing number of joint ventures and foreign-owned firms linked to the encouragement of foreign direct investments by the Chinese government. The goal was to attract the transfer of advanced technologies and develop a skilled Chinese workforce. Multinational corporations (MNCs) have had important implications for the Chinese labor market. They have become attractive for young, well-educated, skilled, and hard-working Chinese graduates. As these MNCs pay high salaries and provide career opportunities to their employees, the selection process has been very competitive, such that young graduates doing jobs below their level of qualification in foreign-owned hotels and restaurants can also be found doing cleaning and catering work.

Chinese management was influenced by the Soviet system until the beginning of the open door policy in 1978. With the introduction of free market principles, the Chinese had to look to the West for examples of best practices in management. Findings from a comparative study of British and Chinese companies revealed some similarities and several differences in management between the two countries (Easterby-Smith et al. 1995). As Branine

(2011: 223) wrote: "Most of the similarities were found in planning and career development procedures, while there were differences in terms of criteria for promotion, job rotation, recruitment and selection, and the role of trade unions." Another study found in 1995 that, despite the economic reforms in China, there was little evidence of changes in management policies (Brown and Branine 1995). The reason was that the Chinese government tried to introduce economic reforms in a way that would not change the ideological orientation of the country. State control over organizations was retained despite the growth of the private sector.

Between the 1950s and the beginning of the 1980s, the enterprise was a unit within the centralized planning system. As Southworth (1999: 325) wrote: There was "no need for marketing, financial controls or human resource management—three of the most striking skill shortages in China today." In fact, the party selected employees for important positions in the departments of the plants and supervised economic policies that had to be followed by those in a position of authority (Warner 1995). The consequence was that Chinese managers avoided any critical remarks on their leaders' decisions. Even after the economic liberalization, the party has remained powerful in managerial decision processes. Though managers are in charge of the day-to-day activities, the party committee is still responsible for making policies at the level of the enterprise. Moreover, enterprise managers are most often members of the party (Branine 2011: 225).

According to Branine (2011), some cultural aspects that influence the practice of management in China are the Chinese respect for age, family loyalty, mutual assistance, and obedience to law. Chinese managers tend to accept what their leaders tell them and treat their employees like members of one family. Moreover, they avoid conflicts and loss of face. China has been managed for centuries by a central authority and local bureaucracy so that Chinese norms and values have their roots in the country's history and the influence of Confucianism. This political ideology influences work behavior even if MNCs and MBA graduates from universities abroad have introduced management policies and practices from the UK or the U.S. In Chinese foreign trade corporations, individual commitment has been introduced despite the influence of a collectivist culture (Brown and Branine 1995, Tong and Mitra 2009). It seems, however, that managerial practices and policies had to be adopted more and more with the introduction of economic reforms and growing business needs from the 1970s onwards. Today, managers of MNCs are "hailed by the media as good models to be followed by domestic firms in China" (Cooke 2004: 31). The spread of MNCs in China has been accompanied by the implementation of quality management and human resource management (HRM) practices (Warner 2004). As foreign trade and foreign investment are important for parts of the Chinese economy, management theories from Western universities had to be learned and implemented after the fall of the Iron Curtain in Europe, according to Fukuda (1989: 49).

India

India's economy is one of the strongest worldwide because of a large reserve of skilled manpower. The major growth sector is the service sector and in particular IT software services. After 40 years of centralized economic planning and the fall of the Iron Curtain, the Indian government introduced liberal economic policies. This strategy has attracted increasing foreign direct investment (FDI). MNCs brought with them a transfer of technology, knowledge, and skills from the industrialized North. As most foreign direct investment was destined to export production, this sector grew from 6 percent in the 1980s to 20 percent in the mid-2000s (Branine 2011: 476). Economic reforms have meant an increase of urban employment especially in IT services and MNCs. India, with the second largest population in the world after China, has seen a growing self-employed population leaving agriculture to work in the informal sector. A growing number of active job seekers can be found among young and qualified people who are no longer ready to work in the large agricultural sector of the country. Women do jobs from home (creating textile products and wearing apparel) or work in the informal sector. Women are underrepresented in many sectors of the economy since Indian males are reluctant to recruit them (cf. Budhwar and Sparrow 2002). This behavior is "influenced by the traditional roles of women and men in Indian society, where men are the breadwinners and women are housewives" (Branine 2011: 482).

In 2000, more than 15,000 MNCs were in India (cf. Budhwar 2001). The English-speaking skilled workforce provides efficient work for rather low wages. Basu (2007: 674) wrote: "World-class businesses that have emerged in knowledge-based industries are transforming India into a key global player." Nevertheless, these jobs are for a tiny minority of the Indian workforce.

Much of the British system of management was transmitted to India and in particular into the administration of the civil service. Therefore, Indian managers are influenced by Indian and Western values (Budhwar 2001: 83). As a result of their education and training in Western countries or in Indian management schools, influenced by Western education, Indian managers have adopted Western management practices. However, this management behavior is characterized by Indian social relationships, family values, and religious beliefs. According to Budhwar et al. (2008: 84), "these two sets of values co-exist and are drawn on as frames of reference depending on the nature of problems that people face." Kakar et al. (2002: 241) could find four types of management systems in India: 1) Family owned, more or less large companies that are linked to foreign companies, which practice a management style influenced by Western and Indian practices; 2) Smaller indigenous family owned plants that follow Indian practices and whose managers are authoritarian and paternalistic; 3) Sub-offices of MNCs that are managed according to the management practice of the head office; and

4) Small plants owned by young dynamic professionals whose management style is still to be defined but is dependent on the experience of the owners. Moreover, management styles differ between private and public sectors. According to Suar et al. (2006: 96), private sector companies operating in a competitive market economy "emphasize high task, close relationships, participation, and caring for employees." Instead, the public sector is "isolated from market pressures, (is characterized by, U.S.) low task, impersonal work environment, and bureaucratic set-up with too many rules and regulations for employees without actual practice" (2006: 96).

Sinha (1995) describes Indian management style as "bureaucratic and authoritarian," but also "nurturant-task." Branine concludes that "Indian managers are said to have preference for *authoritative* rather than *authoritarian* management because they are strict and demanding but caring and supportive just like the paternalistic head of an Indian family" (2011: 485, emphasis in original). And he continues: "The family-owned business houses, which have dominated the Indian economy since the time of British rule of India, inherited a management system that was based on bureaucratic procedures, hierarchy, status consciousness, and mechanisms of control." (485) The centralization of power makes collaborative team efforts and criticism rather seldom. Informal meetings may however help to find solutions depending on the management situation and the manager.

The number of Indian managers that have been educated at Western universities or in Indian institutions of higher education influenced by Western systems is increasing. If they work in family companies, they use this knowledge that is different from the traditional values of the Indian families. Moreover, the spread of MNCs has contributed to the development of a different management system where these graduates are able to realize their management practices learned in higher education. Nevertheless, most of American companies have transferred their management practices to India with minor changes (cf. Budhwar and Björkman 2003, Saini and Budhwar 2004). Kakar et al. argue (2002: 241): "Indian management culture . . . among all of India's various cultures, is arguably the most exposed to forces of modernization and globalization."

African Countries

African labor markets can be described by high unemployment rates, declining public sector employment, an increasing informal sector, a low participation of women in formal employment, the emigration of skilled labor, and shortages of educated workers. The increasing youth unemployment led to loan programs in order to permit self-employment and education in special trades that are in demand. Yet, in many African countries, the informal sector has become the only way to earn a living. Today, the unemployed, the young, women, and increasingly college and university graduates use the informal sector as a source of income so that the working life for many Africans is insecure.

Because of the brain drain to Europe and the U.S., there is a shortage of skilled workers in many organizations. Managers may lack management education but also the opportunity to learn how to do. The practice of management in sub-Saharan Africa seems to be an administrative process that is culturally influenced. This process has been described as centralized and bureaucratic (cf. Kamoche et al. 2004, Khan and Ackers 2004, Okpara and Wynn 2008). The centralization of management is linked to the power distance maintained by African managers. A significant part of bureaucracy reflects the management style of the former English and French colonial administrations. The politicization of management can be explained by the close link to governments and their use of control mechanism. Family inspired management, what is called "*ubuntu* management," reflects the important cultural influence of African traditions on management practices.

In sub-Saharan Africa, managers are respectfully obeyed without any questions on their decisions. Employees are dependent on their managers so that they lack the authority to do anything without their approval (Aryee 2004). Employees are passive as they are powerless and helpless without the decision of their superiors who are not contradicted. Detailed instructions given by managers inform employees what to do even when they have done the job many times before. This attitude can be explained by social values as the belief in seniority, social class, and social divisions in status. Authority is only delegated to relatives and trusted friends (cf. Kiggundu 1989). Managers are protected by a system of friends and relatives around them to cover their actions even if they reveal incompetence.

According to Branine, public sector management in Africa is characterized by often unproductive and ineffective procedures so that civil servants "seem to take pride in filling in forms, pilling up files on their desks and making clients wait outside their offices" (Branine 2011: 417). And he continues: "Often, matters that require urgent attention are delayed for weeks on a pretext of non-availability of resources and/or insufficient information to accomplish a given task" (2011: 417). In public organizations, managers are usually appointed by the state because of their political loyalty. They may find it difficult to maintain principles of objectivity regarding discipline and promotion because of political pressures.

It seems that there is a consensus that African management is more people-centered and "less rational" than Western models. This fact is best expressed by the African concept of *ubuntu* (Kamoche et al. 2004). Kamoche wrote (xvii): "*Ubuntu* is said to signify an indigenous African philosophy of management which captures the complex social relations between people and the idea of caring for others as though they were members of one's own family." This orientation of management may thus be considered a communal approach. It is based on the assumption that everyone is linked to other people in all his/her activities. *Ubuntu* emphasizes the importance of the family and the ethnic group, respect for age and seniority. A younger person will thus not oppose an elder colleague, as the latter is considered as wiser and more experienced. Managers also take care of the material and personal needs of their employees. The African community is characterized according to Branine (2011) by teamwork and collaboration asking for consensus in decision-making so that managers may be authoritarian but they will look after their employees as members of their families. To conclude, one can argue that the implementation of Western management discourse in sub-Saharan Africa is confronted in this continent with strong cultural traditions.

Arab Countries

The labor markets of Arab countries are characterized by government controls in public and private sectors. Arab labor markets are categorized by a high level of youth unemployment, a declining level of public sector employment, an abundance of unskilled and uneducated workers, an increasing employment of women, and the emigration of skilled and professional labor in the form of brain drain. In the Gulf States most of the employees in private sector organizations are foreigners. Nationals do not like to do manual labor but prefer to work for the government doing managerial and professional jobs. Foreign workers, often from Asian countries, are employed for a given period and then sent home.

Unemployment is a major challenge in Arab countries. The population is very young but the economies of these countries are unable to create jobs for these unskilled or even skilled job seekers. Employment policies aimed at creating employment for this workforce have so far been unsuccessful.

Until the mid-1990s, most of the enterprises in the Arab world were owned and controlled by the state. Most often these enterprises were large but were unable to function efficiently because of an inadequate management, a limited qualified workforce, and over-employment (Branine 2011: 447). Economic reforms in the 1990s intended to privatize state-owned enterprises and encourage private sector investments. The private sector should create new jobs but the closing down and the privatization of companies led to job losses. The public sector continues to be the main employer in Arab countries. Jobs in the private sector are considered not desirable as wages are poor and the employees are badly treated: In private sector companies, the owner *hires and fires* at will and may not respect the existing regulations.

Almost all major MNCs can be found in the Gulf States. Often, they have brought in their own managers and experts as expatriates but they have also employed skilled and hard-working foreign laborers in the absence of enough employees among the host country nationals. With the exception of Tunisia and Egypt, most of the Arab States outside the Gulf region couldn't attract FDI in industry and manufacture.

There has been a rise in female employment in Arab countries. Many well-educated women work in service sectors such as education, health, and public administration. There has also been a rise in the number of women entrepreneurs.

Managerial behavior in the Arab states is influenced by cultural and political factors. Islam, state control, and Western influence are important in shaping current management practices (cf. Weir 2001, Ali 2004, Kuran 2004). These studies reveal that inherited management policies are derived from traditional values and the former colonial administration. From 1960 to 1980, the adopted management practices were copied either from the Soviet Union or from the capitalist UK and U.S. Both approaches have also been influenced by Arab traditions and by Islamic principles of management and work behavior (cf. Branine and Pollard 2010).

The management style of the region can be characterized as authoritarian, centralized, paternalistic, and bureaucratic. Authoritarianism has created a tradition of management where people try to be obedient and where managers tell their subordinates what to do and how to do it. As Branine wrote (2011: 450): "Arab managers do not like to be criticized by their superiors and they tend to be aggressive and offensive to their subordinates, and very defensive when challenged by their colleagues." Moreover, managers in the Gulf States are accustomed to obedient foreign workers who risk punishment or deportation. If subordinates are from the same family, they are consulted and discussions are organized. Managers tend to be paternalistic to nationals or members of their family. They value loyalty and run their organizations as family units in the private sector. Yet decisions are taken at a formal and centralized level. Authority is seldom delegated because of low trust between the managers and their subordinates.

The government appoints senior managers of state-owned companies or public sector institutions on the basis of their loyalty or their links to the ruling families. These managers are expected to do what the government wishes or they will lose their power and status. This means that senior managers try to have good relationships with the government. Managers in the region are known for using bureaucratic procedures to impose their authority. They use top-down bureaucratic mechanism and neglect interpersonal communication.

Examples of adopted socialist management systems can be found in Egypt, Algeria, Syria, and Libya. State-owned enterprises had to accept socialist planning mechanisms, but they were abandoned after the fall of the Iron Curtain. Many of the Arab Gulf States have adopted capitalist modes of production and employment. Western management practices have been adopted in the 1990s with free market economic reforms. MNCs have introduced their own management practices so that national managers have been exposed to Western policies. Expatriates have created awareness of the necessity to use Western management theories (cf. Suliman 2006, Yahiaoui and Zoubir 2006). Management theories have been taught in institutions of higher education but the importance of Islam and traditional values do not facilitate the task of adaptation of neoliberal principles to local situations.

Some of these traditional values that Branine evokes are the preference of direct, face-to-face communication, status consciousness, high respect for seniority, and getting things done through connections and family relations. The status-conscious culture in Arab countries means that organizations are hierarchical and decisions are centralized. Business deals are conducted in face-to-face meetings at the workplace or outside in an informal environment, such as the café. In a working situation, managers try to avoid direct conflict and confrontations with their employees and with other managers in order to avoid a loss of face. Direct criticism is furthermore prevented as it is seen as an insult. This has consequences on managing human resources and collective bargaining of employees with their employers.

Islamic law regulates in most countries all kinds of relationships between people. Many verses of the *Koran* are about justice in trade and fairness in work relations. Islam encourages people to learn new skills and do good work in order to benefit the community. Yousef (2001: 153) even wrote: "Life without work has no meaning and engagement in economic activities is an obligation." Employment relations thus go beyond the written contract between an employee and an employer.

Eastern Europe and the Former Soviet Union

After the fall of the Iron Curtain, free market reforms were introduced in the liberalized economies of the region. State-owned enterprises were closed and employment declined in manufacturing while it increased in the service sector (cf. Stockhammer and Onaran 2009). All Central and Eastern European (CEE) countries have an agricultural sector that creates jobs for people in rural regions. Employment was created in banking, transport, and hospitality. Labor market trends after 1989 included a shift from state-owned enterprises to privately owned enterprises. Light industry and the service sector are increasing in importance. Mass unemployment and an abundance of high-skilled workers have characterized the region.

The Central and Eastern European countries inherited centralized, bureaucratic, and authoritarian management policies from the planned economies of the Soviet era. Management "was marked by meticulous rule-following, a lack of initiative, and contentment with inferior product quality" (Ardichvili and Gasparishvili 2001: 229). The transition to a market economy meant the introduction of radical structural changes including privatization of public sector companies and reforms of the banking system. The implementation of these strategies has created problematic shifts, as limited management experience was available.

The current situation is based on an intertwining of inherited socialist economic practices and adopted post-socialist capitalistic approaches. The accession to the EU, the influence of foreign direct investment, and the influence of financial and economic crises are shaping the current management systems of the region. As the chapters by Dufy and Heemeryck in this volume show, management in the region is authoritarian but it takes initiatives and experiments with new possibilities. Mrozowicki and van Hootegem

(2008: 199) wrote that managers have "individualized paternalist relations with the best skilled, full-time, core employees, while simultaneously using low wages, overtime and violations of work contracts to minimize employment costs in the segment of lower-skilled, often female, young and contractual workers." Ardichvili and Gasparishvili (2001: 238) wrote that the fall of communism "created conditions for the emergence of more independent, ruthless and isolated business leaders in Russia."

A study on Bulgaria and the Slovak Republic found that a number of problems of management exist in both countries: "Poor communication about corporate policies and strategic directions, one-way (top-down) communication flow, poor feedbacks from superiors, unclear and unfair performance appraisal and feedback, poor coaching and supporting for problem-solving, unclear career paths, poor information disclosure and sharing, unfair rewards and treatment, poor initiative and passive attitudes of employees, weak employee participation . . ." (Branine 2011: 512)

Recent studies (Peiperl and Estrin 1998, Redman and Keithley 1998) found that managers are business-minded but in need of expertise used in free market economies, in capitalist management situations exposed to competitive situations, and in the motivation of employees. Managers in the region have to cope with economic, commercial, and managerial problems they didn't have in the socialist period of the economy. Managers have learned these new capabilities in recently created business schools of the region or in transnational enterprises and their management policies. Ardichvili and Gasparishvili (2001: 230) characterize the situation in the following way: They are "managers who continue to rely more on networks of connections than on superior business performance; and managers who encourage initiative and creativity in their workers co-existing with those who continue to follow the 'don't rock the boat' philosophy of organizational behaviour and management."

South America

The labor market of South America is rather heterogeneous: A third of the workforce finds employment in rural areas and more than 50 percent are "self-employed, domestic workers, unpaid family workers or wage-earning workers in micro-enterprises with up to five employees" (International Labor Organization [ILO] 2006: 7). According to the ILO, the workforce is young, educated, and poorly paid (5). High levels of unemployment among young people characterize the labor markets. Self-employment and short-term employment are widely spread.

Rural-urban migration in recent years increased the number of unskilled and uneducated manual laborers in urban centers. Yet the recent economic reforms have asked for a skilled and professional workforce that the market cannot supply. Youth needs training and vocational education; as a result, several Latin American countries have introduced programs for young people. These programs offer employers different financial incentives in order to attract young employees.

The reforms of the 1990s characterized by the privatization of state-owned companies and a reduction in public spending have had the effect of mass redundancies and a decline in public employment. This trend has led to an increase of informal activities for skilled workers so that the informal sector has become the largest employer in Latin America. Because of high taxation and difficult bureaucratic procedures people prefer the informal sector instead of being registered as self-employed. The income of those who work in the informal sector is very low, and as a result they become vulnerable to social unrest, as in Brazil in summer 2013. Small businesses that are formally registered are exposed to high taxes, competition, limited experience, and poor management practices. Temporary and seasonal contracts are very frequent in South America. To cut costs, enterprises have learned to use these possibilities that permit them to adapt employment to their own needs. In agriculture, most of the jobs are seasonal and short-term: Workers are only employed *en masse* during the harvest time.

MNCs are not as important in South America as they are in Asia, as investments have been based on the production of export commodities for international markets. Only a small group of qualified workers has found employment in these companies. Multinational corporations in agribusiness employ many women; women also work in the service sectors in low-paid jobs. Women are still largely absent from managerial positions in businesses. Despite equal opportunities legislation, women are discriminated against in the workplace (cf. Branine 2011: 539).

Managers in South America use a mixture of national and Western management practices depending on the size of the company. Larger enterprises use to adopt international management practices while smaller companies and organizations of the public sector use local management practices (Parnell 2008, Gomes and Gomes 2009).

The South American approach to management is "person-centred" (Elvira and Davila 2005b: 2267). Managers take care of the welfare of their subordinates and try to maintain a harmonious working environment where the community of workers respects legitimate authority. As Branine wrote (2011: 541): "Organizations are seen as social entities where people get to work together rather than economic entities where people are hired to do jobs to earn a living."

Management in South America is characterized by authoritarian structures inherited from the military governments of the past and the cultural respect for authority. Managerial authority is seldom delegated and promotions are based on vertically organized social networks of family members and group members. Subordinates tend to be passive and dependent and expect their leaders to tell them what to do. Bureaucratic procedures are followed to the letter, as employees have to respect authority in organizations.

The South American economy is dominated by small- and medium-size family enterprises (Rodríguez and Ríos 2009). According to Elvira and Davila (2005b), paternalism and avoidance of conflict with supervisors is widespread. In smaller enterprises, one can find a sense of commitment to the working environment and the organization. National and religious festivities are celebrated in the company and not at home with the family (cf. Gomes and Gomes 2009). In South America, managers prefer face-to-face contact with each other and seek to maintain good employee relations. However, communication is often vertical because of decision flows from the top to down the hierarchy.

In conclusion, this overview on different world regions has focused more on commonalities than on regional differences that continue to exist. In coming years, the trends that have been shown need to be better analyzed by sociologists and anthropologists through more case studies of globalized working situations. Most of the case studies that were mentioned in this overview were done by specialists of intercultural management; there is some need of sociological and anthropological research that respects methods and methodological approaches of the social sciences in order to enlarge the already accumulated knowledge and to better make it correspond to traditions in the fields of economic sociology and anthropology. Furthermore, some of the references used are dated; changes may have taken place in different globalized world regions since they were written. A better focused theoretical approach and comparative methods would permit us to generalize the findings presented above that sometimes seem to be rather superficial, at least for some regions. Concrete empirical situations change gradually so that more research in this field is necessary.

AN OVERVIEW OF THE DIFFERENT
CHAPTERS OF THIS VOLUME

The first part of the book tackles the topic of the globalization of management practices after the fall of the Iron Curtain. The first article written by Nina Bandelj analyzes the rise of management education in post-socialism. Bandelj argues that neoliberal globalization and market-building in post-socialism facilitated the rise of neoliberal management in Eastern Europe. Management schools were established that transmit market-based knowledge to managers who could use these ideas to establish private companies. According to Bandelj, the communist regimes hated and feared management. American and European business schools and funding by USAID and the European Union helped to create management schools in the region and therefore introduced a management culture grounded in neoliberal economics after 1989. In recent years, and perhaps as a response to the economic crisis, management topics based on arts, ethics, and sustainability have enlarged these educational programs in a few institutions.

The following chapter by Antoine Heemeryck analyzes the creation of new working norms and social relations in a company in Poland. He argues that "the transformation of the socioeconomic fabric has been marked by the importation of new methods of organizing work in terms of production, accounting, human resource management." (59) Heemeryck analyzes the gradual internalization of new forms of work organization, far away from the socialist planning. The company he studied was "'imported' from abroad as part of a strategy of wage cuts and increased fiscal earnings. The cheap workforce in Poland permitted to profit from lower production costs." (55) The general manager of the company was a Belgian who served as an intermediary between the company owner and the local staff. Management dissolved the local union, so the younger workers planned to create a union that would not engage in politics. The author writes: "The office employees derive their legitimacy from a close relationship with foreigners; they convey values associated with the new norms of production, unlike the workers who see themselves as repressed." (69)

The chapter by Caroline Dufy tackles the transformation of Russia's banking sector and, in particular, the new risk of lending money, as credit risks were a new phenomenon in post-Soviet Russia. Credit scoring was introduced that involved "computing the data for each applicant numerically in addition to the production of statistics on the relative risks associated with each category of clients." (73) Russia used security services (police officers or members of the intelligence services) from the former Soviet system that accepted new functions in private enterprises. This risk management ideology originated in advanced Western banking systems. The introduction of these techniques was favored by technical assistance from the European Bank for Reconstruction and Development but also from global firms working in the scoring sector. Credit scoring as Caroline Dufy shows "was supported by a discourse of modernization and economic rationalization, one originating from elites who favored the rational representation of their economic activity." (80) These elites accepted former policing methods and practices within the banking system that had become illegal in post-Soviet Russia in order to obtain reliable information on borrowers and avoid bad debts.

The next chapter from Krista Bywater analyzes corporate social responsibility (CSR) as a management strategy that transnational corporations (TNCs) adopt to protect their revenues and the reputation of their global goods and brand. Bywater studied Coca-Cola in India and the use of CSR to address social opposition in the U.S. and Europe. She argues that sociological analysis can make valuable contributions in order to understand this tactic in global management from the side of the managers of the company. She finds in her research that "CSR is used as a diversionary tactic to suppress social movements and limit the work of transnational activist networks in order to legitimize neoliberal economic relations and corporate globalization." (95) A corporation that relies on brand recognition such as Coca-Cola is "vulnerable to social movements that question the safety of products and sustainability of operations." (108) She continues: "Through its CSR policy and initiatives, Coca-Cola has spent millions of dollars to enhance its public reputation and protect its brand. As part of its global management strategy, the company supports a variety of water programs and community initiatives around the world to gain investor, employee, and consumer trust and confidence." (108) Bywater discusses "how the company uses CSR to carefully misdirect public attention away from its controversial behaviors and highlights its environmental and sustainability efforts." (109) With her study, Bywater challenges CSR "as a useful means to limit the harmful effects of corporate maleficence and achieve progressive social change." (109)

The next chapter by Michel Villette analyzes the production process of a corporate document: The Diversity and Social Cohesion Brochure of a French Corporation. This brochure was destined to display an aspect of corporate social responsibility of this plant. Villette argues "that the idea was to weave a pretty fiction on glossy paper." According to him, The utilization of the entire arsenal of rhetorical and graphic artifices served to produce ambiguity and fuzziness that avoided the contradictory interests present, that escaped a factual denial, and that prevented committing the corporation. The diary of the young manager that he presents allows us to understand social processes at work in the company and to uncover the constraints that faced the writer. The diary gives useful information on the activities of the middle and upper management in a TNC's headquarters regarding new management tools that appeared in 2005 such as "social responsibility" and "diversity management." The detailed description uncovers a discourse that shows the particularities of a corporate commitment in favor of diversity and its critical dimensions.

The second part of this edited volume reunites research that tackles the other side of the labor process: not managers but employees and workers who develop strategies in enterprises and plants to improve their working conditions. These pieces of research discuss new forms of resistance against changing and worsening working conditions that are not organized by unions but by the employees or workers themselves on an individual or small group level.

The first article tackles a group of skilled, well-educated professionals belonging to the "new middle class" in Turkey. Even if this group dresses and consumes well, a proletarianization process has occurred. Esin Gülsen evokes characteristics "such as routinization, deskilling, automation, loss of job security, decreased salaries, increased work load, mobbing." (136) The white-collar employees in the service sector that she studies are organized in trade unions, go on strike, and slow down the pace of work. Her study is based on experiences of call center employees and IBM Turkey employees. She finds that resistance can manifest itself in different forms such as individual or collective, open or hidden, passive or active, formal or informal resistance. The intensification of control and surveillance has triggered new challenges of work and new forms of opposition. These employees have used the Internet to disseminate their working conditions and to force the enterprise to accept their demands. The call center employees in particular felt like a racehorse, confronted with an evaluation of its performance. They organized collective calling actions or campaigns on Facebook to support colleagues. As an improvement, they could find a decrease of pressure on workers by managers. The results of Gülsen's study are "that employees do not simply internalize managerial practices and working rules. Instead they develop some formal, informal, individual, or collective resistance strategies against them." (146) Resistance strategies for these employees are still at the beginning but they show a particular social dialogue, often a more individualized one, that is different from former strategies of trade unions.

The next article, written by Julietta Longo, analyzes precariousness and resistance in a supermarket and a hypermarket in Argentina. A high level of unregistered employment, informality, and the predominance of temporary employment and subcontracting characterizes Argentina's labor market. Longo's chapter is based on a case study about one of the largest retail companies in Argentina. Longo studies the embeddedness of precariousness in these workplaces and the form conflicts take. The Argentine unions she studies have abandoned typical union claims and devoted themselves to the provision of services to members. The delegates say that their "main task is to redistribute among its members the benefits obtained by the union, such as holiday discounts, summer camps, and recreational club facilities, diapers for pregnant women, and cultural discounts." (159) According to Longo, a second function of the union is the mediation between the company and the employee. For instance, the delegate has to solve individual problems of workers with dialogues and negotiate between managers and workers. However, for most of these workers, working in a supermarket in a registered job means an improvement over previous working conditions as unregistered workers in small businesses and shops. The main reason for this sort of resistance is that having a secure job is much appreciated in a country with high levels of unregistered employment. As Longo argues: "The common belief is that it is important to take care of your work and meet the requirements requested by supervisors and managers in order to avoid conflicts." (161) And she continues: The existing "discontent is expressed in individual resistances where workers can temporarily crack the corporate hegemony by various actions." (163) These practices are absenteeism, theft, high turnover, refusing to work overtime, coming late, working at a slower pace, and even the implementation of lawsuits against the company. Yet, common resistances are rare even if the non-payment of workers overtime led to a strike in one of the shops and the plant was obliged to react positively to the demands of the workers.

The subsequent chapter tackles seasonal agricultural workers in Chile and was written by Tamara Heran. This mainly female work consists in harvesting and packing agricultural products and is carried out seasonally under precarious and informal conditions. New mechanisms of resistance have emerged in the field of work and in the private sphere. Heran studies forms of resistance that do not involve protests of organizations. Her field-work in the province of Limarí shows that the workers used labor stoppages so that the job would be halted or even stopped for the working day. As payment is by piecework, a disagreement between employers and seasonal workers may lead to a work stoppage. The workers can then wait to negoti-ate the price of the piecework with the employers who are sometimes ready to negotiate since they need these workers. Other workers prefer not to complain because they are afraid of losing their jobs. Abandonment may be another solution that can be associated with more attractive job opportuni-ties at the same moment somewhere else. Mistreatment and meager nutri-tion are further causes of abandonment.

When one regards gender relations in Chile, the increasing employment of women in the 1980s and 1990s has triggered acts of resistance at the workplace as well as in the domestic sphere. Women have increasingly par-ticipated in agricultural wage labor so that household chores would have to be shared in another way than before with the help of husbands and family members. Insofar women have conquered ground in terms of gender equal-ity but their search for social justice is still limited, as Heran argues.

Patrick Bond's chapter on South Africa describes a struggle that is linked to the color divide of this country: the African miner strike in 2012 when dozens of miners were killed. This strike triggered a strike wave through late 2012 so that by March 2013, "the state and most large farmers agreed to a 52 percent increase in the daily wage." (213) The World Economic Forum's *Global Competitive Report* had already placed South Africa in 2012 "in the world's number one position for adverse employee-employer relations." (213) After the Marikana strike, political strategies of the ANC and the plant "all proved inadequate to restore legitimacy." (213) As a union official argued: "There have not been any significant changes in the last 12 months regard-ing the issues that labour was protesting for . . . Workers are still living in shacks, in the hostels. . . ." (214) Bond also cites a mining industry executive: "Unfortunately very little has changed from a visible point of view. I think what has changed and it's not that visible is that stakeholders have recog-nized and have accepted that there's a need to do things differently." (215)

The last chapter of this book is dedicated to small independent presses that have been created in France in the last 20 years in the field of the social sciences. These presses represent pockets of resistance to the neoliberal eco-nomic pressures. As Sophie Noël argues, "they exemplify the possibility of alternative ways of doing business in the cultural field." (220) These pub-lishers promote an "economic world reversed" as Bourdieu (1996) wrote. They occupy a niche characterized by a political commitment. Most often, these presses are not-for-profit organizations and challenge the excesses of neoliberalism. The owners' discourse is characterized by their fragile posi-tions so that they downplay commercial considerations even if they have to accept the rules of the market in which they operate. They try "to avoid two ills: renouncing their principles or exhausting themselves."

CONCLUDING REMARKS

So far I have summarized the findings of the different articles and included these results in a vision of management practices in the current global post-neoliberal economy that focuses on various cultural influences on these economic practices. In particular, efforts have been made to demonstrate, on the one hand, possibilities of resistance of the labor force and, on the other, strategies transnational enterprises use in order to perpetuate their economic interests. Behind an often rather consensual discourse described in some chapters, one can find strategies of enterprises, such as CSR, that strengthen the argument of the improved conditions of employers and the weakening situations of employees under the socioeconomic globalization processes of the last 20 years.

The main challenge for the next years seems to be the changing role of labor unions: Will their role continue to decline or will they be able to voice the growing disapproval of an economy where economic profits are the main arguments of employers and shareholders? Will the huge group of unemployed people all over the world lead to changes in economic policies of global enterprises and mean changed roles for both global management and local employees and laborers in the coming years? As the South African example has shown, other possible relations between labor and companies exist that have a much more dramatic character. One may ask if this particular case is an exceptional one and if these South-African minors, this disillusioned workforce, may become a potential reality in other countries influenced by the global economy. Political unrest based on high youth unemployment is an actual challenge in several countries and regions, such as North Africa or Southern Europe. The possible unstable situation of these regions will continue to challenge global political relations but also the global economy. Decisions that will be taken in MNCs will continue to have consequences for regions and subcontinents.

This book has tried to show some of the challenges and their possible solutions. Further studies are needed on concrete empirical situations so that political and economic efforts can find solutions to challenges of globalized economies and societies. These problematic questions can no longer only be known by elites; globalization and its communication instruments render populations everywhere on the globe capable of understanding certain societal trends. Politicians are thus asked to react to these challenges and to find solutions together with economic actors in a responsible manner for a common future to the mutual benefit of both groups of the labor process. It seems to me that this was already discussed in Mauss's (2012) *Essai sur le don* from the 1920s, where he argued that economies should not only be governed by profit but that economies are there to function for the welfare of their populations. It seems as if this viewpoint is voiced in recent social movements such as the *Indignad@s* in Spain, the *Indignés* in France, and the Occupy movement in the U.S. and many other countries. These movements may become potential forces of probably necessary societal transformations in today's globalized societies if the trade unions join their organizational force and their *voice* (Hirschmann) with these rather unlinked social movements that have the sympathy of parts of the global critical thinking on important societal challenges.

NOTES

1. My particular thanks go to Nina Bandelj for valuable and constructive comments on an earlier draft of this introduction.
2. This process has been called "marketization." See for instance: http://wirtsoz-dgs.mpifg.de/dokumente/Programm_Marketization_of_Society.pdf, accessed on September 26, 2013.
3. See for instance: http://www.tandfonline.com/doi/abs/10.1080/147084704086 68871?journalCode=rmli20#.UjbCerxyWpI; https://www.cassknowledge.com/sites/default/files/article-attachments/%27Moving%20Management%20-%20 Theorizing%20Struggles%20Against%20the%20Hegemony%20of%20Man agement.pdf, accessed on September 26, 2013.
4. See for instance: https://www.cassknowledge.com/sites/default/files/article-attachments/%27Moving%20Management%20-%20Theorizing%20 Struggles%20Against%20the%20Hegemony%20of%20Management. pdf, accessed on September 26, 2013; http://www.sagepub.com/upm-data/ 27357_02_Cunliffe_Ch_01.pdf, accessed on September 26, 2013.

REFERENCES AND FURTHER READING

Albers, Detlev, Stephen Haeler, and Henning Meyer (eds) (2006) *Social Europe: A Continent's Answer to Market Fundamentalism.* London: European Research Forum at London Metropolitan University.
Ali, Abbas J. (2004) *Islamic Perspectives on Management and Organization.* Cheltenham: Edward Elgar.
Anquetil, Alain (2008) *Qu'est-ce que l'éthique des affaires?* Paris: Vrin (Chemins philosophiques).
Ardichvili, Alexander and Alexander Gasparishvili (2001) "Socio-cultural Values, Internal Work Culture and Leadership Styles in Four Post-communist Countries," *International Journal of Cross Cultural Management* 1 (2): 227–242.
Aryee, Samuel (2004) "HRM in Ghana," in Ken N. Kamoche, Debrah Yaw, Frank Horwitz, and Gerry Nkombo Muuka (eds) *Managing Human Resources in Africa,* 121–134. London: Routledge.
Ascencio, Chloé and Dominique Rey (2010) *Etre efficace en Chine: Le management à l'épreuve de la culture chinoise.* Paris: Pearson.
Atzeni, Mauricio (2010) *Workplace Conflict. Mobilization and Solidarity in Argentina.* Basingstoke: Palgrave Macmillan.
Bäckstrand, Karin (2006) "Multi-stakeholder Partnerships for Sustainable Development: Rethinking Legitimacy, Accountability and Effectiveness," *European Environment* 16 (5): 290–306.
Banerjee, Subhabrata Bobby (2008) "Corporate Social Responsibility: The Good, the Bad and the Ugly," *Critical Sociology* 34 (1): 51–79.
Basu, Parikshit K. (2007) "Critical Evaluation of Growth Strategies: India and China," *International Journal of Social Economics* 34 (9): 664–678.

Bourdieu, Pierre (1996) *The Rules of Art: Genesis and Structure of the Literary Field* (tr. Susan Emanuel). Cambridge: Polity Press.

Bouffartigue, Paul and Sophie Béroud (2009) *Quand le travail se précarise quelles résistances collectives?* Paris: La dispute/SNEDIT.

Branine, Mohamed (1997) "Change and Continuity in Chinese Employment Relationships," *New Zealand Journal of Industrial Relations* 22 (1): 77–94.

Branine, Mohamed (2011) *Managing across Cultures: Concepts, Policies and Practices.* London: Sage.

Branine, Mohamed and David Pollard (2010) "Human Resource Management with Islamic Management Principles—A Dialectic for a Reverse Diffusion in Management," *Personnel Review* 39 (6): 712–727.

Braun, Werner and Malcolm Warner (2002) "The 'Culture-Free' versus 'Culture-Specific' Management Debate," in Malcolm Warner and Pat Joynt (eds) *Managing across Cultures: Issues and Perspectives*, 13–25. 2nd ed., London: Thomson Learning.

Brown, David H. and Mohamed Branine (1995) "Managing People in China's Foreign Trade Corporations: Some Evidence of Change," *The International Journal of Human Resource Management* 6 (1): 159–173.

Budhwar, Pawan S. (2001) "Doing Business in India," *Thunderbird International Business Review* 43 (4): 549–568.

Budhwar, Pawan S. and Ingmar Björkman (2003) "A Corporate Perspective on the Management of Human Resources in Foreign Firms Operating in India," International HRM Conference, 4–6 June, Limerick, Ireland.

Budhwar, Pawan S., Habte G. Woldu, and Emmanuel Ogbonna (2008) "A Comparative Analysis of Cultural Value Orientations of Indians and Migrant Indians in the USA," *International Journal of Cross Cultural Management* 8 (1): 79–105.

Budhwar, Pawan S. and Paul R. Sparrow (2002) "An Integrative Framework for Determining Cross-National Human Resource Management Practices," *Human Resource Management Review* 12 (3): 377–403.

Capron, Michel and Françoise Quairel-Lanoizelée (2004) *Mythes et réalités de l'entreprise responsable. Acteurs, enjeux, stratégies.* Paris: La Découverte.

Chen, Min (2004) *Asian Management Systems.* 2nd ed., London: Thomson Learning.

Chieng, André, Philippe d'Iribarne, and Richard D. Lewis (2006) "Cultures d'entreprises," *Revue des deux mondes* 2 (Feb.): 93–155.

Child, John (2002) "Theorizing about Organization Cross-Nationality: Part 1, an Introduction," in Malcolm Warner and Pat Joynt (eds) *Managing across Cultures: Issues and Perspectives*, 26–39. 2nd ed., London: Thomson Learning.

Cooke, Fang Lee (2004) "HRM in China," in Pawan S. Budhwar (ed.) *Managing Human Resources in Asia-Pacific*, 17–34. London: Routledge.

Crouch, Colin (2011) *The Strange Non-Death of Neo-liberalism.* Wiley: Cambridge.

Davis, Gerard F. (2009) *Managed by the Market: How Finance Reshaped America.* Oxford: Oxford University Press.

Deresky, Helen (2001) *International Management: Managing across Borders and Cultures.* London: Prentice-Hall.

D'Iribarne, Philippe (2007) *Successful Companies in the Developing World: Managing in Synergy with Cultures.* Paris: Agence Française de Développement.

D'Iribarne, Philippe and Alain Henry (2003) *Le Tiers-monde qui réussit: nouveaux modèles.* Paris: O. Jacob.

D'Iribarne, Philippe, Alain Henry, Jean-Pierre Segal, and Sylvie Chevrier (1998) *Cultures et mondialisation: gérer par-delà les frontières.* Paris: Ed. du Seuil

Dossani, Rafiq (2008) *India Arriving: How this Economic Powerhouse is Redefining Global Business.* New York: AMACOM, American Management Association.

Easterby-Smith, Mark, Danusia Malina, and Yuan Lu (1995) "How Culture Sensitive is HRM? A Comparative Analysis of Practice in Chinese and UK

Companies," *The International Journal of Human Resource Management* 6 (1): 31–59.

Elites managériales et mondialisation (2005) *Entreprises et histoire* 12 (41): 15–119.

Elvira, Marta M. and Antonio Davila (2005a) "Culture and Human Resource Management in Latin America," in Marta M. Elvira and Antonio Davila (eds) *Managing Human Resources in Latin America: An Agenda for International Leaders*, 3–24. London: Routledge.

Elvira, Marta M. and Antonio Davila (2005b) "Special Research Issue on Human Resource Management in Latin America," *International Journal of Human Resource Management* 16 (2): 2164–2172.

Fleming, Peter and Graham Sewell (2002) "Looking for the Good Soldier, Svejk: Alternative Modalities of Resistance in the Contemporary Workplace," *Sociology* 36 (4): 857–873.

Fougère, Martin and Nicodemus Solitander (2009) "Against Corporate Responsibility: Critical Reflections on Thinking, Practice, Content and Consequences," *Corporate Social Responsibility and Environmental Management* 16: 217–227.

Fourcade, Marion and Rakesh Khurana (2013) "From Social Control to Financial Economics: The Linked Ecologies of Economics and Business in Twentieth-Century America," *Theory and Society* 42: 121–159.

French, Ray (2007) *Cross-Cultural Management in Work Organisations.* London: CIPD.

Fukuda, John K. (1989) "China's Management Tradition and Reform," *Management Decision* 27 (3): 45–49.

Godong Bend, Serge Alain (2011) *Implanter le capitalisme en Afrique: Bonne gouvernance et meilleures pratiques de gestion face aux cultures locales.* Paris: Karthala.

Gomes, Ricardo Corrêa and Luciana de Oliveira Miranda Gomes (2009) "Depicting the Arena in which Brazilian Local Government Authorities Make Decisions: What is the Role of Stakeholders?" *International Journal of Public Sector Management* 22 (2): 76–90.

Graeber, David (2010) "Les fondements moraux des relations économiques," *Revue du MAUSS* 2 (36): 51–70.

Hampden-Turner, Charles and Fons Trompenaars (1993) *The Seven Cultures of Capitalism: Value Systems for Creating Wealth in the United States, Britain, Japan, Germany, France, Sweden and the Netherlands.* New York: Doubleday.

Hickson, David J. and Derek Salman Pugh (2001) *Management Worldwide: Distinctive Styles among Globalization.* 2nd ed., Harmondsworth: Penguin.

Hofstede, Geert (1980) *Culture's Consequences: International Differences in Work Related Values.* London: Sage.

Hofstede, Geert (1991) *Culture and Organizations: Software of the Mind.* London: McGraw-Hill.

Hofstede, Geert (1998) "Think Locally, Act Globally: Cultural Constraints in Personnel Management," *Management International Review*, Special Issue, 98 (2): 7–26.

House, Robert J., Paul J. Hanges, Mansour Javidan, Peter Forfman, and Vipin Gupta (2004) *Culture, Leadership and Organization: The GLOBE Study of 62 Societies.* London: Sage.

International Labor Organization (ILO) (2006) *Decent Work in the Americas: An Agenda for the Hemisphere, 2006–15*, Report of the Director General, 16th American Regional Meeting, Brasilia, May. Geneva: ILO.

Jamali, Dima and Ramzi Mirshak (2007) "Corporate Social Responsibility (CSR): Theory and Practice in a Developing Country Context," *Journal of Business Ethics* 72: 243–262.

Javidan, Mansour and Ali Dastmalchian (2009) "Managerial Implications of the GLOBE Project: A Study of 62 Societies," *Asia Pacific Journal of Human Resources* 47 (1): 41–58.

Kakar, Sudjir, Manfred F.R. Kets de Vries, and Pierre Vrignaud (2002) "Leadership in Indian Organizations from a Comparative Perspective," *International Journal of Cross Cultural Management* 2 (2): 239–250.

Kamoche, Ken N., Debrah Yaw, Frank Horwitz, and Gerry Nkombo Muuka (eds) (2004) *Managing Human Resources in Africa*. London: Routledge.

Kanter, Rosabeth M. (1995) *World Class: Thinking Locally in the Global Economy*. New York: Simon & Schuster.

Khan, Alhajie Saidy and Peter Ackers (2004) "Neo-pluralism as a Theoretical Framework for Understanding HRM in Sub-Saharan Africa," *International Journal of Human Resource Management* 15 (7): 1330–1353.

Kiggundu, Moses N. (1989) *Managing Organizations in Developing Countries: An Operational and Strategic Approach*. Hartford: Kumarian Press.

Kiggundu, Moses N. (1991) "The Challenges of Management Development in sub-Saharan Africa," *Journal of Management Development* 10 (6): 32–47.

Khondker Habibul H. and Ulrike Schuerkens (2014) "Social Transformation, Development, and Globalization," *Sociopedia article*, International Sociological Association.

Kuran, Timur (2004) "Why is the Middle East Economically Underdeveloped? Historical Mechanisms of Institutional Stagnation," *Journal of Economic Perspectives* 18 (3): http://www.aeaweb.org/articles.php?doi=10.1257/0895330042162421, accessed on April 27, 2014.

Lammers, Cornelius J. and David J. Hickson (1979) *Organizations Alike and Unlike: International and Inter-institutional Studies in the Sociology of Organizations*. London: Routledge & Kegan Paul.

Laurent, André (1983) "The Cultural Diversity of Western Conceptions of Management," *International Studies of Management and Organization* 13 (1–2): 75–96.

Lewis, Richard (2004) *When Cultures Collide: Leading, Team-working and Managing across the Globe*. London: Nicholas Brealey.

Lituchy, Terri R., Betty Jane Punnett, and Bill Buenar Puplampu (eds) (2013) *Management in Africa: Macro and Micro Perspectives*. New York: Routledge.

Lodge, George and Craig Wilson (2006) *A Corporate Solution to Global Poverty: How Multinationals Can Help the Poor and Invigorate Their Own Legitimacy*. Princeton: Princeton University Press.

Majumdar, Sumit K. (2012) *India's Late, Late Industrial Revolution: Democratizing Entrepreneurship*. Cambridge: Cambridge University Press.

Mauss, Marcel (2012) *Essai sur le don. Forme et raison de l'échange dans les sociétés archaïques*. Paris: Presses Universitaires de France.

Mendonça, Manuel and Rabindra N. Kanungo (1996) "Impact of Culture on Performance Management in Developing Countries," *International Journal of Manpower* 17 (4/5): 65–75.

Moran, Robert T., Philip R. Harris, and Sarah Virgilia Moran (2007) *Managing Cultural Differences: Global Leadership Strategies for the 21st Century*. 8th ed., London: Routledge.

Moon, Jeremy (2007) "The Contribution of Corporate Social Responsibility to Sustainable Development," *Sustainable Development* 15: 296–306.

Mrozowicki, Adam and Geert van Hootegem (2008) "Unionism and Workers' Strategies in Capitalist Transformation: The Polish Case Reconsidered," *European Journal of Industrial Relations* 14 (2): 197–216.

Mulholland, Ken (2004) "Workplace Resistance in an Irish Call Centre: Slammin', Scammin' Smokin' an' Leavin'," *Work, Employment and Society* 18 (4): 709–724.

Newell, Peter and Jedrzej George Frynas (2007) "Beyond CSR? Business, Poverty and Social Justice: An Introduction," *Third World Quarterly* 28 (4): 669–681.

Nolan, Peter (2001) *China and the Global Business Revolution*. London: Palgrave.

O'Leary, Greg (ed.) *Adjusting to Capitalism: Chinese Workers and the State*. Amonk: M.E. Sharpe.

30 *Ulrike Schuerkens*

Okpara, John O. and Pamela Wynn (2008) "Human Resource Management Practices in a Transition Economy: Challenges and Prospects," *Management Research News* 31 (1): 57–76.

Parker, Martin (2002) *Against Management: Organization in the Age of Managerialism*. Cambridge: Polity.

Parnell, John A. (2008) "Strategy Execution in Emerging Economies: Assessing Strategic Diffusion in Mexico and Peru," *Management Decision* 46 (9): 1277–1298.

Peiperl, Maury and Saul Estrin (1998) "Managerial Markets in Transition in Central and Eastern Europe: A Field Study and Implications," *The International Journal of Human Resource Management* 9 (1): 58–78.

Pfeffer, Jeffrey (1994) *Competitive Advantage through People: Unleashing the Power of the Workforce*. Boston: Harvard Business School Press.

Punnett, Betty Jane (2012) *Management: A Developing Country Perspective*. London: Routledge.

Redman, Tony and Don Keithley (1998) "Downsizing Goes East? Employment Restructuring in Post-socialist Poland," *The International Journal of Human Resource Management* 9 (2): 274–295.

Rist, Gilbert (1996) *Le développement. Histoire d'une croyance occidentale*. Paris: Presses de Sciences po.

Rodríguez, M. Darío and René Ríos (2009) "Paternalism at a Crossroads: Labour Relations in Chile in Transition," *Employee Relations* 31 (3): 322–321.

Sabeg, Yazid and Laurence Méhaignerie (2004) *Les oubliés de l'égalité des chances. Participation, pluralité, assimilation ou repli*. Paris: Institut Montaigne.

Saini, Debi S. and Pawan S. Budhwar (2004) "HRM in India," in Pawan S. Budhwar (ed.) *Managing Human Resources in Asia-Pacific*, 113–139. London: Routledge.

Schein, Edgar H. (2004) *Organizational Culture and Leadership*. 3rd ed., San Francisco: Jossey-Bass.

Scherer, Andreas Georg and Guido Palazzo (2011) "The New Political Role of Business in a Globalized World—A Review of a New Perspective on CSR and its Implications for the Firm, Governance, and Democracy," *Journal of Management Studies* 48: 899–931.

Schuerkens, Ulrike (2001) *Transformationsprozesse in der Elfenbeinküste und in Ghana: Eine historisch-vergleichende Analyse des Verhältnisses von Lebensgeschichten und strukturellen Wandlungsprozessen*. Münster: Lit.

Schuerkens, Ulrike (ed.) (2008) *Globalization and Transformations of Local Socio-Economic Practices*. London: Routledge.

Schuerkens, Ulrike and Habibul Khondker (2014) "Social Transformations and Sociology of Development," *Sociopedia*, International Sociological Association.

Schuler, Randall S., Susan E. Jackson, and Yadong Luo (2004) *Managing Human Resources in Cross Border Alliances*. London: Routledge.

Selmer, Jan (2001) "Adjustment of Western European vs. North American Expatriate Managers in China," *Personnel Review* 30 (1): 6–21.

Sinha, Jai B.P. (1995) *The Cultural Context of Leadership and Power*. New Delhi: Sage.

Somers, Margaret R. and Fred Block (2005) "From Poverty to Perversity: Ideas, Markets, and Institutions over 200 Years of Welfare Debate," *American Sociological Review* 70 (2): 260–287.

Southworth, David B. (1999) "Building a Business School in China: The Case of the China Europe International Business School (CEIBS)," *Education + Training* 41 (6/7): 325–331.

Stockhammer, Engelbert and Özlem Onaran (2009) "National and Sectoral Influences on Wage Determination in Central and Eastern Europe," *European Journal of Industrial Relations* 15 (3): 317–338.

Sparrow, Paul, Randall S. Schuler, and Susan E. Jackson (1994) "Convergence or Divergence: Human Resource Practices and Policies for Competitive Advantage Worldwide," *The International Journal of Human Resource Management* 5 (2): 267–299.

Srinivas, Kalburgi M. (1995) "Globalization of Business and the Third World: Challenges of Expanding the Mindsets," *Journal of Management Development* 14 (3): 26.

Suar, Damodar, Hare R. Tewari, and Kostubh R. Chaturbedi (2006) "'Subordinates' Perception of Leadership Styles and their Work Behaviour," *Psychology and Developing Societies* 18 (1): 95–114.

Suliman, Abubakr Moryeldin Tahir (2006) "Human Resource Management in the United Arab Emirates," in Pawan Budhwar and Kamel Mellahi (eds) *Managing Human Resources in the Middle East*, 59–78. London: Routledge.

Sztompka, Piotr (1991) *Society in Action: The Theory of Social Becoming*. Chicago: University of Chicago Press.

Tang, Jie and Anthony Ward (2003) *The Changing Face of Chinese Management*. Working in Asia Series. London: Routledge.

Tayeb, Monir H. (2003) *International Management: A Cross-Cultural Approach*. London: Harlow Prentice-Hall: Financial Times.

Tayeb, Monir H. (2005) *International Human Resource Management: A Multinational Company Perspective*. Oxford: Oxford University Press.

Tong, Jin and Amit Mitra (2009) "Chinese Cultural Influences on Knowledge Management Practice," *Journal of Knowledge Management* 13 (2): 49–62.

Torrington, Derek (1994) *International Human Resource Management: Think Globally, Act Locally*. Hemel Hempstead: Prentice-Hall.

Trompenaars, Fons (1993) *Riding the Waves of Culture: Understanding Cultural Diversity in Business*. London: Economist Books.

Trompenaars, Fons and Charles Hampden-Turner (2004) *Managing People across Cultures*. Oxford: Capstone.

Tsui, Anne S., Sushil S. Nifadkar, and Amy Yi Ou (2007) "Cross-national, Cross-cultural Organizational Behaviour Research: Advances, Gaps, and Recommendations," *Journal of Management* 33 (3): 426–478.

United Nations Industrial Development Organization (UNIDO) (2009) *Position Paper on Corporate Social Responsibility*. New York: United Nations.

Utting, Peter (2002) "Regulating Business via Multi-Stakeholder Initiatives: A Preliminary Assessment" in UNRISD *Voluntary Approaches to Corporate Responsibility*, 61–126. Geneva: NGLS.

Verver, Michiel and Heidi Dahles (2013) "The Anthropology of Chinese Capitalism in Southeast Asia," *Journal of Business Anthropology* 2 (1): 93–114.

Warner, Malcolm (1995) *The Management of Human Resources in Chinese Industry*. Basingstoke: Macmillan.

Warner, Malcolm (ed.) (2003) *Culture and Management in Asia*. London: Routledge Curzon.

Warner, Malcolm (2004) "Human Resource Management in China Revisited: Introduction," *The International Journal of Human Resource Management* 15 (4): 617–634.

Warner, Malcolm and Chris Rowley (eds) (2011) *Chinese Management in the 'Harmonious Society': Managers, Markets and the Globalized Economy*. London: Routledge.

Weir, David (2000) "Management in the Arab Middle East," in Monir Tayeb (ed.) *International Business: Theories, Policies and Practices*, 501–509. London: Prentice-Hall.

Weir, David (2001) "Management in the Arab World: A Fourth Paradigm?" Paper submitted to EURAM Conference, 2 Dec., Sophia Antipolis, France.

Whitley, Richard D. (1992) *Business Systems in East Asia: Firms, Markets and Societies*. London: Sage.

Wilk, Richard (1996) *Economies and Cultures*. Boulder, CO: Westview.
Yahiaoui, Dorra and Yahia H. Zoubir (2006) "Human Resource Management in Tunisia," in Pawan Budhwar and Kamel Mellahi (eds) *Managing Human Resources in the Middle East*, 233–249. London: Routledge.
Yousef, A. Darwish (2001) "Islamic Work Ethics: A Moderator between Organizational Commitment and Job Satisfaction in a Cross-Cultural Context," *Personnel Review* 30 (2): 152–169.
Zeffane, Rachid and Robert Rugimbana (1995) "Management in the Less-Developed Countries: A Review of Pertinent Issues, Challenges and Responses," *Leadership and Organization Development Journal* 16 (8): 26–36.

Part I

Empirical Case Studies on the Implementation of the Globalized Management Discourse

2 The Rise of Management Education in Post-Socialism

Nina Bandelj

INTRODUCTION

Central and Eastern Europe have been fundamentally transformed since the fall of the Berlin Wall in 1989 and the subsequent collapse of communism throughout the region. One of the central transformations has been the institutionalization of free markets, which coincided with neoliberal globalization. In this chapter, I examine the processes, which, I argue, significantly contributed to market building in post-socialism but also facilitated the rise of neoliberal management in this region.

Market building is not a natural and spontaneous process that just happens when market institutions are put in place to create incentives for profit-maximizing actors. Much scholarship has emphasized the role of states in building markets as well as the role of international organizations, including the IMF and the European Union. However, while states and international organizations are clearly important in market transition, the institutionalization of a new economic order also requires the socialization of actors into new rules of behavior. Basically, if cadres are to become managers, they need to learn management. A crucial way to do so is by establishing management schools that transmit market-based knowledge to actors who can use it to restructure state-owned enterprises and establish new private companies.

Socialist command economies were focused on planning and controlling rather than managing (Kornai 1992). Management was not seen as a profession requiring formal education, so there was no reason to have management schools. According to Michal Čakrt (1993: 63), a Czech professor, "the communist regime hated and feared management." Even the word itself was considered "a word of capitalism." In what follows, I trace how the introduction of management education behind the Iron Curtain has been heavily influenced by Western countries because of dependency on the international funding organizations, as well as on American (and to some extent European) business schools and faculty. I argue that this kind of introduction of management education into post-socialist countries has also contributed to the transposition of a particular kind of management culture grounded in neoliberal economics and finance. However, in recent years, the

Central and East European Management Development Association (CEE MAN), the first and biggest regional professional organization dedicated to the advancement of management education, has started to "promote leadership for change, global competitiveness and social responsibility, innovation and creativity, and respect for cultural values" (CEEMAN 2013a). In addition, the oldest management school in the Central and East European region located in Slovenia has engaged in efforts to implement a management education program based on arts, ethics, and sustainability. I find this consistent with a discourse linked to a broader global movement for responsible management education, supported by the Principles for Responsible Management Education initiative of the United Nations Global Compact, which attempts to counter the neoliberal global management discourse.

RISE OF MARKET AND MANAGEMENT CULTURE

Scholars have asserted that the economic logic of rationality, market, and, most recently, finance, has become a prevalent way of how people make sense of their lives. In sociology, George Ritzer (1993) developed the influential idea of the McDonaldization of society, arguing that the organizational innovations championed by the McDonalds corporation have come to define how contemporary society is run outside of the corporate world and spilling over, for instance, to health care, education, tourism, and criminal justice. While the emphasis on efficiency, calculability, predictability, and control through automation seems to go hand-in-hand with Weberian rationalization and bureaucratization of the world, Ritzer, as did Weber, also warned of "irrationality of rationality," especially its dehumanizing nature. Similarly interested in pinpointing the shifts in contemporary business culture, Luc Boltanski and Eve Chiapello (2007) examined French management texts from the 1960s and the 1990s to identify a "new spirit of capitalism," as labeled in the book's title. This new spirit advocates self-management and versatility in the workplace and sees managers as coaches who get the workers to do what is needed by convincing them that the firm's interests are also their own interests. The normative order upon which this kind of capitalism rests is that of connections and networks, and a successful actor is one with many contacts and much flexibility and mobility.

An increasingly vigorous line of inquiry has also been preoccupied with the contemporary rise of market fundamentalism or a belief in "the moral superiority of organizing all dimensions of social life according to market principles" (Somers and Block 2005: 261). Margaret Somers and Fred Block (2005) coined the term "ideational embeddedness" to explain how market fundamentalist ideas have radically transformed our knowledge culture. The concept is used to capture that the economy is embedded within the "ideas, public narratives, and explanatory systems" that serve to create the necessary conditions for certain ways of organizing the economy to be normalized.

The authors compare two cases of welfare revolutions in England and in the United States in different historical periods, which were both preceded by the "triumph of market fundamentalism as a new ideational authority," but otherwise exemplified difference on every other significant explanatory factor. In their account, culture in the form of ideas is not only a part of the context in which economic processes are inserted but has a causal influence on constituting market outcomes.

In the wake of financial crises of 2008, scholars also turned to examining financialization as a major driver of societal transformation. Gerald Davis (2009) argues that finance has come to take center stage and defines how corporations and individuals behave. In this finance-centered system, the overriding concern of corporations is not productive activity but shareholder value, and individuals come to increasingly rely on financial markets, and not employment in corporations, for security and wealth creation.

In a recent study, Marion Fourcade and Rakesh Khurana (2013: 121) examine how contemporary business school development in the U.S. "marked the decisive ascendancy of economics, and particularly financial economics, in business education over the other behavioral disciplines." Fourcade and Khurana argue that education currently provided in American business schools has been characterized by "'Chicago-style' economic approaches offering support for deregulatory policies and popularizing narrowly financial understandings of the firm," (p. 122) which scholars have dubbed a neoliberal approach. Similarly, I argue that the rise of management schools in Central and Eastern Europe has played a prominent role in supporting a particular kind of post-socialist economic subjectivity that is grounded in the principle of neoliberal management.

MANAGEMENT EDUCATION IN POST-SOCIALISM

> [The] assumption that if individuals internalize the costs and benefits of their decision everyone will respond to price stimuli is nothing but an article of faith. Powerful cultural barriers must be broken and well-entrenched habits must be eroded if people are to behave like market actors. . . . Modernization, the process by which individuals became acculturated to market relations, took decades or longer in Western Europe. Moreover, whereas, as Lenin once remarked, any cook can be taught to administer a socialist economy, the market economy is a world of accountants, stockbrokers, investment planners, and financial wizards. It takes time for cooks to become MBAs.
>
> (Przeworski 1991: 158)

Taking Przeworski's (1991) point quite literally, it is important to recognize the role of management education in helping post-socialist economic actors to learn how to become market players and, consequently, help to build capitalism from the bottom up. Most research on market transition has emphasized the role of states and international organizations in this process (e.g. Jacoby 2004, King and Sznajder 2006, Bandelj 2008, Hamm et al. 2012), as well as firms (e.g. Stark and Vedres 2010, Nee and Opper 2012). While ethnographic research examines the making of various aspects of post-socialist identities (Dunn 2004, Brubaker et al. 2008, Imre and Verstraete 2009, Shevchenko 2009, Swader 2013), emphasizing the importance of management education is a piece that is missing in existing accounts of how Central and East European countries managed to create market-based economies over a very short span of time. Moreover, while there exist some studies that pay attention to management schools in post-socialist Europe, they are limited to descriptions of the teaching experiences of Western professors in Central and Eastern Europe (Elbert 1996), descriptions of initial management-education programs and schools that developed after the collapse of the system (Fogel 1990, Drew 1994, Purg 1997, 1999), and suggestions for the reform of these programs (Madhavan and Fogel 1992, Kenny and Trick 1994). Extending this research, the aim of this chapter is to examine how creation of management education in post-socialism has facilitated the introduction of neoliberal management because of the substantial dependence of East European schools on resources from the West. Still, as I discuss preliminarily in the second part of the chapter, the recent years have seen some new management education initiatives in Eastern Europe that attempt to provide an alternative to the neoliberal management discourse.

DATA AND METHODS

The data come from a variety of quantitative and qualitative sources, including case studies of the first business school in the region, International Executive Development Center (IEDC) in Slovenia, and the central regional professional management organization CEEMAN; an open-ended survey of 32 school administrators conducted by CEEMAN in 2003; content analysis of 56 school websites collected in 2006; and informal interviews with organizational leaders, administrators, and faculty, and participant observation at one of the schools intermittently between 1993 and 2003, when I worked as a summer management program manager and lecturer.

   The CEEMAN survey includes 32 administrators from Belarus (1), Croatia (1), the Czech Republic (1), Estonia (1), Georgia (2), Hungary (2), Latvia (4), Lithuania (2), Poland (4), Romania (4), Russia (7), Slovenia (2), and Ukraine (1). The questionnaire was emailed to representatives of the school (usually dean's assistants) from the CEEMAN directory list to gather information for preparation of the 2003 CEEMAN conference on Business and Business School Cooperation. The response rate for private establishments in Central and Eastern Europe was 69 percent, with 32 surveys returned. The survey asked some basic demographic information and then focused on most important cooperative relationships that their schools were currently engaged in with: (1) National or international governmental agencies; (2) Domestic or international NGOs; (3) The research or educational programs of other schools, such as joint degrees; or (4) Any other type of institutional cooperation. For each of the cooperations that the schools listed, they were asked to provide a brief description, names of institutions or individuals involved, start year, expected duration, how initial contacts were established, reasons for entering the cooperation, what benefits they gained from it, and what some of its disadvantages might be.

The sample for website analysis includes 56 schools including Belarus (3), Croatia (4), the Czech Republic (8), Estonia (2), Hungary (3), Georgia (2), Kazakhstan (2), Latvia (4), Lithuania (2), Poland (13), Romania (3), Russia (7), Slovakia (1), Slovenia (1), and Ukraine (4), collected in 2006 by the author and research assistants. Given that a reliable listing/directory of management schools, such as those that can be found for the U.S. or Western Europe, does not exist for post-socialist countries, we started with the CEEMAN Membership Directory (CEEMAN 2013c), listing a total of 36 private management schools. My research assistants and I complemented that with the two most prominent online directory sources, the Central and East European Education Directory Online (four schools added) and the Hobson MBA Central Online Directory (seven schools added). We then cross-checked our list with the membership lists of regional management associations (BMDA, CAMAN, FORUM, RABE) and with the EFMD, AACSB, and AMBA (Association of MBAs) directories. This generated six additional schools. Finally, we used the Google search engine (using the words "management school" and country name) to identify any additional private management schools in the region for all of the 17 countries included in the analysis. Through this search we found three additional schools, yielding a total of 56 schools. Using content analysis of these school's websites was a way to have access to the self-presentation of schools and gather institutional foundation data, mission and activities, and evidence of connections to other entities (i.e., other schools in the region or abroad, corporations, and professional organizations) as revealed in written descriptions or graphic display of affiliations in the form of names and logos.

FROM PLANNING AND CONTROL TO MANAGEMENT

Before the breakup of socialism, business and management schools did not exist in the East European region. Socialist command economies were focused on planning and controlling rather than managing. As one administrator suggested, management was not seen as a profession requiring formal education, so there was no reason to have management schools. According to Michal Čakrt (1993: 63), a Czech professor, "the communist regime hated and feared management." Even the word itself was considered "a word of capitalism." Notably, post-socialist countries have adopted the

English expression, *management*, and by using that label carved out space for a new organizational phenomenon and new forms of economic behavior.

By the late 1980s, communist rulers in several Central and East European countries introduced some economic reforms, which included experimentation with economic decentralization and liberalization (Bandelj 2008). This was the context in which the first management school was formed, called International Executive Development Center (IEDC), established in 1986 in Slovenia. Slovenia was then part of Yugoslavia, which had its own form of socialism, workers self-management. This means that the economy wasn't centrally planned like in Soviet Union and its satellite states but was more decentralized, while retaining collective ownership of assets (Horvat 1976). Given such an organization of a socialist economy in Yugoslavia, it may not be surprising that its most advanced region, Slovenia, with significant integration in Western trade networks by the 1980s, gave rise to the first entity that offered Western-style management training and that later evolved into a full-fledged management school, IEDC-Bled School of Management.

In 1986, Professor Danica Purg, a political scientist who taught self-management in the socialist Slovenia, was appointed by the Slovenian Chamber of Commerce as the new director of an entity that provided courses to leaders of economic enterprises in former Yugoslavia. Purg changed the name of this entity into International Executive Development Center (IEDC) with the goal to develop an educational institution that would truly serve the needs of executives and help them restructure socialist enterprises (Purg and Filipović 1993). According to Purg, she did not receive any official approval for her plan from the Communist Party and many were suspicious about her efforts. She remembers the day when she started the job as "a cold day" not only because it was in February but also because of the general atmosphere she encountered. As Purg proceeded with her goals, she did not face any direct political resistance from Party officials. This may be because Purg quickly garnered support from some of the key members of the Slovenian business elite by taking the time to go and personally speak to 25 top executives of the largest Slovenian companies, asking them to suggest the kind of knowledge and training they thought they needed in the process of transforming their enterprises. Even if the image of the Iron Curtain suggested strict separation of the capitalist West and communist East, several Slovenian companies had well established trading relations with the West before 1989 and so had come into contact with Western managerial practices. They were on board with Purg's plan to offer management courses so that their support boosted the legitimacy of the effort in the eyes of the communist elite. Moreover, according to Purg, the officials went along naïvely because they could not fully envision the consequences that IEDC activities would have on broader Slovenian economic transformations.

As a charismatic and highly entrepreneurial individual, Purg took the initiative to visit prominent West European management schools and attend international conferences, where she gathered information on management education. One of the first places she visited was the oldest European management school, INSEAD in France, where she asked the dean to recommend a professor who would be interested in teaching at IEDC "not for money but for the experience." INSEAD's dean at that time recommended one of the school's professors, a German by origin, who was intrigued by the possibility to teach in the East. He became the first visiting professor at IEDC and asked for no payment for his teaching there.[1]

FOREIGN INFLUENCES ON MANAGEMENT EDUCATION IN EASTERN EUROPE

Given the reform context in Slovenia before 1989, the establishment of the first management school in Central and Eastern Europe did not face any outright political resistance. Still, a management school in post-socialism could not operate without resources, including required financial capital but also faculty to staff courses and aid in curriculum development.

As in the case of IEDC, the establishment of other private management schools in Central and Eastern Europe faced a lack of domestic donors who would contribute private financial resources. As Eyal, Szelenyi, and Townsley (2001) noted, capitalism was being built without capitalists in Eastern Europe. After all, private property was abolished during communism so that individuals could not amass wealth and make a contribution to management schools as is common practice in the West. Charging high tuition fees was not feasible for the lack of private wealth as well as the fact that students were not used to paying for education, which was provided for free by the state during socialism. Therefore, it comes as no surprise that the first management schools in Central and Eastern Europe relied heavily on financial support from foreign actors, which became broadly available after the official collapse of communist regimes. West European and North American governmental and non-governmental organizations were quite keen on supporting management schools as part of the effort of economic restructuring after communism. One of the prominent financial sources was the PHARE program of the European Union. This program was one of three pre-accession instruments financed by the European Union to assist the applicant countries of Central and Eastern Europe in their preparation to join the European Union (EU 2013). Initially created to facilitate reforms in Poland and Hungary, The Poland and Hungary Action for the Restructuring of the Economy (PHARE) has since included most of Central and East European countries. The objectives of PHARE included mostly institution building and promoting convergence with the EU legislation, but its TESSA fund for Training and Education in Strategically Significant Areas was also available to support management programs. The International Trade School (ITS) in Warsaw, Poland, was among those receiving this assistance in 1994 (GSBE-HSICF 2006).

In some other cases, international funds were received from the United States Agency for International Development (USAID). Recipients of these funds included The Institute for Business and Public Administration from Bucharest (ASEBUSS) established in 1993 and KIMEP, the Kazakh Institute for Management, Economics, and Strategic Research, where getting USAID funds was facilitated by the fact that an American became its executive director in 1994 (KIMEP 2006). Other schools that received assistance from USAID included CMC (Czech Management Center), European School of Management (ESM) in Tbilisi, Georgia, IAB-International Academy of Business in Kazakhstan, Kaliningrad International Business Institute (KIBI) in Russia, and UIB-University of International Business, Kazakhstan.

To receive assistance from PHARE or USAID, the budding management schools in Central and Eastern Europe had to propose programs and structures approved by these organizations and often needed support from Western educational institutions in this process. For instance, IMC partnered with the University of Pittsburgh, the Czech Management Center with Tulane University, and the International School of Management in Lithuania with the Norwegian School of Management. In fact, provision of joint degrees with business schools from the West was quite widespread. This brings us to another crucial set of resources needed for the establishment and operation of management schools in Central and Eastern Europe: faculty and curricula.

Faculty and Curricula

"By far the most critical difficulty in the transfer of business education to the reforming economies is the lack of qualified, trained faculty to teach executive education and MBA programs" (Madhavan and Fogel 1992). Next to financial capital, management schools in Central and Eastern Europe needed academics and professionals able to develop a management curriculum and conduct instruction on market economies and private enterprises. These were offered not as part of regular university programs but mostly as courses that practicing economic actors, who had already finished their university education during socialism, could take to upgrade their knowledge, including executive training programs and the flagship management education program, the MBA. This was the case also for IEDC.

As noted above, Purg managed to lure an INSEAD professor to come and lecture without a fee and become the first IEDC professor of management. Later on this person recommended other colleagues from INSEAD. Moreover, Purg established connections to faculty at IMD, one of the top European business schools, located in Lausanne. She relied on a network of her husband, who was a Dutch professor of management. Twenty-five years later, in 2013, among the 26 professors listed on the IEDC's website as many as 20 are still visiting professors from places like INSEAD, IMD, Richard Ivey School of Business from Canada, and IESE, a top Spanish business school.

In one of the first reports on budding management education in Central and Eastern Europe, Drew concluded that "several North American and West European management schools [had] assisted in the foundation of Western-style management schools in Central and Eastern Europe" (Drew 1994: 7) by establishing joint degrees or lending their faculty to come and teach courses, which significantly shaped the type of curriculum that these schools offered. My data also show that *all* of the first 30 schools established from 1986 to 1993, for which I have survey and/or online information, involved foreign faculty in their courses and help from foreign business schools in designing the curriculum. While initially foreign faculty were the only ones who could teach courses on market economy subjects (given that this knowledge was not accumulated, but prohibited, during socialism), it became then clear that the lists of foreign faculty also enhanced the legitimacy of schools. As the officials of the Leon Kozminski Academy of Entrepreneurship and Management in Warsaw wrote on their website, "the Academy has a 50 percent rule for the participation of foreign professors in programs taught in English. At least 50 percent of the professors come from the United Kingdom, USA and Canada" (WSPIZ 2006). Statements such as these signal that having foreign faculty, especially from places with a long management education history such as the U.S., has been a sign of prestige and an important promotion tool to attract prospective students.

The role of Western actors was crucial in professionalizing management education in Eastern Europe. Most of the East European schools quickly tried to become members of either AACSB International—The Association of Advanced Collegiate Schools of Business, International, with headquarters in the U.S.; the Executive MBA Council, also based in the U.S.; and/ or EFMD, the European Forum for Management Development based in Brussels. The AACSB is a non-profit organization of educational institutions, corporations, and other organizations devoted to the promotion and improvement of higher education in business administration and management. As its website purports, "[the] Association's growing membership outside the U.S. provides new opportunities and challenges for AACSB International as it expands its role as a source of information, training and networking for management educators" (AACSB International 2005). The Executive MBA Council offers a professional forum to schools with MBA programs in order to "strengthen the bonds among Executive and Professional MBA Programs throughout the world and [contribute] to the advancement of executive education" (EMBA 2005). EFMD is

[an] international membership organization, based in Brussels, Belgium. With more than 600 member organizations from academia, business, public service and consultancy in 70 countries, EFMD provides a unique forum for information, research, networking and debate on innovation and best practice in management development. EFMD is recognized globally as an accreditation body of quality in management

education and has established accreditation services for management schools and management school programmes, corporate universities and technology-enhanced learning programmes.

(EFMD 2013b)

As of 2011, 50 schools from Central and Eastern Europe and the former Soviet Union were EFMD members, including some public universities that offer MBA programs. However, by 2010, only one of the post-socialist private school members had also received EFMD's accreditation EQUIS ("the world's leading international accreditation of business schools," EFMD 2013a), namely the Leon Kozminski Academy from Poland, which was granted the seal in 2005. As one academic director from a school that seriously considered trying for EQUIS explained to me,[2] it has been very difficult for private schools in Central and Eastern Europe to pass the requirement of having a requisite number of home faculty with appropriate distinctions, given that they have relied so heavily on visiting professors from the West. He added that the appeal of possessing the EQUIS accreditation could be explained by the considerable legitimacy this seal provided to potential students when they selected the school to attend. Moreover, it contributed to an increase in the overall reputation of a school in the national and international community.

The influence of Western institutions is also obvious on management schools' websites. Of the 56 schools whose websites I reviewed, 29 provided some indication of foreign connections on the first page of their website, mostly by displaying the logos of their Western partners or from international associational memberships. Additionally, 25 out of 48 schools that included this information either on a survey or website mentioned that they had already established joint programs (most often MBA programs) with North American or West European schools. Overwhelmingly, the schools report that many professors who teach in their courses come from foreign countries (44 out of 45 schools). Moreover, schools highlight other cooperations with foreign actors or international organizations in fields such as curricula development, joint research projects, and community initiatives. This was mentioned by 37 out of 56 organizations on their websites and by 30 out of 32 organizations that responded to the survey. Based on this evidence, I conclude that management education would have not taken hold in post-socialism as quickly as it did and in the form it did were it not for the significant role of foreign actors. One might wonder whether such emphasis on the foreign influence is unique to post-socialist Europe. After all, American influence already weighed heavily on the institutionalization of management education in other parts of the world, given that the very first management school originated in the U.S. and was established in 1881, when James Wharton commissioned the Wharton School of Finance and Economy at the University of Pennsylvania. The establishment of the University of Chicago Graduate School of Business followed in 1898. In

Western Europe, a small number of business schools were established in the early 20th century and their growth intensified from the 1950s onwards (Engwall 1992). The Masters of Business Administration (MBA), the signature product of business schools, was first offered in 1908 at the Graduate School of Business Administration at Harvard. The first European MBA program was established at INSEAD, a prominent French business school, in 1958 (Daniel 1998). According to Hedmo et al. (2006: 314), the establishment of business education in Western Europe was influenced by the U.S. as "some programs arose from collaboration between European management education providers and their US partners; others were formed as the European management education providers imitated well-known programs or widespread models and guidelines." Furthermore, Fourcade and Khurana (2013: 211) have shown, for the U.S. from the 1960s onwards, the rise of "the Chicago-style" economic approaches in business schools, "offering support for anti-regulatory approaches and popularizing narrowly financial understandings of the firm . . . that sociologists have described as characteristic of the modern neo-liberal regime." Hence, the links between American and West European business schools helped spreading a broadly legitimated neoliberal management education in the West, followed by its import into Eastern Europe some 30 years later, when management education took off in that region.

There are nevertheless some notable differences between the rise of management education in the "Old" and the "New" Europe. Most obviously, it is the sheer scope of foreign influence that is remarkable in the post-socialist region, including the phases of institutional entrepreneurship, resource provision, peer awareness, and professionalization. The strength of this foreign influence can be explained, on the one side, by the introduction of management into a context where all market institutions had still to be built and, on the other side, by a process that happened in a time of international foreign investment expansion in the late 1980s, when established management education organizations in the West were actively looking for targets abroad. This development is very different from management education in the 1950s. Moreover, the world system of power relations between regions cannot be ignored (Wallerstein 1974). The diffusion of management education from the U.S. to Europe encompasses processes between major world powers. In contrast, post-socialist countries may be characterized as developing states situated in the semi-periphery according to Wallerstein's notions. The dependency relations that others have documented for industrial processes (Frank 1969, Cardoso and Falletto 1979) come to the fore also in management education as part of a cultural and socioeconomic globalization process. The unequal power relation between the influencer and the influenced, especially after the fall of communism, has led to a receptive local environment of political and economic power and legitimacy and therefore to a lower, although by no means absent, domestic resistance among the new political elites.[3]

In brief, management education in post-socialism occurred at a juncture when North American and West European business schools are in bloom and, along with the rise of neoliberal globalization in the late 1980s, ready to provide their products to international audiences. They find Eastern European elites in a dire need for financial, professional, human, and instructional resources to impart management knowledge on fledging market actors.

Nevertheless, a picture of direct transposition of Western-style management to Eastern Europe needs to be balanced by management education efforts developed within the region and, in particular, through the role of CEEMAN, the key regional management development association. This is where I turn next.

ROLES OF REGIONAL PROFESSIONAL ASSOCIATIONS: BEYOND NEOLIBERAL MANAGEMENT?

In the process of building management education in post-socialism, the newly established schools within the region also created a regional Central and East European Management Development Association, CEEMAN, "established in 1993 with the aim of accelerating and improving management development in Central and Eastern Europe" (CEEMAN 2013a). CEEMAN activities include annual conferences and deans and directors meetings, the organization of the IMTA (International Management Teachers Academy) for educators in the region, and case-writing seminars and competitions. As I attended the first few CEEMAN conferences in Slovenia in 1993 and in Poland in 1994, I could observe networking and sharing of experience among participants, which is a central function that this professional organization initially played and one clearly laid out in CEEMAN's Charter: "to provide a network and meeting place for management and business schools from Central and Eastern Europe in order to promote cooperation in the following fields: school organization and management; research projects and programmes [sic]; faculty development, exchange of teachers, students and staff; organization of conferences, round tables and meetings; development of curricula; exchange of information and ideas" (CEEMAN 2013a). Sixty-three participants, including representatives from Croatia, Estonia, Hungary, Latvia, Lithuania, Poland, Romania, Russia, the Slovak Republic, and Slovenia attended the 1994 conference. There were also attendees from Western Europe and the U.S., including a representative of the Eastern European Enterprise Network from the College of Business Administration at the University of Maine, an official from the International Labor Office in Geneva, three from two management schools in France, and one from Germany. The registration fee for the conference could be waived or reduced in cases of need, in particular for East European participants.

CEEMAN established soon its own International Quality Accreditation system (http://www.ceeman.org/accreditation) in order to grant "a seal of approval" to management schools that abide by certain criteria, including specific admission requirements, student size and profile, faculty size and profile, program contents, infrastructure, international orientation, and business community relations. Through its accreditation activities, CEEMAN played a role in enforcing professional norms and structuring the management education field in the post-socialist region. The director of CEEMAN informed me that the association developed its own accreditation system because it had been very hard for East European schools to get accredited by Western management accreditation agencies, which many attempted several times. Some of the reasons were lack of own faculty, reliance on visiting faculty from abroad, and underdeveloped research activities.

Initiatives launched by the regional associations, such as CEEMAN, have attempted to lessen the foreign influence, develop management programs that are designed specifically for post-socialist conditions, and aim to train professors from the region to lead such courses. For instance, with support from the Open Society Institute headed by George Soros, CEEMAN launched in 2000 the International Management Teachers Academy (IMTA) with the explicit purpose to train junior management faculty from post-socialist countries in the field of management (CEEMAN 2013b). In 1998, CEEMAN established its own accreditation label, the International Quality Accreditation (IQA) to "help schools in Central and Eastern Europe to do the things they need to do to improve business education in this part of the world" (Kudar 2011), according to the words of the IQA director, Randy Kudar. However, at the point of writing, all but one faculty member teaching these junior management professors from Central and Eastern Europe come from the West, from IMD (Switzerland) and IESE (Spain) business schools. The president of IQA and its director are based at the ESMT—European School of Management and Technology in Germany (and formerly at IMD Lausanne) for the first and Richard Ivey School of Business in Canada for the second. These efforts at self-sufficiency of management education in formerly socialist countries co-exist with the development of management education as a transnational global project (Hedmo et al. 2006).

Moreover, in recent years, the Central and East European Management Development Association (CEEMAN) has tried to "promote leadership for change, global competitiveness and social responsibility, innovation and creativity, and respect for cultural values" (CEEMAN 2013a). Consistent with these activities, IEDC managed to attract funding to hold the "Sustainable Development Chair," financed by Coca-Cola Company, and is currently trying to obtain necessary financing for the "Arts and Leadership Chair" (IEDC 2013). IEDC has supported business ethics as part of its required curriculum since 1991 (Delo 2013). More recently, IEDC has advocated for "using art as tool of personal leadership development" and has offered an Arts and Leadership module to its MBA students, which connects art and leadership to personal development in order to foster reflection, critical thinking, and creativity. Artists are invited as lecturers/

performers in the program, including film directors, orchestra conductors, musicians, actors, poets, and sculptors. The faculty director responsible for the arts and leadership module is himself a concert pianist and professor of leadership. It is also clear that this initiative is strongly supported by IEDC Dean Professor Purg, who commented in a recent interview for *The Financial Times* (April 8, 2013):

> I am inspired by art. Bringing the arts and business together has long been a passion of mine. I feel art is essential to having rich experiences, a life full of meaning. I have always wanted to impart this to those with whom I work: our students, staff and faculty. The integration of art and art experience in education has been a focus of our school from its beginnings, but especially for the past 10 years. The inspiration for this approach to leadership development is a deep-rooted belief that art helps us. As the celebrated professor Edgar Schein said: "Art is helping us to see more, hear more, and to feel more."

IEDC and CEEMAN are also actively cooperating with the United Nations Global Compact (UNGC). This initiative (http://www.unglobalcompact.org) is the world's largest global corporate responsibility and sustainability initiative. According to UNGC, "Academia adds critical dimensions to the Compact's operations. Through research and educational resources, this sector can increase knowledge and understanding of corporate citizenship. In addition, academia plays an important role in shaping future business leaders and educating them on the importance of responsible citizenship" (UN Global Compact 2013).

The Slovenian chapter of the UN Global Compact was established in 2007 at the initiative of Professor Purg. In early 2013, it was announced that Professor Purg took over as Chair of the PRME—Principles for Responsible Management Education initiative of the UN Global Compact, as the first person from Central and Eastern Europe. At the occasion of her election, Purg said, "in times of economic crisis, accompanied by the crisis of values, ethics, morals and responsible leadership become especially important" (Delo 2013).

In sum, there exists some evidence that management education promoted by CEEMAN and practiced at IEDC goes beyond neoliberal managerialism with a self-interested focus on profit-making. The focus on responsible leadership, sustainability, and business ethics has been made central to CEEMAN's and IEDC's agenda. Admittedly, we should not automatically assume that it is also prevailing among East European management schools more generally and that it is easily translatable into managerial behavior. Still, given that professional organizations structure the organizational field (DiMaggio and Powell 1983) in which individual management schools are located, we can take this as a sign of possible diffusion of these sustainability principles across the organizational field.

CONCLUDING REMARKS

The establishment of management schools at the end of the Central and East European socialism was a sign of social change in the region. The first management school was established in Slovenia a few years before 1989, and, in hindsight, could be seen as a harbinger of the large-scale socioeconomic transformations to come. Soon after the collapse of communist regimes, after the fall of the Berlin wall, management education institutions proliferated throughout the region. Today, the main regional management association, CEEMAN, has more than 200 members, and there exist other regional management development organizations, including the Baltic Management Development Association, BMDA (69 members by 2012), the Polish Association of Management Education, FORUM (22 members by 2012), the Russian Association for Business Educators, RABE (128 members by 2006), and the Central Asian Foundation for Management Development, CAMAN (56 members by 2001). Management programs, in particular MBA degrees, are also offered in public universities. Similar to the West (Khurana 2010), the demand for MBA degrees has increased in Central and Eastern Europe since the early 1990s. While data on the total number of people graduating from these management schools is not available, the numbers are not trivial: The dean of IEDC-Bled School of Management told me in 2005 that 33,500 managers have attended the school's programs between 1986 and 2004. To put this in context, one has to know that the school offers only graduate-level education and executive management programs, has just 30 permanent employees, and is located in one of the smallest post-socialist countries with less than 2 million inhabitants. As studies in West European and American business schools are still very expensive for East European standards, and many programs in Eastern Europe are modular and allow full time employment, they are quite attractive to potential students.

My evidence from case studies, surveys, content analysis of online material, and participant observation has shown that the rise of management education in post-socialism was mainly influenced by a variety of foreign actors. Aid from USAID and the European Union, the integration into American and European professional management associations, and connections to business schools from these countries have helped spread not only management education but its neoliberal managerialism kind that was on the rise in the late 1980s. The establishment of management education in post-socialism happened concurrently with the embrace of "Chicago-style" economic approaches in American business schools (Fourcade and Khurana 2013) and the rise of market fundamentalism (Somers and Block 2005) and financialization (Krippner 2005, Davis 2009), which took off after the codification of neoliberal principles in the Washington Consensus in the late 1980s (Gore 2000). This process went hand-in-hand with the more or less wholehearted embrace of liberal market models in post-1989 Central and Eastern Europe (Srubar 1996, Orenstein 2009, Stuckler et al. 2009).

Whether this "dependency" of post-socialist management education on the West may be waning in the next years remains an open question. The schools have matured and are able to secure more domestic resources, in terms of finances, faculty, and curriculum. Moreover, the financial crisis of 2008 and a subsequent world economic crisis have stimulated a broader awareness of the importance of a new kind of leadership, sustainability, and corporate responsibility. The Central and East European Management Development Association has embraced these standards and is promulgating them throughout the region, with IEDC Bled School of Management as its leader. Given the appointment of IEDC Dean as a Chairperson of the United Nations Global Compact PRME, these efforts have been connected to a wider scale movement for responsible management education. To what extent these standards will remain largely professed but on paper, or will serve to undermine the prevailing neoliberal management discourse, is an open question that awaits the test of time.

NOTES

1. His teaching at IEDC was modular, for one to two weeks at a time, so that he kept his position and salary at INSEAD.
2. Field notes, IEDC-Bled School of Management, summer 2006.
3. Danica Purg recalled one case in Russia where an entrepreneur was trying to establish a private business school in the early 1990s but could not get it off the ground because he lacked local political support.

REFERENCES

AACSB International (2005) "About Us." Online at http://www.aacsb.edu/about/default.asp, accessed on March 21, 2005.

Bandelj, Nina (2008) *From Communists to Foreign Capitalists*. Princeton, NJ: Princeton University Press.

Boltanski, Luc and Eve Chiapello (2007) *The New Spirit of Capitalism*. Translated by Gregory Elliott. London, UK: Verso.

Brubaker, Rogers, Margit Feischmidt, Jon Fox, and Liana Grancea (2008) *Nationalist Politics and Everyday Ethnicity in a Transylvanian Town*. Princeton, NJ: Princeton University Press.

Čakrt, Michal (1993) "Management Education in Eastern Europe: Toward Mutual Understanding," *The Academy of Management Executive* 7 (4): 63–69.

Cardoso, Fernando H. and Enrique Falleto (1979) *Dependency and Development in Latin America*. Berkeley, CA: University of California Press.

CEEMAN (2013a) "About CEEMAN." Online at http://www.ceeman.org/about-us, accessed on July 1, 2013.

CEEMAN (2013b) "IMTA- International Management Teachers Academy." Online at http://www.ceeman.org/programs-events/imta-international-management-teachers-academy, accessed on July 1, 2013.

CEEMAN (2013c) "Meet our Members." Online at http://www.ceeman.org/about-us/ceeman-members/ceeman-institutional-members, accessed on July 1, 2013.

Daniel, Carter A. (1998) *MBA: The First Century*. Cranbury, New Jersey: Associated University Presses.

Davis, Gerald F. (2009) *Managed by the Market: How Finance Re-Shaped the Market*. Oxford, UK: Oxford University Press.

Delo (2013) "Danica Purg izvoljena v Zdruzene narode." January 23, 2013, online edition. Online at http://www.delo.si/gospodarstvo/posel/danica-purg-izvoljena-v-zdruzene-narode.html, accessed on February 20, 2013.

DiMaggio, Paul and Walter Powell (1983) "The Iron Cage Revisited: Institutional Isomorphism and Collective Rationality in Organizational Fields," *American Sociological Review* 48 (17): 147–160.

Drew, Stephen (1994) "Executive Development Observations: Prague 1993," *Journal of Management Development* 13 (3): 4–15.

Dunn, Elizabeth (2004) *Privatizing Poland: Baby Food, Big Business, and the Remaking of Labor*. Ithaca, NY: Cornell University Press.

EFMD (2013a) "Equis." Online at https://www.efmd.org/accreditation-main/equis, accessed on July 1, 2013.

EFMD (2013b) "What is EFMD." Online at https://www.efmd.org/index.php/what-is-efmd, accessed on July 1, 2013.

Elbert, Norbert (1996) "Management Education in Postsocialist Hungary: Observations on Obstacles to Reforms," *Journal of Management Education* 20 (1): 70–79.

EMBA (2005) "What We Do?" Online at http://www.emba.org/about_whatwedo.htm, accessed on March 23, 2005.

Engwall, Lars (1992) *Mercury Meets Minerva. Business Studies and Higher Education. The Swedish Case*. Oxford, UK: Pergamon Press.

EU (2013) "Phare Programme." Online at http://europa.eu/legislation_summaries/enlargement/2004_and_2007_enlargement/e50004_en.htm, accessed on July 1, 2013.

Eyal, Gil, Ivan Szelenyi, and Eleanor Townsley (2001) *Building Capitalism without Capitalists*. London, UK: Verso.

Financial Times (2013) "Interview with Danica Purg." April 8, 2013.

Fogel, Daniel (1990) "Management Education in Central and Eastern Europe and the Soviet Union," *Journal of Management Development* 9 (3): 14–20.

Fourcade, Marion and Rakesh Khurana (2013) "From Social Control to Financial Economics: The Linked Ecologies of Economics and Business in Twentieth Century America," *Theory and Society* 42 (2): 121–159.

Frank, Andre Gunder (1969) *Capitalism and Underdevelopment in Latin America: Historical Studies of Chile and Brazil*. New York: Monthly Review Press.

Gore, Charles (2000) "The Rise and Fall of the Washington Consensus as a Paradigm for Developing Countries," *World Development* 28 (5): 789–804.

GSBE-HSICF (2006) "History." Online at http://www.wshifm.edu.pl/history.php, accessed on March 9, 2006.

Hamm, Patrick, Lawrence King, and David Stuckler (2012) "Mass Privatization, State Capacity, and Economic Growth in Post-communist Countries: Firm- and Country-Level Evidence," *American Sociological Review* 77 (2): 295–324.

Hedmo, Linda, Kerstin Sahlin-Andersson, and Linda Wedlin (2006) "The Emergence of a European Regulatory Field of Management Education," in Marie-Laure Djelic and Kerstin Sahlin-Andersson (eds) *Transnational Governance: Institutional Dynamics of Regulation*, pp. 308–328. Cambridge, UK: Cambridge University Press.

Horvat, Branko (1976) *The Yugoslav Economic System: The First Labor-Managed Economy in the Making*. White Plains, NY: International Arts and Sciences Press.

IEDC (2013) "History of IEDC." Online at http://www.iedc.si/about-iedc/history, accessed on May 8, 2013.

Imre, Aniko and Ginette Verstraete (2009) "Media Globalization and Post-socialist Identities." *European Journal of Cultural Studies* 12 (2): 131–135.

Jacoby, Wade (2004) *The Enlargement of the European Union and NATO*. Cambridge, UK: Cambridge University Press.

Kenny, Brian and Bob Trick (1994) "Developing Management Education in the Former Communist Countries of Europe," *European Business Review* 94 (1): 30–39.

Khurana, Rakesh (2010) *From Higher Aims to Hired Hands: The Social Transformation of American Business Schools and the Unfulfilled Promise of Management as a Profession*. Princeton, NJ: Princeton University Press.

KIMEP (2006) "The Kazakhstan Institute of Management, Economics, and Strategic Research." Online at http://www.kimep.kz/, accessed on March 9, 2006.

King, Lawrence P. and Aleksandra Sznajder (2006) "The State Led Transition to Liberal Capitalism," *American Journal of Sociology* 112 (3): 751–801.

Kornai, Janos (1992) *Socialist System: Political Economy of Communism*. Princeton, NJ: Princeton University Press.

Krippner, Greta (2005) "The Financialization of the American Economy," *Socio-Economic Review* 3 (2): 173–208.

Kudar, Randy (2011) "How Well are Accreditations Reflecting New Challenges." Online at http://video.ceeman.org/lectures/226/2010_ceemanddm_caserta_kudar_accee, accessed on May 11, 2011.

Madhavan, Ravindranath and Daniel Fogel (1992) "In Support of Reform: Western Business Education in Central and Eastern Europe," *Review of Business* 13 (4): 4–10. Online at http://www.freepatentsonline.com/article/Review-Business/12847003.html, accessed on July 1, 2013.

Nee, Victor and Sonja Opper (2012) *Capitalism From Below*. Cambridge, MA: Harvard University Press.

Orenstein, Mitchell (2009) "What Happened in East European (Political) Economies? A Balance Sheet for Neoliberal Reform," *East European Politics and Societies* 23 (4): 479–490.

Przeworski, Adam (1991) *Democracy and the Market*. Cambridge, UK: Cambridge University Press.

Purg, Danica (1997) "Management Development in Central and Eastern Europe," in *The Directory of MBAs*, pp. 30–31. 2nd ed. London: Edward More O'Ferrall.

Purg, Danica (1999) "Management Development and MBAs in Central and Eastern Europe," in *MBA Casebook 2000: Management Degrees at the World's Top Management Schools*, pp. 44–45. London: Hopsons.

Purg, Danica and Nenad Filipović (1993) "Management Development in Slovenia," *EFMD Brussels* 2: 36–37.

Ritzer, George (1993) *The McDonaldization of Society*. Thousand Oaks, CA: Sage.

Shevchenko, Olga (2009) *Crisis and the Everyday in Postsocialist Moscow*. Bloomington, IN: Indiana University Press.

Somers, Margaret and Fred Block (2005) "From Poverty to Perversity: Ideas, Markets, and Institutions over 200 Years of Welfare Debate," *American Sociological Review* 70 (2): 260–287.

Srubar, Ivo (1996) "Neoliberalism, Transformation and Civil Society," *Thesis Eleven* 47 (1): 33–47.

Stark, David and Balazs Vedres (2010) "Structural Folds: Generative Disruption in Overlapping Groups," *American Journal of Sociology* 115 (4): 1150–1190.

Stuckler, David, Martin McKee, and Lawrence King (2009) "Mass Privatisation and the Post-communist Mortality Crisis: A Cross-national Analysis," *The Lancet* 373 (9661): 399–407.

Swader, Christopher (2013) *The Capitalist Personality*. London: Routledge.

UN Global Compact (2013) "Participants & Stakeholders." Online at http://www.unglobalcompact.org/ParticipantsAndStakeholders/academic_participation.html, accessed on May 9, 2013.

Wallerstein, Immanuel (1974) *The Modern World System*. New York: Academic Press.

WSPIZ (2006). "What Makes Us Different?" Online at http://www.kozminski.edu.pl/pl/, accessed on July 1, 2013.

3 New Working Norms and Social Relations in Poland

The Example of a Transnational Company[1]

Antoine Heemeryck

For numerous reasons, Poland represents a very interesting case study for the social sciences. First, the country was under a communist regime for more than 40 years. Second, at the international level, its position depended on issues that opposed two major actors: the Soviet Bloc and Western societies. Since 1989, Poland has been considered a member of the post-communist "transition" economies. In particular, following in the footstep of the U.S., Great Britain, and Argentina, Poland is one of the first East European countries to have implemented "shock therapy," meaning neoliberal policies after 1989. As a result, in addition to erasing its debt to Western countries, the country received immediate massive funding in order to transform its economy following the end of the communist regime. As a result the country rapidly welcomed international economic investors, particularly European and American and a significant number of multinational companies. For this, Poland has been seen as a "good student" by international institutions, unlike other counterparts in the region such as Romania (Heemeryck 2010).

The transformation of the socioeconomic fabric has been marked by the importation of new methods of organizing work in terms of production, accounting, human resource management, and by the introduction of Western management methods. These techniques create a specific rationality in a terminology of power that includes the society as a whole. On a schematic level, one could argue that its main objective has been to submit reality to a cost/benefit calculation. This implies the imposition of a power structure aimed at organizing social relations in the same way that may be considered as a form of domination operating according to a technical register.

These general observations should not obscure the specificities linked to implementing this technology across the whole social spectrum. Among the social fields (in the sense defined by Bourdieu in 1985) impacted by this imposition, companies are the most vulnerable ones submitted to this new wave of profound change.

Once the arena for the forceful exercise of power and the ideology of the party-state, and for those forces that opposed it (in particular the trade union *Solidarność*), Polish companies now represent social environments favorable to the emergence of new global political issues (Bazin and Sélim

2001). Accordingly, one can here observe links between different social groups that would otherwise remain socially and spatially distant. Since it allows for the study of the internalization of the forms of work organization and the contradictions they generate, a company is a relevant framework for the study of contemporary social transformations.

My attempt to at least partially elucidate these dynamics of transformation implies a closer look at the mutations of the means of power legitimization or imposition, of hierarchies and domination through the changes in the political and economic regimes. As such, the tools of political anthropology will be mobilized. In this chapter, I study the internalization of these global movements based on the case study of a company in Poland. After a brief presentation of the company, I first discuss the relationship between the employees and foreign management. Then I explain the forms of crossed allegations, of de-legitimization among the employees, which are structured by the dichotomy of communist versus competent. Finally, I analyze how workers attempt to create a local union to supposedly both shape and strengthen their claims. This research was conducted in collaboration with Sébastien Cordeau as part of a larger study that included the study of two companies, as well as a part of the reconstituted transnational aristocratic elite.[2] Both social anthropologists appear intermittently in this chapter.

This investigation started with a cross-examination of all categories of employees in a specific company and their relations within this framework. From a methodological point of view, the company is considered a social field with a minimum of autonomy (Althabe and Sélim 1998). This hypothesis leads me to take into account the fact that this subject cannot be artificially separated from global society as a whole as it is a mirror image of its evolutions. In return, my interrogation doesn't dissolve it either; my approach follows as a main line the structuration of social relations in this particular company.

It is important to observe that field research of this type is uncommon in Poland. On the contrary, during the period leading up to EU accession, research in social sciences or development addressed subjects such as "the construction of elites" in order to implement "economic mechanisms" or to "assert the interests of Poland in the European Union in preparation for integration." Such research strategies are still popular in Poland.[3] This trend reflects the internalization of a global stigma and therefore a form of domination between countries that still need to integrate into the European Union and countries that are already integrated, the latter being considered socially, morally, politically, and economically legitimate models. From this point of view, post-communism is still dependent on Cold War ideology.

A Belgian entrepreneur created PUP (Production Unit in Poland[4]) in 1993–1994. The company produces lower cost goods (heavy transport equipment) for European Union markets and has 68 employees.

This company, "imported" from abroad as part of a strategy of wage cuts and increased fiscal earnings, is a pertinent example to examine the problem of methods of power legitimation, of their entanglement, and of the relationship to the symbolic figure of the "foreigner." The on-site investigation lasted three weeks in May 2001. Fifteen formal interviews were conducted, and our continued presence in the company offered the opportunity for numerous fruitful discussions with employees.

PUP is currently located between Krakow and Katowice, near the town of Olkusz. To reach the company, it is necessary to drive two kilometers along an old road, where a few old homes are bordered by rather dense vegetation. The road ends at an industrial complex at the outskirts of a small forest. This aged complex is fairly representative of large derelict construction sites that can be found in industrial areas, such as the Upper Silesian basin. PUP is situated there amid buildings that once constituted a Soviet production center. After 1989, the site was dismantled and several buildings sold. This project of industrial dismantlement was, on a broader political level, part of the "shock therapy," the strategy of accelerated privatization carried out by Leszek Balcerowicz (also called the "Balcerowicz plan"). At that time, he was the Minister of Finance in a government led by a well-known former member of *Solidarność*: Tadeusz Mazowiecki.

PUP was not among the first companies operating on the site. In 1995, it was located in Krakow. Given the constant rent increases, the owner and director (Philippe V.), a Belgian citizen and resident, decided to transfer the production unit in order to take advantage of a tax incentive policy.

The owner also benefitted from the opportunity to dissolve the company's union, which was considered too rebellious. From 1997 onward, machines and materials began to arrive from Krakow. From the outset, the company sold most of its products to a Belgian company owned by the director and owner of PUP. A large majority of products manufactured in the factory are exported. "We export to Belgium and the Belgians sell to the French and Dutch. We also sell a little in Poland," testifies an employee of the Polish management. In fact, exports account for over 90 percent of turnover. This Western company, like many others, was created to profit from lower production costs, in particular the cheap workforce. PUP can be considered an extension of the Belgian company. Although legally it is not a subsidiary, both companies have the same owner and founder, Philippe V. In fact, Poland represents an opportunity for companies in Western Europe to generate profits while maintaining a good "brand," "offering" stable paid jobs to a portion of the population in a country that had an official unemployment rate of 18.3 percent in January 2001 and 10.5 percent in November 2012[5] (according to Eurostat).

The company presents itself as a center of production mainly dependent on the Western market, indirectly part of a large Belgian company considered a European leader in its field. Orders keep coming in; the factory produces accordingly. The goods and money flows highlight an objective dependency on the Western European market. Karel B., a young Belgian general manager of the company, represents this "foreign" presence within the company. He is an intermediary between the company owner and the local staff.

COMPANY PRESENTATION AND INTRODUCTION

Three people work in the office section of the company: the executive secretary [Karolina P.], the production manager [Antek R.], and the graphic designer (who is also in charge of administrative tasks) [Monika C.]. The office of Karel B., the Belgian manager, adjoins this area. In the workshop, there are two "teams" of 30 people led by a "team-leader," the equivalent of a foreman/supervisor. Finally, a delivery driver comes once or twice a week before each delivery to Benelux, the multinational firm belonging to the owner of PUP, who buys the products.

Initial Contact with PUP Employees

At our arrival at PUP, Karel B., the manager, awaited us in his office in the early afternoon. After a detailed presentation of the methods of our investigation, Karel B. introduced us to the employees of PUP: first, to those working in what he called the "secretariat" who welcomed us politely. Smiling, the manager told the employees: "Everything is anonymous, so you can talk about all your frustrations." Next, he went along to present the production part of the company. Workers were busy with their tasks in a deafening noise. We followed the production chain while Karel B. was explaining how it functioned and the purpose of the different workshops. The decay and the height of the building, which amplified the noise, were shocking at first. This large space accommodated all the machinery needed for the various stages of production: cutting, welding, painting, and finishing. The space served as storage unit as well, taking over at least a quarter of the area, and used to stock the finished products. The tour ended with the locker room of the company where workers also have their meals. The four people working in the office have their lunch outside of the company premises or in the "secretariat," separated from the workers.

The Figure of the Foreigner

Born in a modest Benelux family, Karel B. (30 years old at the time of the study) graduated with the equivalent of a Higher Technician Certificate (HTC) in management. Free of family obligations, after several years serving in another branch of the Belgian company, he decided to seize the opportunity to become a manager in the Polish branch. The salary, the professional experience, and the "discovery" of Poland were his major motivations. But more than a mere decision, his expatriation has been the hallmark of a career development strategy. Master of his own schedule, it was not uncommon for him to be absent for the day for reasons unrelated to his professional responsibilities. It should be noted here that because of the similarity in age and language with the researchers (he speaks French), he is unsuspicious and confesses that he sometimes partakes in more entertaining activities. Only partially committed to his work, Karel B. represents above all the figure of the foreigner in the company. Although he sometimes addresses the workers during the rare inspections in the production workshop, he usually counts on Antek R. to make sure his instructions are followed; at times, he does directly address the team-leaders in rough Polish. His management position is effective only in the sense that his job provides a link between the Belgian company and the production unit based in Poland. Thus, his presence is a constant reminder to employees that the business depends on a foreign company. It is also remarkable that Karolina P. repeatedly calls him "Big Brother," the executive secretary making reference here to the popular global television show. Whether the reference is *1984* by George Orwell or the *Wielki Brat* television program,[6] the allusion implied by the name is that of a "camera," permanent scrutiny, and constant monitoring. Hence, the executive secretary expresses the position of Karel B. who acts as the eyes of Philippe V.

Polarized Introductions

The beginning of the investigation was marked by the absence of Karel B. The three actors in the office courteously received the first ethnologist (Antoine Heemeryck, called A in order to be distinguished from the second investigator, Sebastian Cordeau, called B); two women (Karolina P. and Monika C.) and a man (Antek R.) operated in this space. These actors were enthusiastic about the investigator (A), to the point that the executive secretary introduced him to the workers without being asked to do so. Karolina P. eagerly invited the observer to follow her to the workers' locker room, which proved to be in an advanced state of decay. It was the moment of the day when shifts changed, so while some were preparing to begin their working day, others hastened to leave. Karolina P. invited the workers to cease their activities for a few moments in order to be introduced to the French social anthropologist. The latter then briefly explained the purpose of the investigation to the workers and spontaneously invited one of them to answer a few questions. Once again, the scene took place in the workers' locker room. The man interviewed (Pavel P.) was in his 40s. When confronted with the possibility of recording the interview, he retorted:

PAVEL D.: *No, no. Eh!* [He turned to the other workers] *you never know where they will send it* [slightly nervous laughing]. (Interviewed on May 7, 2001)

However, he did not express any reluctance in answering the questions. But, the introduction by the secretary gave him an opportunity to harbor both fictitious and real suspicions, explicitly assumed, *vis-à-vis* the claims of the interviewer, which he openly expressed. Furthermore, Karolina P. used my presence to attempt to impose her authority on the workers in a space she otherwise never entered. She interfered in the area reserved for workmen in an authoritarian and demonstrative manner, such as a leader, entitled to go wherever she wants. Presenting both the study and its objectives, which she only superficially understood, she created a situation at the very least difficult for me. Caught in the web of internal relations within the company, the social anthropologist (A) involuntarily found himself immersed in a close relationship with company management. However, it was this same authority that the workers contested in front of him.

The second investigator (A), also French, introduced himself to the workers. The scene took place in the locker room of the workshop. In the center of the room was a desk that was used as table where most of the discussions took place. Surprised by the presence of a "foreigner," workers quickly confronted the social anthropologist with numerous questions and requests for clarification. They were mainly interested in the cost of living in France and, in response to my questions, they asked for clarifications on the possibility of creating a union. But, the conversation quickly turned to a general uproar. Finally, the roles were reversed and the social anthropologist was repeatedly thanked for the information he provided to the workers (workers' wages, bank loan rates in France, etc.). Given that shift change took place, the room was filled with employees leaving their jobs. The following is an excerpt of this first contact.

RAPHAO Z.:   *Here, when I arrived, there was no union. But, before, in the foundry, there had been one.*

PIOTR P.:   *There should be a union in the company, but an independent one, because. . . .*

LESZEK R.:   Cutting him off: *The union should be by sector because if it is within the company, that may create conflicts with the boss.*

PIOTR P.:   *And in France?*

A.H.:   Unions have some power, but there are unions by sector, unions at the national level, and there are also collective agreements. There are quite a few strikes, and they are important. Strikes are popular in France.

PIOTR P.:   *Yes, we know.*

LESZEK R.:   *Sometimes in France, the workers have no contact with the administration. Not even education allows one to reach the ceiling. But if everyone has a university degree then who will work for those who have a university degree? We have to think about it.*

PIOTR P.:   *How much does a French worker make?*

A.H.:   If one works 35 hours a week, because usually it's 35 hours or 39 hours in France, one makes approximately 1,000 €.

PIOTR P.:   *What is the cost of living for a Frenchman who benefits from social housing? The rent? The phone? The electricity? That is*

	the basis for life. Even the car is not essential. How much is it in a month? Is € 1,000 per month enough for a living?
A.H.:	Yes, a living. But, that kind of a living depends on the situation.
LESZEK R.:	*It is tragic compared to Poland and to our wages.*
A.H.:	Is the situation difficult in Poland?
LESZEK R.:	*I earn 1,200 zlotys[7] per month. The flat costs 700, the telephone 100, the electricity 60, the nursery 200. For the rest, there is no money, there is no more [money]. It's my wife who earns the money for our food.*
PIOTR P.:	*Are loans in France high? What is the rate for.* . . . (Interviewed on May 7, 2001)

The question of the presence of a union in the company was not without influence on the positions adopted by the actors. They made a comparison between their standards of living as workers in Poland and those of French workers. In order to do so, they first had to identify themselves with the figure of the foreigner. Thereafter, I could share a close relationship with the workers.

When entering into the office, the social anthropologist (A) attracted furtive dirty looks from Karolina P., the executive secretary. Later, on some occasions, she was uncooperative with the interviewer, for example, when he asked for access to the archives, access already authorized by the general manager and the owner. Often, without ever obviously displaying any ill thought, she would delay the delivery of documents (about the company statutes, the turnover, etc.). This behavior, along with signs of hostility, was observed only toward the second investigator; but in the same way workers did not show much enthusiasm with the first social anthropologist. In the office, the opinions about the investigators being in special relationships with different members of the company were so opposed that sometimes they wondered if they really worked together and on the same issue.

This differentiated introduction of both investigators was based on a previously established strategy. Accordingly, the first social anthropologist was meant to launch his research mission from the management level of the company and then gradually extend it to the workers. As for the second social anthropologist, he was supposed to follow the opposite route. This configuration determined the relationships with PUP employees. First, it indicated the determination of Karolina P. to become a part of this configuration, and to prove to social anthropologist (B) her power over the workers, which in fact, turned out to be rather ineffective. Her legitimacy was based on her proximity to the foreigner. Because he had been introduced by the executive secretary, social anthropologist (B) found himself symbolically confined by the workers to a close relationship with management. As for the second social anthropologist (A), because his introduction did not implicate the intervention of the secretary, he found himself assigned to a position of mediation between "foreigner," "Westerner," or even "European" and the workers, because the "foreign" face of the direction had no contact with this class of employee. Also, as we already noticed, social anthropologist (A) appeared to be a source of information about France and the "West," and a foreign listener to the workers' demands. By introducing himself to the workers, social anthropologist (A) inadvertently denied Karolina P. the possibility of using a form of legitimacy that she used with the other investigator (B).

This methodological experience proved to be fruitful for the investigation as it triggered a differentiation in the positions adopted by the actors in relation to the two social anthropologists. For the most part, the employees participated in the investigation and therefore identified themselves with the two young French investigators.[8]

THE RELATIONSHIP WITH FOREIGN MANAGEMENT

During our initial contacts, Karel B. and Philippe V. seemed to fear the reaction of the employees to the introduction of the investigators in the company.

> *They'll say: "Ah! Foreigners again."* (He adds speaking of the director) *He is afraid that the workers will complain about their conditions. In addition, he is afraid that it creates a bad atmosphere in the workshop, and you are French, they will ask you how you are paid in France, and they will complain about their work, you must say nothing about France or else you must reduce wages* [the real ones in order to mention lower, fictitious ones].
>
> (Karel B., interviewed on May 9, 2001)

These remarks have strong West/East overtones; they indicate the opposition between "Western Europe" and "Eastern Europe," what we call the autochthonous/allochthonous relationship. We, "French," and he, a "Belgian," are opposed to them, "the East." In fact, Karel B. plays the card of factitious complicity. These remarks show that the direction is clearly aware of the demands of the lower levels of hierarchy, demands they (Karel B. and Philippe V.) attempt to contain in one way or another, thus far successfully. Certainly it would have been impossible for us to censor the employees' remarks and impossible to accomplish our investigation under such conditions. In addition, the management team obviously overestimated the catalytic effect of a social-anthropological investigation of labor relations.

In the workshop, Karel B. communicated only with the team leaders, whom he likes. The flow of information between the workshop and the management in Belgium showcases the team leaders. Antek R., head of production, and Karel B., director and manager, are the ones who stay in contact with the workers. Karel B. has a poor command of Polish. In addition, all procedures besides those mentioned above—delivery of wages, payment for extra hours—that could lead to having contact with workers are provided by the Polish office employees. Karel B. carefully avoids this contact, mainly because it represents potential opportunities for the lower echelons of the company to express their demands. One can note that these "fears" refer to individual workers with whom the social distance is greater. Under such circumstances, which elements could the employees mobilize in order to legitimize the position of the foreign manager?

Post-communism as Crisis

When questioned about the evolution of Polish society, employees most often compared their current situation to the situation in other Polish companies and/or the situation of PUP when it was still in Krakow. They highlight the failures of the companies in which they worked, unemployment, and low wages.

Piotr P., laborer, 26 years old, is married and has two daughters. He has a small company that offers repair services for almost 2 years. He attempted several professions (26, he says, in trade, plumbing, auto mechanics, etc.) in the *Małopolska* area. He talks about his past professional experience and at the end concludes with a voice full of dismay:

> *I have not earned a lot of money what is the most depressing thing.* By contrast, he summarizes the current situation in these words: *I am satisfied with this job because my boss gives me a good salary. In addition, he pays on time, and for all these reasons, he is legit. Those who own a firm understand their boss. Everyone wants to earn more, but the situation is as it is. It's good to have a job. The conditions are not the best. But, I also have to work here because I have a wife and children. I want to have enough money to support my family. The biggest change is that I make more money, and that makes me happy.*
> (Interviewed on May 14, 2001)

Salaries paid on time, a salary rate that is relatively high compared to the local labor market: All these are key issues for those interviewed. These elements differ from other companies, all Polish, in which Piotr P. has worked. We remark that Piotr P. expresses a symbolic similarity with the director of PUP, since he is also the only worker who owns a business. His comments compare the past (in the other companies) to the present (PUP).

Let's listen to Monika C., graphic designer, single, 27 years old, who lives in Krakow and has worked for PUP for two and a half years.

MONIKA C.: *I used to work for a Pole. He owned a construction company. This company had a lot of financial problems and everything fell apart, it went bankrupt with a lot of debts and problems.*

A.H.: Is it better to work for a foreign-owned company?

MONIKA C.: *The most positive aspect is that a lot of orders come from the Benelux countries. Orders come three months in advance. So,*

> *I'm not afraid that the company will disappear or that orders will stop coming in, and that I lose my job. This is very important because I know that the biggest problem for Polish companies is selling products, and above all, maintaining customers, because of strong competition. Overall, there is stagnation in Poland and there is strong competition to sell anything. I think the main advantage of our company is that we are able to sell our products.* (Interviewed on May 21, 2001)

The explanation is admittedly more detailed here, but it is clearly in the exteriority, "the West," that the legitimate power stands. This sort of dependency is justified by wage stability and job security that exists in this particular company. It is what differentiates the plant, in the eyes of the employees, from companies operating on the Polish market. Fears of unemployment, as well as of insufficient wages, are an ever-present concern. Also, Polish companies are, for these actors and in relation to their past, synonymous with "insolvency," "bankruptcy," and limited funds. One could summarize the actors' remarks in an opposition between, on one side, the "bleak" Polish situation, and on the other side, the "good working conditions" and "good salaries" that come from working for a foreigner and from being "connected" to the European market. This type of remark is present throughout the whole staff of the company.

The social actors involved in the company clearly identify and manifestly acknowledge the positive aspects of PUP: What exactly qualifies the situation of this company as catastrophic then? What are the elements associated with this view?

The interviews emphasize two main factors: the State and "foreign investments," which highlight the dependency on the symbolic figure of the foreigner. We are going to examine them in the following section of this study.

An Illegitimate Political Sphere

Let us consider the example of Raphao Z.

RAPHAO Z.:   *Since 1989, there have been changes because foreign investors have entered our market. Before 1989, people used to work less. Now we must work harder because the competition is strong. Now we must respect our work because there is unemployment, there is less work.*

A.H.:   What changes have you experienced since 1989?

RAPHAO Z.:   *Nothing has really changed at the political level, but there is more stress and depression because we always have to think about our future.*

A.H.:   Do you have the impression that the government is working to change this situation?

RAPHAO Z.: *No, we earn low wages and leaders earn huge sums of money.* (Interviewed on May 15, 2001)

We can clearly see, on the one hand, the association between foreign investment and changes and, on the other, politics in Poland that "do not really change." The divide between before and after 1989 emerges as well. On the one side, "people worked less" before and on the other "now we must work harder," "we must respect our work." The State's political idleness results thus in questioning the unequal distribution of wages.

Let us now go back to Monika C. and see how she approaches the topic.

But, unemployment is the worst! And we see that the government doesn't do anything about it. Naturally, they say they do a lot, but in reality they do nothing! There is no positive effect. For example, they eliminate some taxes. I don't know. I'm not good at economics. I do not know what they could do to improve this situation. They could use some tools to deal with this situation. Obviously, they could do much more. But, now they only do what they have to do. If they do this it's because they have a personal interest in it all. I consider it all extremely negative.

A.H.: Do you believe that there are not any positive changes?

No, for example the reduction in work hours doesn't make sense. Maybe it was propaganda, to show that they did something in this area. The reduction is like showing people who don't know anything about it that they did something in this area. My opinion? This is completely the opposite, because it is absolutely not beneficial for working people nowadays.

(Interviewed on May 10, 2001)

According to the remarks of Monika C., state political action is associated with the personal interests of the agents who run this institution. The "necessary" reforms are "propaganda" that deceives the Polish and are "totally negative." The political sphere is thus indicted and relegated to a negative sphere.

Let us now consider Marcek B. This workman is one of the eldest and most senior employees. His remarks are different from those of other actors, who, given their age, did not experience the changes in the Polish society in the same way.

MARCEK B.: *Since 1989, I have only gone on vacation once. It's harder, the flat is expensive. Before, I was able to support myself, but that was the minimum. Now it is very difficult with 1,200 zlotys per month. . . . I am very angry with Solidarność. They promised a*

> lot, and did nothing. Thanks to us, they have everything. They
> are workers who took advantage of other workers and now
> they ignore us. You know, I earn 1,200 zlotys per month, my
> daughter has an engineering degree and she has been looking for
> a job for two years. (Interviewed on May 17, 2001)

The remarks of this man reflect a sense of historical regard on a most significant span of time. The *Solidarność* trade union is accused of having taken over the efforts produced by the workers when communism fell, only to "ignore" them afterward. Let us note that, since the mid-1980s, some members of the union have recycled themselves into politicians, thereafter applying a policy of strong liberalization in response to donor agencies (Wedel 1998). It is worth noting that, for all employees, wages are higher at PUP than at other Polish companies, although the amounts are not substantially enough for the workers.

We thus see that the symbolic and real domination of the Polish state on the economy, on companies, and on the legislation affecting the labor market in general is negative in those employees' imagination. To be more precise, we are talking here about an indictment of the elite. The representation of the state is twofold. On one hand, the state is "privatized" and monopolized by an elite whose policy is based on its own self-interest. On the other, the state represents a form of power to which one addresses complaints expecting it to meet demands. In contrast, the "foreigner" that, according to the employees' remarks, dominates both in the company's hierarchy and Polish economy, is seen positively because he is different from the "disastrous" situation in Poland. This foreigner assures the company's survival and provides the employees' livelihood.

What is the relationship between the owner (Philippe V.), the general manager (Karel B.), and the rest of the employees? We turn to a discussion of these aspects in the next part.

"Communists" versus "Competent": Forms of Hierarchical Legitimation

The allochthony/autochthony framework seems to be the result of social relations within PUP. Exchanges with Belgium and the "West" are locally reconstructed in interpersonal relations. However, other elements complete this ensemble. The construction of this "space of communication" (Althabe 1990) appears as well in relation to history. The "young"/"old" ratio looms in this configuration. However, this description remains schematic and the actors' remarks concerning their relationships with other employees and/or classes of employees need to be reconsidered starting with management.

The three office members come from the "countryside," in their own words. Their fathers, more often than their mothers, studied in Krakow but quit school before the degree equivalent to the bachelor's level. The father of Monika C. "installed toilets for the government." Antek R.'s father worked at the Lenin factory in *Nowa Huta* as a "worker," his son initially claimed. In fact, his father held the position of production manager, which implies a certain social power in the political hierarchy. Karolina P. never knew her father. She lives alone with her mother in Krakow.

First, let us consider Karolina P., the secretary of PUP and an employee since June 1994, almost since the creation of the plant.

> *I have a lot of contacts with "Big Brother"* [Karel B.]. *I also discuss frequently with my very good friend. But I do not have as much contact with the team leader. As for the workers, there is only contact when I give them their wages; and the same with the companies that we do business with. I am responsible for ordering materials.*
>
> (Interviewed on May 11, 2001)

Karolina P. claims to have a close relationship with Karel B. as well as with Monika C. while she keeps the workers at a symbolic distance. Our observations categorically contradict this assertion. Indeed, Karel B. only addresses office employees in English, and Karolina P.'s knowledge of this language seems very poor in comparison with that of Antek R., the production manager. Additionally, the data submitted by phone to Karel B. and then to the owner of the company, are not transmitted by Karolina P. but by Antek R. Somehow excluded from the management of the company, that is embodied in the relation Karel B./Antek R., Karolina P. has built in her relationship with Karel B. a closeness with the "foreigner," apart from the hierarchical work structure.

Her relationship with the graphic designer is part of a very different configuration. In fact, they have known each other for a long time. Moreover, the secretary is the one who contacted Monika C. when the position she currently occupies became vacant. As for her relationship with other companies, she only deals with administrative procedures. In fact, Antel R. manages all orders and sales, and everything connected to these operations (customs duties, purchase of materials, etc.). However, he only collects data and transmits them to Karel B. All decisions on sales are the prerogative of the owner of PUP, who also owns the multinational that purchases virtually all products for resale primarily in France and the Netherlands.

Karolina P. tried to obstruct the work of one of the investigators (B) through a few "harmless" actions. For instance, during the interview with Monika C., she interrupted us on several occasions in a courteous fashion such as: "I apologize, but we must have lunch," and this, a few minutes before they usually leave for lunch. Monika C. expressed surprise on the reaction of her "friend," followed by an apologetic phrase that was addressed to the social anthropologist. In fact, Karolina P. quickly realized that the social anthropologist was less naïve than she had imagined at the outset of the investigation.

Situations that cast doubt on her assertions led to some unusual reactions on her part, which even her friend, Monika C., noticed. The reaction of Karolina P. was undoubtedly influenced by the fact that Karel B., while using the French language with the researchers, raised a barrier between him, the investigators, and the other employees. In fact, Karolina P. found herself excluded from the group of "foreigners."

Let us now consider Monika C. and see how she describes her relationship with the owner of PUP.

A.H.:   Have you had any difficulties with Philippe?
MONIKA C.:   *No, but once there was a small problem. It was a long time ago, everything has since changed. But, we happened to be late on the orders. There were a number of reasons: he was not very satisfied. Of course, he commented on it. Well, I've never had major conflicts with him. Sometimes there are product errors so he comments on it. He would be very angry if something is not done as it should be.*

We see that the actions of Philippe V. are, for this employee, legitimate.

MONIKA C.:   *All entrepreneurs try to avoid paying overtime, because employees should do their tasks on time, and if they do not succeed, they must do so during overtime. All employees have a job to do during the week, and if they fail to do it then, they have to come in on Saturdays.* (Interviewed on May 10, 2001)

For Monika C., the inappropriate attitude of employees explains the legitimate approach of entrepreneurs in the working world in general, and of Philippe V. in particular. Speaking of a "Polish mentality" in the company, Monika C. says:

> *I find that the younger generation is very different from the older one. For example, those who worked under communism were sure to keep their jobs, felt safe, and did not think they would stop working even for a day. Now, there is a very strong competition. They see the future and have different aspirations than the older generations. They must have more and more qualifications; they must be competent.*
>
> (Interviewed on May 10, 2001)

A dichotomy between "young" and "old" emerges in these sentences. On the one hand, young people with more "skills" and "qualifications" face "competition," on the other, "older" people who "worked under communism" "felt safe" (job security). However, they all live in the same context and, as shown in the example of Marcek V., they all are confronted to the competition of the labor market.

Let us now turn to Antek R., the production manager, a 29-year-old man, married, who arrived at PUP in October 1999. A graduate of the Polytechnic University of Krakow, his experience of the working world is limited to three companies including PUP. His first company was his post-graduation internship. His career began in 1997 as a salesman before becoming responsible for transport operations and logistics. Low wages and lack of opportunities for advancement pushed him to change jobs.

ANTEK R.: *I found my second job in a newspaper ad. Well, it was my wife who found it and asked me to call. I had not obtained a pay rise, and had stayed on in the same position for a year and a half. I had other preoccupations; I wanted to work in industry, maintenance, robotics, and automation. I wanted more experience, a change in posts, and to have more responsibility.*

A.H.: What problems did you have in your profession?

ANTEK R.: *I have a lot to say about the manager (laughs). In every job, there are problems. For me, it's with the workers, because of their mentality; they come from public companies and were not prepared.*

A.H.: For what?

ANTEK A.: *Ah! All these changes. . . . Before, they did one thing at a time, now they must do two or three. They never paid attention to the machines. The biggest problems revolved around the machines, so I had to start over again.* (Interviewed on May 12, 2001)

Antek R. arrived at the company a little less than 2 years ago, approximately 10 years after the fall of the former socialist regime, which puts the "mentality" to which he refers relatively far back in time and in his experience. In addition, he never officially worked under the communist regime. These remarks refer to a widely accepted judgment of the difficult transition from a job that is stable and without pressure in the production line to another one constrained by profitability requirement and volatility of the labor market. However, PUP workers are mostly under the age of 30. Therefore, the professional achievements of this category of employees refer to the 1989–1999 period. Antek R.'s allegations are fictitious. They show a desire to keep distance to the employees at the bottom of the companies' hierarchy, assigned to communism. This past relationship with communism is associated with an image of inferiority at the national level, as well as the international one. Antek R. justifies his apparent superior position within the framework of the idealized transformations of Western norms and rules of production.

His remarks on Karel B. were always sarcastic and elusive. For instance, he said: "He works so much" and "He's very punctual," when, in fact, Karel B. wasn't actually at the company. The supposed relationship of the social anthropologists with the general manager deterred him from clearly expressing a disapproval or contempt on Karel B.'s minimal involvement in the actual management of the company.

We also observed the employees' aversion to the stereotypical image of the "worker" from the former "socialist" regime. This recurring image is pertinent since it refers to a past situation. We judge the willingness of Karolina P. and Antek R. to distance themselves from the workers as a position strictly in opposition to the "egalitarian" ideology they project on the workers. This "egalitarian" ideational production that brings together "managers" and "workers," has always been contested, but it serves here as a corollary legitimizing the "new values" carried on by these actors. The emphasis on the communist mentality claimed by Antek R. is accompanied by the reference to a reified past (communism) in the present-day activities. Everything is based on a general assumption explained by Bernard Pudal: "(The) necessary relationship between Communism and the working class is a bias . . . which only ratifies the dominant representation that communism gave of itself" (Pudal 2000). This discourse is all the more legitimate since it is socially accepted (Kuk 2001).

The Workers and the Union

The main features of this company are associated with the absence of a trade union and the significance of this situation for employees. On this particular issue, Karel B., the manager, observes:

> There was a union, but we fired it [laughs]. With the union, we could not fire people. . . . So, we fired the union, but some groups persist amongst the workers.

Interviewed on May 14, 2001

The dissolution of the local union seems to be initiated by company management. In coming to power, *Solidarność* lost much of its legitimacy that was based on its opposition to the communist system. The coalition, in office until 1995, included the AWS (*Akcja Wyborcza Solidarność* [Solidarity Electoral Action]), a party that emerged from the internal rupture of *Solidarność*, and the UW Liberal Party (*Unia Wolnosci* [The Freedom Union]). The loss of legitimacy is exemplified by Lech Walesa's withdrawal from the political landscape. At the moment, the opponent that had justified its existence disappeared, the union lost its own credibility in defending workers' interests. Many of the workers who experienced difficult times before 1989 consider *Solidarność* today as a group of opportunists who defended their own interests and not those of the workers. In other words, workers feel now betrayed.

The youngest workers, those who were not employed before 1989, plan to create a union. However, in their mind, *Solidarność* is associated with politics. Most of them say they are not interested in politics or that they will take an interest in politics after retirement. They discuss the possibility of a national union created by the business sector. Indeed, the dissolution of the local union forces them to return to this "solution" that seems strategically more viable. One often hears the insinuation that a local union might create antagonisms with the "boss" (Philippe V.), which would be troublesome since the latter is "legitimate." These assertions articulated to social anthropologist (B) show that the investigation was instrumentalized as support for demands that include, among other things, wage increases. The attitude of Karel B. when he requested that the investigators should not mention the wage issue and labor rights in France can now be explained. A conflictive relationship appears between workers and the manager, expressed as a rapport of demand/repression. With the workers on their side, the investigators were placed in a position of mediators with the foreign management. Conscious of the relative benefits of their employment, the employees remained cautious.

The case of this company is symptomatic of the general situation of trade unions in Poland, which are, as elsewhere in Europe, in a situation of decline (see the decreasing number of members[9]). If the workers accepted *Solidarność* participation in the first governments, the support from a segment of this union for privatizations clearly separated it from its labor base. It should be emphasized that in 1989 *Solidarność* was a social movement comprised of highly different categories of actors, both workers and intellectuals, with diverging interests. These differences became visible after the fall of the communist regime in 1989 and resulted in internal cleavages and occasionally in volatile conflicts. This development occasioned the fragmentation of this union, as well as major strikes in the country. The projects and questions of PUP's workers are a response to this general situation within the framework of local constraints.

CONCLUSION

To summarize, Karel B. symbolizes the employees' dependency on foreigners. The fact that he resides outside the overall Polish economic situation gives legitimacy to his position. The office employees derive their legitimacy from a close relationship with foreigners; they convey values associated with the new norms of production, unlike the workers who see themselves as repressed, assigned to "communism" and incompetence. The integration of the new working norms, including management, is a tool for the hierarchical legitimization for this category of actors. This form of domination is an instrument they use in order to justify their position in the company and in society. Given the absence of unions in the company, eliminated by the owner, the investigation of the two social anthropologists could develop into a support for the workers' political and salary demands, as they could not find other ways to express them within the company. Simultaneously, this fact gave them the opportunity to compare their situation in PUP with their previous work experience. In a way, the workers legitimized Karel B.'s position as a foreigner. However, they remained hopeful that a union would represent their demands. The management fully grasped this fact in a country where a part of a union turned into a political party and quickly dissociated itself from the workers in the name of solidarity. But, the requests have remained existent within the local framework of constraints and aim at negotiating rather than engaging an open conflict within the company.

We, the social anthropologists, also observed that the dependency on foreigners has helped neutralize the subordination to the state, held responsible for the "disastrous" situation in Poland. The employees' allegiance to management is coupled with allegations against the ruling groups. Domination has thus been reinvested in the imaginary. At a more general level, since the fall of the Berlin Wall, successive governments in Poland have allied themselves with Western creditors while trying to impose an autochthonous power. These actions have always been considered as great challenges.

The ambiguous ideological shift to the West is thus one of the topics that the employees can use to make sense of their social relationships (Bandelj 2008). The overall changes in Poland have resulted in a conversion of the imagined political-economic superiority of liberal capitalism over communism to a mode of domination/justification of power and of hierarchy. This superiority has been shown in the eyes of the social actors by the collapse of the Soviet bloc in 1989 but also by policies pursued by governments thereafter. "Shock therapy" placed Poland and its economy in a position of subordination to the new global ideological and political-economic system.

NOTES

1. This chapter was originally published in French (Heemeryck 2008).
2. This study was led by Laurent Bazin. I gratefully thank him for the numerous relevant advice and the constant attention he gave to this work (Cordeau and Heemeryck, 2001).
3. For a comprehensive review on this subject please refer to Kovacs (2002), Keen and Mucha (2003), Mucha (2003).
4. Except the public figures, all the names used in this article are fictitious.
5. The statistics referring to unemployment are questionable as long as they do not accurately, if at all, reflect the poverty, the precariousness, the exclusion, and the stigma they are associated with. Please refer to Bafoil (1999), Bafoil and Matuchniak-Krasuska (1999), Matuchniak-Krasuska (1999).
6. This reality show with varying names (*Loft Story/Secret Story* in France, *Big Brother* in the Netherlands) has been successful in numerous countries all over the world.
7. One Zloty is equivalent to 0.24 €.
8. Our approach is directly inspired by the reflections of G. Althabe (1969). His epistemological reflections are presented in Althabe and Sélim (1998).
9. In 1990, the unionization rate was 28 percent whereas in 2010 it reached 14.6 percent (OECD.Stat Extracts databases).

REFERENCES

Althabe, Gérard (1969) *Oppression et libération dans l'imaginaire. Les communautés villageoises de la côte orientale de Madagascar.* Paris: François Maspero.
Althabe, Gérard (1990) "Ethnologie du contemporain et enquête de terrain," *Terrain*, 14: 126–131.
Althabe, Gérard and Monique Sélim (1998) *Démarches ethnologiques au présent.* Paris: L'Harmattan.
Bafoil, François (1999) *Chômage et exclusion en Europe postcommuniste. Allemagne de l'Est et Pologne.* Paris: L'Harmattan.
Bafoil, François and Anna Matuchniak-Krasuska (1999) "Marché du travail et chômage en Pologne. La construction des politiques publiques de l'emploi," in François Bafoil (ed.) *Chômage et exclusion en Europe postcommuniste, Allemagne de l'Est, Pologne,* pp. 201–223. Paris: L'Harmattan.
Bandelj, Nina (2008) *From Communists to Foreign Capitalists.* Princeton: Princeton University Press.
Bazin, Laurent and Monique Sélim (2001) *Motifs économiques en anthropologie.* Paris: L'Harmattan.
Bourdieu, Pierre (1985) "The Genesis of the Concepts of Habitus and of Field," *Sociocriticism* 2 (2): 11–24.
Cordeau, Sébastien and Antoine Heemeryck (2001) *La Pologne postcommuniste: dépendance et formes de domination. Essai d'ethnologie de l'entreprise.* Master's thesis in ethnology. Université des sciences et technologies de Lille 1: Lille.
Heemeryck, Antoine (2008) "Une analyse des rapports hiérarchiques dans une firme multinationale de Pologne : légitimation des effets micro-politiques du marché," *Anale al facultatea Spiru Haret. Seria sociologie-psihologie,* ed. fondaţia Romania de maine, 2–3: 35–51.
Heemeryck, Antoine (2010) *L'importation démocratique en Roumanie. Une perspective anthropologique sur la construction d'une société post-dictatoriale.* Paris: L'Harmattan.
Keen, F. Mike and Janusz Mucha (eds) (2003) *Sociology in Central and Eastern Europe: Transformations at the Dawn of a New Millennium.* Westport: Praeger.
Kovacs, Éva (2002) "What's New in East-Central European Sociology?" *Regio—Minorities, Politics, Society*—English Edition 1: 89–111.
Kuk, Leszek (2001) *La Pologne du postcommunisme à l'anticommunisme.* Paris: L'Harmattan.
Matuchniak-Krasuska, Anna (1999) "Exclusion et pauvreté en Pologne," in François Bafoil (ed.) *Chômage et exclusion en Europe postcommuniste, Allemagne de l'Est, Pologne,* pp. 271–287. Paris: L'Harmattan.
Mucha, Janusz (2003) "Polish Sociology 1990–2000: Society after a Breakthrough, Sociology in Evolution" in Mike F. Keen and Janusz Mucha (eds) *Sociology in Central and Eastern Europe: Transformations at the Dawn of a New Millennium,* pp. 117–132. Westport: Praeger.
Pudal, Bernard (2000) "Politisation ouvrière et communisme," in Michel Dreyfus, Bruno Groppo, Claudio-Sergio Ingerflom, Roland Lew, Claude Pennetier, Bernard Pudal, Serge Wolikow (eds) *Le siècle des communismes,* pp. 513–522. Paris: De l'Atelier.
Wedel, Janine (1998) *Collision and Collusion. The Strange Case Western Aid to Eastern Europe 1989–1998.* New York: St. Martin's Press.

4 A New Model of Risk Management: Credit Lending to Small and Middle Enterprises

Calculations, Guarantees, and Information Gathering in 21st Century Russia[1]

Caroline Dufy

The Russian banking sector's appetite for credit followed the stock market crash of 1998 that dried up profit opportunities on the public debt markets. The decade following 2000 was marked by an explosion in lending. The volume of credit extended to the private sector more than doubled from 1999 to 2006 rising from 13.1 percent to 30 percent of gross domestic product (GDP).[2] In this context of credit-led growth, risk control became a central issue in a rapidly expanding banking system still heavily influenced by the Soviet heritage of centralized, planned finance. Credit risks were thus a new phenomenon[3] in post-Soviet Russia. Legal risks were also significant given the liberal legislation implemented during the transition period and the new creed of promoting small businesses favored by lax regulations placing few restrictions on the creation of economic activities. The result was an increase in the number of dummy corporations complicating debt collection. Repeated severe banking crises, in 1998, 2004–05, and, in particular, 2008, revealed the uncertainties characterizing the banking sector's adjustment to economic instability and market expansion (Dufy 2008). In this context, how did the Russian banking system attempt to mitigate risks and deal with uncertainty, while simultaneously continuing to expand? What measures did banks implement to improve their individual and collective knowledge about their borrowers and prevent default?

This research is based on a field survey carried out in Russia between 2006 and 2009 based on approximately 30 interviews carried out in lending institutions in Moscow and Yekaterinburg.[4] I concentrate on analyzing these issues more specifically in the case of lending to small and medium-sized enterprises (SMEs) (Figure 4.2). These entities present difficulties with regards to statistical calculations due to their heterogeneous nature, their uncertain profitability, and the particularities of their activity (Ferrary 1999). Indeed, the division of labor in banks traditionally distinguishes between the administration of loans to businesses and that of lending to households (Figure 4.1). Regarding the former, risks are more complex and harder to grasp, guarantees are more difficult to implement, and the outstanding amounts are higher than those of consumer credits.[5]

Nevertheless, the drastic reduction in the official bad debt levels illustrates that radical changes have taken place in Russian risk management. The rate of overdue loans in bank portfolios fell from 13.4 percent in 2000 to 2.6 percent in 2006[6] (Barisitz 2008). Simultaneously, the expansion of the market, the growth in banking networks, and their regional expansion has required the development of procedures for the economic and legal identification of loan applicants (Laferté 2010). One of the most frequently discussed solutions in the literature on modern banking systems is credit scoring (Ferrary 1999, Leyshon and Thrift 1999, Poon 2009, Carruthers and Cohen 2010). This involves computing the data for each applicant numerically in addition to the production of statistics on the relative risks associated with each category of clients. Thus, it enables interpersonal ties to be discarded and standardizes the credit relationship. Following 2000, credit monitoring spread very rapidly within the Russian banking sector (Guseva 2008, 2010). Such solutions rely on an intrinsic economic rationality that justifies the automation of credit lending. However, the research developed here, like similar studies, shows that credit management instruments do not eliminate measures of discretion (Ferrary 1999). Moreover, a now substantial literature has shown the minor relevance of scoring for the assessment of default risks (Carruthers and Cohen 2010).

This contribution is based on the central thesis that the effectiveness of these tools lies more in their function of monitoring banks than in their supposed predictive value (Lascoumes and Le Gallès 2004, Power 2004). Beyond this already-established result (Carruthers and Cohen 2010), the issue here is one of demonstrating the way in which the banking sector organizes the overall monitoring of risk within a system in which the actors are strongly interdependent and simultaneously possess very diverse professional identities and strategies. In fact, the introduction of risk management tools aims at building a hierarchical banking system controlled by a supervisor, the Central Bank of the Russian Federation (CBRF) through financial indicators including prudential ratios. Commercial banks adapt to this constraint by creating internal and private risk management tools that benefit from commercial secrecy: credit-scoring programs. How do banks cope with these new constraints? How are used these new tools? I show that the widespread existence and the crucial role within Russian banks of security services perfectly demonstrates that risk credit scoring programs are not able to cope alone with default risks in credit lending. However, they are key factors in the bureaucratic consolidation of the expanding banking system.

CALCULATION TOOLS AND RISK MANAGEMENT

Credit scoring is a tool used by banks and lending institutions in order to assess the solvability of their borrowers. Technically, it transforms information of different sorts (qualitative and quantitative) supplied by borrowers, into a single figure—credit scores—ranking applicants for credit according to the risk of their defaulting. Accounting or financial information; data from firm's credit ratings, from information about guarantees, or debt servicing analysis; and credit histories may be used if considered requisite information. Standardization of credit applications by these means reduces processing costs as well as response times to clients, providing a significant competitive advantage.

Credit rating assesses the solvability of bond issuers and the liquidity of bonds issued and quoted on financial markets. In contrast to credit scoring, credit ratings are generally rendered public. This activity is consolidated at the international level in the hands of a few actors, in particular Standard and Poor's, Fitch, and Moody's.

Prudential ratios are indicators used by supervising bodies to monitor the exposure of commercial banks to various risks such as credit risks, market risks, or liquidity risks. As regards credit risks, prudential ratios measure, for example, the risk-weighted volume of credits as a function of a bank's assets. In modern financial systems, a two-level structure is an essential part of financial stability. A supervisor, most commonly a central bank, monitors the risks incurred by the commercial banks. For the last 20 years, the work of the Basel committee, comprising representatives from the central banks of around 30 countries, has promoted the development and widespread dissemination of tools for managing financial risks internationally, among which are prudential ratios or commonly named the Basel ratios.

CONSTRUCTING A COLLECTIVE RISK MANAGEMENT SYSTEM: AN IMPOSSIBLE UNDERTAKING?

Setting up a banking system with a two-level hierarchy involves commercial banks being subjected to supervision. However, the authority of the Russian supervisor over commercial banks is the result of a political balance of power; significant internal pressures favored the central bank only at the end of the 1990s. The delayed way in which credit histories were developed in the Russian market illustrates perfectly this marked reticence on the part of commercial banks. We demonstrate that their autonomization strategy was based on privatizing indicators and information about their clients' credit risks.

The CBRF acquired its independent status *vis-à-vis* political interference as early as 1995. However, close links existed between the banking elites and the Yeltsin government whose 1996 presidential campaign they heavily financed. This relationship afforded them a great deal of protection from public oversight throughout the 1990s. This latitude was then wiped out by the failure of entire sectors of the banking world with the crisis of Russian government bonds and the stock market crash of 1998 (Buyske 2007). The stability of the financial sector as such became a major priority of financial regulation. For a long time, the Russian banking system was characterized by a polarized structure, on the one hand, the profusion of small regional banks with relatively weak capitalization and limited territorial networks developed. These coexisted, on the other hand, with a handful of enormous federal banks often state owned or controlled absorbing the greater part of public savings and spreading it around the entire country. The most powerful widespread network remains that of the successor to the Soviet Savings Bank, the Sberbank. Overall, the Russian banking system in 2010 comprised nearly 1,200 banks whose survival and access to savings depended on the extent of their financial standing and thus their grip on the Russian territory (Central Bank of the Russian Federation (CBRF) 2006, 2007, 2008).[7]

In order to establish its legitimacy and control over these heterogeneous organizations, the central bank took advantage of the movement towards financial regulation being encouraged at the international level. In 2002, the Russian Federation adopted international agreements known as the Basel Agreements and imposed prudential ratios on the Russian financial sector. These strengthened and lent greater sophistication to the instruments available to central bankers to manage the risk posed by commercial banks. The translation of these external standards was achieved by enacting a large number of directions from the central bank. According to Anton P.[8], a credit manager in the economic department of the local branch of a federal bank in Yekaterinburg:

> *We get instructions (from the central bank) for everything: what we can accept as guarantees, what we can't, guarantees which are hard (the most secure ones), those which are soft (the least secure ones), how we monitor each one of these.*
>
> (Interviewed on June 24, 2008, Yekaterinburg)

Thus, the context of international financial regulation is a favorable trend used by the CBRF to make internal sanctions effective and encourage compliance with instructions. Indicators are used by the CBRF through on-site inspections and off-site supervision operated both in planned and unplanned ways. Ninety percent of all supervisory personnel are located in the regions (CBRF 2008); the arsenal of measures used by the supervisor ranges from reprimands and penalties to the withdrawal of the operating license, which is a powerful deterrent. In the second part of this decade, around 500 licenses were annually withdrawn on the basis of CBRF controls.

However, within this vast movement to stiffen financial controls, international banking circles managed to gain responsibility for the procedures assessing the risks that they themselves incur. The CBRF failed to impose any particular system for measuring risk or any standardized, collective instrument. The central banks' macro-prudential supervision of financial systems was thus disconnected from micro-prudential assessment of the risks associated with individual borrowers. Nonetheless, the supervisor required credit organizations to provide themselves with internal methods of risk evaluation and obliged creditors to collect economic, legal, and financial information on applicants prior to lending. The level of overall risk disclosed by each bank determines a minimum level of reserve requirements. These reserves can vary from nil percent for lending of very high quality, up to 100 percent for the most risky lending; these risk categories are determined by a small number of explicit criteria, such as the number of days of late payments.[9]

The banks' room to maneuver is also displayed in the negotiated implementation of the supervisory procedures provided by the central bank. The work done by local bank employees in order to achieve formal compliance with regulatory requirements is sometimes quite far from any substantial, *deep* compliance as understood on the basis of established principles (Power 2004). Artëm D., the director of the well-appointed local subsidiary of a small regional Siberian bank, claims a specific identity as a private banker, as well as a great deal of operational autonomy with regards to a supervising body that had little legitimacy for a long while and who employs now agents described as poorly qualified and badly paid. The personal dimension of the lending relationship is obscured in the reporting destined for the supervising authorities:

> *For us the balance sheet (of a client's business) is not a priority; obviously, we look at it but it's secondary. The first thing we do is to look at the person in front of us, whether the applicant is a capable businessman and then we look (at the balance sheet). We have subjective criteria and we base our work on reality. And then for the central bank, we write up a nice little tale ('narisuem krasivye istorii').*
>
> (Interviewed on June 26, 2008)

The distinction that this interviewee draws between the profession of private banker and the employees of the public supervising body is used to distance him from this form of supervision. In a meeting that took place before the financial crisis, Artëm D. argued:

> *There is a comprehensive monitoring every two years; otherwise there are partial and thematic controls (e.g. foreign currencies). But, it's still a bureaucratic institution, cumbersome and conservative; these guys are not highly qualified, not well paid, so if they could hire people from commercial banks, well in that case yes . . . but, for the time being, these guys come along, we take them for a ride to some extent. You just have to get them onto something; in any case, that's what they are there for. They have to find something, and they just don't see all the rest. The central bank is an enormous bank; it's colossal in terms of personnel. And then again it depends on the region. In the Tiumen oblast (the region bordering on the east, C.D.), they are more easygoing, but here no.*
>
> (Interviewed on June 26, 2008, Yekaterinburg)

The preference of most Russian banks for a private oversight of risks explains the difficult and tardy creation of a central agency on credit histories. This project was evoked as early as in the mid-1990s in Russia. Usually, a unified system of credit histories is intended to favor the development of retail lending, while simultaneously reducing the cost of collecting information for the banking system. However, in the case of Russia, the opposition of the banking sector, officially based on the concern for the protection of personal data, but in reality more on a strong internal mistrust between banks, frustrated this project until the end of 2004 (Guseva 2008). The December 30, 2004, law set up credit bureaus as private entities.

As reported by Timofei M., a lawyer and initiator of this project, in an interview carried out in June 2009, in Moscow, the collection of credit histories was intended to replace the gathering of illegal data or even the creation of ad-hoc blacklists between banks. This procedure encountered a very marked reticence on the part of banks in a highly concentrated market:

> *The three largest banks and all the major banks were in general afraid that their data would be used by other banks. . . . In fact, some databases such as that of the GIBDD (Gosudarstvennaâ Inspekciâ Bezopasnosti Dorožnogo Dviženiâ,* State Inspectorate for Road Traffic Safety*) or other databases can be found on the market* (despite it being illegal, C.D.).
> (Interviewed on June 30, 2009, Moscow)

The distrust of the banking sector was also directed towards the financial information services sector. Timofei M. continued to argue:

> *In the mid-1990s, there were ratings agencies that wanted to do the same thing (create credit history bureaus). . . . This didn't work because the banks mistrusted them. You know that in the banking sector, there is a tradition of secrecy, so banks were very reticent.*
> (Interviewed on June 30, 2009, Moscow)

This opposition was lifted thanks to the creation of a competitive market of private companies. In fact, the newcomers in this market were heterogeneous and segmented. Some foreign agencies entered the market and developed along the lines of the North American model of professionalization of financial information services, as was the case, e.g., for Equifax. But the dominant banks on the market, such as Russkij Standard Bank or Sberbank, concerned with retaining control of their data, set up their pocket structures that communicated data solely to partner banks. Despite this late creation, the market for credit histories experienced rapid expansion. In 2009, there were 27 agencies, six more than in 2006. Registered information was quite rapidly growing by more than 150 percent in 2006, bringing the number of informational items registered up to 35 million (CBRF 2008).

One major actor, the Credit History Bureau, imposed himself, promoted by legal circles, placed under the aegis of the Association of Russian Banks, and owned by banking shareholders. Timofei M., who was previously mentioned, initiated this commercial company. He explained its success with this dual identity:

> *So we went in a different direction, and we created it under the aegis of the Association of Russian Banks. Since they were members, they knew who we were and they trusted us more.*
>
> (Interviewed on June 30, 2009, Moscow)

The legitimizing discourse emanating from these actors associated modernity, legality, and economic development based on credit. Garegin A. Tosunyan, President of the Association of Russian Banks, one of the founders of this initiative, explained in an interview published in the printed press[10]:

> *Unfortunately, even today, there are clients, even those with an economic background, who request not to be registered with the Credit History Bureau when they apply for a mortgage loan. . . . In the West, a lot of doubts emerge about someone with whom you engage in a financial transaction and yet who has no credit history. . . . This is why we must understand this very simple truth: you can't do business and have no credit history.*[11]

At the same time, the way in which information is collected and transmitted revealed the arbitrages obtained in order to accommodate banking secrecy. Legislation obligates banks to communicate their data on debtors to credit bureaus for both individuals and legal entities, but this procedure is subject to the borrowers' explicit agreement. The entity collecting this data can then transmit it to affiliated potential creditors. Nevertheless, the transparency of the information communicated to credit organizations is asymmetrical: The file establishes the legal identity of debtors on the basis of their passport number and on personal, residential, and insurance data. It specifies the amounts, costs, and conditions of the credits already held. For legal entities, it additionally includes information about legal decisions affecting them, but it does not reveal the name of the existing creditors.

The implementation of a collective risk management system took much longer than the adoption of credit scoring programs, which spread rapidly among Russian banks. The latter enabled to overcome the immense distances within the Russian territory by helping strengthen the control head offices have over local subsidiaries and agencies (Leyshon and Thrift 1997). Economic rationalization and bureaucratic rationalization thus appeared to be tightly interwoven. Credit scoring programs facilitate hierarchical control, but as I demonstrate below they simultaneously create strong tensions for banking staff at the local level.

MANAGING THE ORGANIZATION THROUGH CREDIT REPORTING

The risk management ideology[12] that produced credit scoring originated in advanced Western banking systems, as exemplified by the direct transliteration of the English word (*scoring*) into Russian. The introduction of these tools of calculation transpired with technical assistance from international organizations, such as the European Bank for Reconstruction and Development (EBRD), but also owing to leading global firms such as Experian, Equifax, and Scorto, which actively marketed these programs in Russia after 2000 (Mays 2001).[13]

Devised for the most part to manage the risks of private actors, they are also used by Russian banks for SMEs and individual entrepreneurs. However, the form of this tool varies considerably depending on the size of banks. The most rudimentary systems, found in small regional banks, are point systems and consist of Excel databases that attribute points according to a series of criteria, such as the financial situation, profitability, liquidity, indebtedness, or the financial reputation of business clients. The final score authorizes (or not) lending. In contrast, major federal banks use much more sophisticated IT programs, constructed on the basis of locked algorithms and devised by head offices with the support of external companies specialized in scoring software.

Nevertheless, in these cases, this quantitative information is not communicated to the client. Prior to the financial crisis of 2008, numerous studies showed that the reliability of financial risk assessment should not be overestimated (Carruthers and Cohen 2010). Scoring is used for other functions: It favors the adoption of a system for collecting reliable data. However, my research findings show that credit scoring plays an essential role in strengthening and consolidating banking hierarchies at the beginning of the 21st century in the Russian context marked by rapid expansion over an extensive territory. In fact, these tools are commercial secrets, as mentioned in interviews and are jealously guarded on by banking hierarchies who have privatized these tools. The imposition of standardized procedures, whose application can be monitored at all levels, enabled head offices to combat the extreme regional segmentation of banking networks that dominated in the 1990s and that entailed average transaction times of between four and six weeks for all interbank transfers depending on the regions (Clément-Pitiot and Scialom 1995).[14] Standardizing procedures allowed banks to impose at a low cost an administrative hierarchy between head offices and local branches and to create within banking groups a standardized decision-making system controlled by head offices. In this process, credit scoring organizes hierarchical segmentation and structures a delegation system where the competent decision-making level is determined on the basis of the size of the loan under consideration. In fact, each bank's IT architecture provides each territorial branch with a specific volume of credit allowances corresponding to its size in the global network of the firm. Moreover, adapting scoring programs for internal use and specific institutional particularities renders impossible the transfer of the tool between banks. These imperatives explain the massive and rapid spread of credit scoring for all types of clienteles, including SMEs. Credit scoring was supported by a discourse of modernization and economic rationalization, one originating from elites who favored the rational representation of their economic activity (Carruthers and Cohen 2010). Risk management allowed the importance of personal knowledge to be downplayed when extending credit: Lending could be separated from personal relationships and corruption, supposedly rampant in Russian economic relationships (Ledeneva 2002, Buyske 2007).[15] For bank employees, the main difference between modern banking and non-bank lending was precisely this new approach to risk that substituted statistical consolidation for individual judgment. As Anton P. (mentioned above) explained in June 2008, on the subject of loan sharks, who have the unusual nickname of *lombardies* in Russian:

> *Concerning loan sharks, the difference from us is that they don't do any risk analysis. But, these days, there are hardly any left.*
> (Interviewed on June 24, 2008, Yekaterinburg)

While the same discourse on modernization is also heard from those dealing directly with clients, in contrast there is fierce resentment of the top management's monitoring of local branches. Credit managers engage in practices to ease supervision and reassert their own power when extending credit. Various strategies are used, including disparaging the tool in light of requirements on the ground, parallel procedures at lower levels, or work carried out upstream in order to make the real data match up with the thresholds and norms imposed by credit scoring.

Many credit managers in major federal bank branches argue that credit scoring is only moderately useful, presenting it as unsuited to local specificities. This is equally true for directors of small regional banks who strive to differentiate themselves from the major Moscow banks and draw their legitimacy from their contacts with clients in the field. For Igor O., a young legal affairs manager in a small regional bank in the Yekaterinburg region:

> *They buy that* (credit scoring programs, C.D.) *in the West. They are standards. Obviously, they can adapt them with parameters to fit regional criteria. There is statistical information too. Besides, the Sverdlovsk region is one of the foremost regions for delays in payment. That means there's twice as much work, you have to do a credit score and then also have an appropriate form of analysis. Otherwise, I personally can't see too well why we should go to the market if we can't offer anything* (more to clients, C.D.). *Compared with Moscow, we can offer something else, people expect something else.*
> (Interviewed on June 26, 2008, Yekaterinburg)

This discourse of a clearly felt opposition between Moscow and the regions is juxtaposed with the segmentation of risk perceptions between management and local personnel. To my question, Marina S., a young, female business credit analyst in the Yekaterinburg branch of a federal bank, replied in astonishment:

> *Credit scoring? Up there* (Moscow, C.D.), *yes, it probably exists. Here, we don't have it. In fact, credit scores offer fewer guarantees, because nobody goes out and takes a look. In Moscow, they arrive at conclusions solely by analyzing documents.*
> (Interviewed on June 27, 2008, Moscow)

Checking the status and the state of guarantees entails fieldwork. As a result, branch-based credit analysts see the local level as the most competent one for correctly analyzing risks and understanding the gap between documents and reality. Anton P., the credit manager quoted earlier explained:

> *Everyone knows well that a business doesn't win by paying taxes, and that there are a few who take us for a ride with their accounts (narisovat' shemy,* literally "they paint us pictures," C.D.).
> (Interviewed on June 24, 2008, Yekaterinburg)

The mechanized, standardized system of analysis is experienced as poorly adapted to local behavior. Numerous institutions modify these tools that are often seen as too inflexible. This is the case for the K Bank that specializes in micro-credits for businesses and was set up with the help of the EBRD and European banking shareholders. For Elena P., a young female credit analyst for SMEs in Yekaterinburg, the realities of the local clientele must be taken into account. One of the solutions adopted consisted of falsifying the information supplied:

> *Our bank has adopted this technology* (credit scoring, C.D.). *Generally, banks extend credit on the basis of the official accounts. Our bank was the first to extend credit on the basis of real accounting data* (and not just official data, C.D.).
> (Interview on April 27, 2007, Yekaterinburg)

In response to the rigidity of the new norms introduced by banking head offices, credit managers in local branches achieve more wriggle room for themselves by paralleling at local level the decision-making processes and structures set up by levels higher up in the bureaucratic ladder. Taking these additional requirements into account involves additional documents that must be verified and certified, and it adds a supplementary level of supervision. Anton P. explained this again:

(The Credit Committee) is in Moscow, we are a Moscow bank, but in fact, along with Oleg N. [his friend and director of the regional subsidiary, C.D.], *we set one up here comprised of the director of the security department, the director of the legal department, the director of the economic department, the risk manager, the director, and the deputy director.*
(Interviewed on June 24, 2008, Yekaterinburg)

The increasingly anonymous nature of decision-making entailed a professional repositioning by intermediaries that had multiplied in the non-banking credit system characteristics of the 1990s. *Brokers*, as some of these operators designate themselves, no longer market to SMEs or individual entrepreneurs their own personalized knowledge of private lenders. Instead, they market their expertise in procedures for extending credit. In fact, obtaining financing, which is, for the most part, short-term in nature, implicates borrowers in very frequent and time-consuming procedures of document collection and of putting together credit applications for a large number of financial intermediaries.[16] According to data collected from 2000 to 2004 from more than 800 small Russian businesses in 64 Russian regions, slightly less than 40 percent of lending was for a period of six to 12 months, 20 percent was for one to three years and only 4.6 percent was for more than three years. Sixteen percent of businessmen made no applications for bank loans (Dolgopyatova and Ivasaki 2006).

Valeriya I., a young woman, a former entrepreneur in small retail clothing, set up business as a credit broker by professionalizing her knowledge of lending networks, previously acquired for her own purposes. She puts together credit applications and explains how she works with banking personnel beforehand in order to gain approval by banks for her clients' applications:

They tell you on the phone (bank employees, C.D.), *to embellish (narisovat') your application. You have to do this, or you have to have a certain level of revenues. . . . So afterwards, I pass this information on* (to my clients, C.D.). *Sometimes they do it themselves and fiddle with the figures. It can even happen that way; they dress up the accounts so that it goes through. They know what has to be done. . . .*
(Interviewed on June 28, 2008, Yekaterinburg)

The justification offered by Valeriya I. for her role as intermediary is of a mixed nature. As regards borrowers, it is a deep knowledge of the procedures for compiling a credit application, while for lenders it is personalized guarantee against defaults of payments. Her remarks stress her role as guarantor, insuring trust, which parallels procedures for calculating risk numerically. Valeriya I. continued saying:

It works because I guarantee people. Credit, especially for large sums, still has a personal dimension; nobody will look at your application if

nobody knows you. Nobody will examine your application. . . . When all is said and done, I get to know one or two people, and since I can recommend people, I say yes, I know that guy and I recommend them. And I tell the bankers, "I'll vouch for them," you can give them credit.
(Interviewed on June 28, 2008, Yekaterinburg)

Paradoxically, this personalized picture of the decision making process is not incompatible with a discourse about risk analysis, which runs throughout the remarks of actors who base their reputation on informal ties. However, these individuals do not have decision-making powers over lending, nor are they in control of the repercussions in cases of default of payment.

I also carry out my own little analysis of risk myself. At the beginning, I believed everything people told me, but I have learned and I know what's going on now. I know pretty well what to expect from people. I've learned to assess the businesses that have the best prospects and I recommend them or not, based on that.
(Interviewed on June 28, 2008, Yekaterinburg)

However, these intermediaries may find that they are called upon to be liable in the case of overdue loans. Valeriya I. made this clear, touching wood, and crossing her fingers:

Thanks God, since I started, I've only had one payment default case.
(Interviewed on June 28, 2008, Yekaterinburg)

The lending decision-making in banks thus leaves room for personal ties. Personal knowledge of clients may even be explicitly promoted by banking management in order to retain customer loyalty and through the requirement for all new borrowers to open a bank account. Moreover, personalization was an integral part of the autonomous, private, economic, and legal information systems adopted by banks in Russia in the 1990s. This specific institutional structure indicates an awareness of the low level of reliability that the scoring systems offer when it comes to assessing risks. It emphasizes both the incomplete nature of risk calculation tools, as well as the need to continually check that they are keeping up with developments in the business world.

INTELLIGENCE IN RUSSIAN BANKING: BETWEEN WESTERNIZATION AND A SPECIFIC FORM OF INFORMATION GATHERING

Three key departments are responsible for collating and examining credit applications. The economic department is responsible for evaluating economic and financial risks. The legal department checks whether documents, supplied by applicants, comply with legislation and investigates fraud and fake identity risks. The security department (*otdel bezopasnosti*) is the third actor whose approval is crucial to obtain consumer credit, as well as commercial lending. In the banks studied, the members of this department had in common that they had previously belonged to police or legal agencies such as former police officers, bailiffs, or members of the intelligence services who, on retirement or in order to increase their income, obtain new employment in the banking sector. The intelligence role carried out by the security department, and its place in lending activity is fundamental during the phase of enquiries. Security department personnel are in fact involved during two phases of this procedure: prior to the extending of credit and also during the collection phase.

In a context of recurrent mistrust of documentary information supplied to lenders, the function of the security department is intelligence in the broader sense. Credit professionals regularly repeat: "You have to check things out;" "You can't trust documents;" "They give us a load of bull." Officially constituting a documented credit application involves a parallel intelligence operation in the broader and unofficial sense into the applicant's personal data. Carried out by the security department, this operation updates and checks the data supplied by the applicant, supplementing their details in a way extending beyond the official documentary framework required for calculating risk indicators. These functions, undertaken in a privatized manner within Russian banks, may also be outsourced to so-called collection agencies (*kollektorskie agenstva*). Here, banks acknowledge the deficiencies of risk management instruments within a context in which information is incompletely standardized.

In particular, security department personnel carry out prior verification of the information supplied and its degree of correspondence to realities in constant movement, regularly moving back and forth between records, the assets, and the borrowers' legal situation. They base their work on the declarations made by future borrowers about their assets, on the reality of control procedures in the companies concerned, and on the status, situation, and real value of assets pledged. As Anton P. observed:

> *There is the official part and the unofficial part, but it is all regulated by written requirements. The unofficial part is that the security people (bezopasniki) will go and check whether the applicant is indebted to other banks, whether his criminal liability has already been a matter of concern . . . because with documents you can't trust them entirely. Sometimes, you get people who spin you a nice little tale (narisuu't krasyvye istorii).*
>
> (Interviewed on June 24, 2008, Yekaterinburg)

But this work is also carried out in the perspective of exercising preventive pressures to strengthen payment discipline, by collecting information on the behavior of borrowers and their guarantors, as well as on any deviancies on

Figure 4.1 In this high street window, a clear distinction is made between business clients facing left and households on the right. Credit is advertised as deliverable within the hour. © DR.

Figure 4.2   'Credit for SMEs, at Rates Reduced to 7% per year', as Shown by this Advertisement in the Streets of the Urals city of Ekaterinburg. © DR.

record in domains as wide as criminal convictions, highway misdemeanors, or failure to meet military obligations. The narrative offered by Dmitri N., a legal affairs manager highlights this double function. Verification is carried out on phone by banks for individuals as well as for businesses and for organizations:

> *And we telephone, we try to contact people close* (to the borrowers, C.D.). *Often we call the wife, to ask her if she is aware of the loan, whether he has other loans with other banks. . . . And then after this, we get hold of other phone numbers, which the applicant has not given us, to check. We ask the neighbors, to see if the information is verifiable. Often they too can give us good information.*
> (Interviewed on June 24, 2008, Yekaterinburg)

The same interviewee explains that for businesses, in contrast, a visit is involved:

> *If it's for a corporate entity, it's a bit different, we visit, but not for individual borrowers. The amounts involved are more significant and the risks too. . . . In these cases, we also telephone the neighbor and the employees to find out if the firm really operates. We check everything and we report our conclusions to the credit committee.*
> (Interviewed on June 24, 2008, Yekaterinburg)

Regular on-the-spot checks take place in particular because of the need to assess the state of real estate and property securities that may be offered up by companies as collateral for each loan. Checking out real estate does not present too many problems, but this is not the case for collateral ones such as goods or industrial machinery. In this case, site visits enable the verification of the existence and the state of the property pledged to secure the loan. However, the main resource these security department personnel can privately provide to banks is the access they offer stemming from their strong social networks to information gathered by professionals who monitor and control social deviance. This illegal access is justified in the eyes of local actors by the ease with which official economic and legal data can be falsified in the Russian context and by their incomplete nature. In fact, complex property schemes and dummy corporations are sometimes used to hide fraudulent activity.[17] Therefore, security departments carefully investigate the match between legal statuses and the actual management line in the company. In the opinion of an American consultant in development banking, Gail Buyske, this practice is linked to the nature of information in former socialist economies:

> *This use of security services is not typical in developed economies. . . . However, it is a standard operating feature of banks throughout the countries of the former Soviet Union, which have had to develop their own source of information. The development of credit bureaus, which were introduced in Russia in 2005 should lead to increasing use of this more formalized source of borrower information.*
>
> (Buyske 2007: 177)

This necessarily autonomous gathering of information by banks is in particular supposed to enable credit managers to unmask cases of fraud, in which corrupt civil servants have falsified official documents. In this perspective, banks obtain databases of diverse natures and origins. For credit managers, these constitute tools that are more credible than risk management instruments. The information gathered about borrowers is of a composite nature: civil, penal, military, fiscal, land registry, private or public, it may be legal or illegal, free of charge or paid for. Set up by private security companies, these databases are partly constituted from information illicitly provided by members of public security services. The Internet also plays an essential, complementary role, this time legal, as a supplier of information of a highly varied nature. The Internet allows numerous checks to be performed on borrowers.

In contrast to the documentary information collected together in the credit application, users don't question the reliability of these sources of information. The only limits mentioned were their comprehensiveness and whether they were up to date. On the contrary, the effectiveness of these databases is sometimes thought to be too selective. The interviewees stress the necessarily limited influence these databases should have on their task of selecting borrowers. Igor O., the previously mentioned legal specialist, explains the useful limits of this information:

> We have entered into an agreement with this company that has offered us these (illegal, C.D.) databases. But, the problem with them is that if individuals fall in, it's hard to get out. There are all sorts of things in this blacklist, traffic misdemeanors . . . , delays in payment, even for a few kopeks. So, if you do an objective credit scoring with this list, you find yourself looking at 70–80 percent of loan rejections for physical persons.
>
> (Interviewed on June 26, 2008, Yekaterinburg)

For client managers, databases are a substitute for personal contacts in the public security sector. They avoid referring to these services on a daily basis in order to accumulate information and save time. As one independent collector reported:

> As for the databases we use, they are still accessible today, but it is harder to buy them. Besides, there are quite a lot of frauds where they sell you used databases, and you have to check them out. They are still useful. Recently, I carried out a search on the basis of no more than a surname, I spent an hour and a half on it, and I found the borrower's address, his mother's address, the name of his girlfriend, and some of his friends. To get this information, we looked at his land registry record, his cars, etc. It's quite rapid and straightforward. Had we used our administrative resources, we would have ended up with the same result, but it would have taken three months.
>
> (Interviewed on December 16, 2008, Yekaterinburg)

The privatized intelligence system used by the banks helps limit the power of credit analysis by introducing a different occupational culture into the banking sector. Between Pavel B. and Dmitri N., mentioned earlier, the contrast is striking. Dmitri N., a legal department manager, is in his 20s. He dresses casually—jeans, no jacket. He has worked in six banks in the last four years. Pavel B., his colleague, 10 years older, is in charge of the security department in the same bank. He is a former police officer and presents a professional, plasticized business card. The legal department has one person in addition to Dmitri N., whereas the security department has five members, and is heavily influenced by police culture and methods. Pavel B. explained:

> (In this department, C.D.), two people take care of mortgages, one looks after debt recovery procedures, and one looks after private individuals' applications for consumer credit. In the department, there are five of us, two of whom are former police officers. In the end, we do the same thing (as the legal department, C.D.), we work in exactly the same way

(as in the police force, C.D.), *but we work for a private company. And there again, it's a distinctive mentality, that's all there is to it.*
(Interviewed on June 24, 2008, Yekaterinburg)

The economic information gathering by internal security departments has been viewed by some actors and analysts as a Russian particularity linked to the high levels of uncertainty that prevail in business and economic life and that can only be partly overcome by identification tools (Buyske 2007). In this perspective, the collection of information is thought to contribute towards a form of re-personalization and re-embedding of lending operations within these traditional social ties and at the same time as a return to informal methods in lending. In fact, the same actors who recovered and guaranteed debts in the prior informal non-banking credit system that dominated in the 1990s carry out the management of overdue payments. However, the viewpoint defended here is quite distinct: The expansion of the role of personal information does not go hand in hand with a return to a face-to-face lending relationship. On the contrary, it takes to its logical conclusion the system of monitoring and controlling economic and legal identities within a framework that also gives police methods an increasing role in banking (Favarel-Garrigues, Godefroy, and Lascoumes 2009). As such, we are not looking at the persistence of interpersonal ties in the lending relationship, but indeed we can see the establishment of new tools for risk mitigation whose utility is derived from the limited reliability of quantitatively based methods of assessing financial risk.

Security department personnel also have an internal monitoring role. They supervise the internal operations of the organization and additionally act as the middle office, responsible for preventing the corruption of lending managers. This specific institutional development is the result of a decade of upheavals that led to the dispersion of the professionals managing and monitoring social deviancy, at a time when, in contrast to other professions, the skills and contacts acquired by professionals were highly sought after by economic actors (Favarel-Garrigues 2007). This institutional configuration should therefore not be seen as a cultural propensity within Russian society for surveillance or as a reified Soviet heritage. It may be transient since the re-employment of police officers in the banking sector remains an accepted practice while many actors in the field are calling for a much needed legal regulation of these practices while displaying strong demands for the professionalization of their activities.

CONCLUSION

In just a few years, a new model of risk management has imposed itself within the Russian banking system. This economic rationalization affects the banking system as a whole, from regional banks to the Central Bank, whether it takes the form of credit scoring at the bank level or that of prudential ratios at a macro level. This development, though not without any tensions, was achieved as a result of the congruence of two strategies: the need for management bodies to consolidate their rapidly growing banking organizations and the political will of the Central Bank to impose its authority on actors who were highly autonomous throughout the 1990s. In this context, risk management instruments appear less as reliable indicators of credit risk than as tools for the organizational governance. Their informational status, experienced as both partial and relative, incentivized banking organizations to set up private structures capable of closing the circuit of information on borrowers. However, the rapid progress of sharing arrangements for personal credit data might reduce the vestiges of policing methods and practices within the banking system.

NOTES

1. This chapter was previously published in French in *Genèses* 84 (September) 2011: 25–46: "Faire crédit aux PME; calcul, garanties et collecte de l'information dans la Russie des années 2000."
2. The fall in interest rates over this period was much faster than that of the inflation rate. The sharp drop in lending rates occurred between 1999 and 2006: They fell from 13.6 percent in 1999 to 4.1 percent in 2006.
3. For more in-depth analyses of the restructuring of the banking sector during the period of the economic transition, see Johnson (2000) and Buyske (2007).
4. This qualitative survey was carried out from 2006 to 2009 in credit organizations and banks in the Moscow and Yekaterinburg—that is situated some 1000 miles east of Moscow and is the fourth-largest city in Russia—regions. It is based on 34 qualitative interviews of managers in different size and types of banks, as well as on an analysis of documentation such as banking laws and professional works and journals on credit activities in Russia. This research also profited from research collected by the ANR (*Agence nationale de la recherche*, French National Research Agency) team project to which it belongs. Research Agreement n° NPP18 "Legal Regulations and Economic Development in Countries in Transition: Institutional Reforms, Policies for Justice and the Transformation of Economic Practices in Post-communist Countries." Coordinator: Thierry Delpeuch (*Institut des sciences sociales du politique-École normale supérieure Cachan* [ISPENS]). The research team on Russia included Gilles Favarel (*Centre d'études et de recherches internationales* [CERI-CNRS]), Aurore Chaigneau (*Université de Paris-Ouest-Nanterre-La Défense, Centre d'études juridiques européennes et comparées*), and Caroline Dufy (*Institut d'études politiques [IEP] de Bordeaux, Centre Émile Durkheim [CED], Université de Bordeaux*). My personal gratitude goes to Alexei S., Serguei N., and Oxana P. for their photographic contribution to this research.
5. MEs remain quasi-anonymous clients able to select from a wide range of banking services offered, while the reputation and market position of large-scale organizations constitute definite protection against default, according to surveys.
6. Official default rates may well underestimate the real value of bad debts that were already thought to be running at more than 7 percent before the 2009

crisis, according to some sources. However, the high level of variation in observations remains significant (Bonin, Hasan, and Wachtel 2008).

7. Despite financial instability, the number of credit organizations fell from 1,349 to 1,189 from 1999 to 2006 (CBRF 2008).

8. Fictive names are used here to refer to interviewees in order to protect their anonymity, in accordance with the ethics of ethnographic work. Besides, any details allowing for the identification of the firms concerned have been avoided.

9. Chapter III, Central Bank Instruction no 254P of March 26, 2004 on the "Regulation for the Formation by Credit Organizations of Compulsory Reserves in the Case of Losses and the Constitution of a Debt."

10. All translations from Russian to English were carried out by the author.

11. Interview with Garegin A. Tosunyan, *Novaja Gazeta*, on October 20, 2008.

12. This influence was more widespread than the slow development in Russia of foreign banking capital as compared with the situation in Central and Eastern European countries. Its share of banking sector asset holdings grew from 10 percent in 1999 to 12 percent in 2006 (Bonin, Hasan, and Wachtel 2008).

13. Among the numerous existing tools, some programs marketed in the U.S. and imported to Russia are capable of calculating, for example, the probability of a company's becoming insolvent within 12 months, and within 24 months as well as the probability of a 50 percent fall in the balance sheet within 12 months, or the detection of fraud and contradictory information supplied by the borrower. Other programs are designed for particular sectors, such as energy, real estate, or retailing (Mays 2001).

14. During the 1990s, the system of direct multilateral compensation between banks was still very rudimentary. All bank transfers had to pass through the central bank. In the absence of any automatic procedure for compensating inter-company debts, only the gross positions of actors were known and not their net positions (Clément-Pitiot and Scialom 1995).

15. These practices developed above all during the 1990s in the context of industrial and financial groups promoted by the government in order to favor access to credit for the largest enterprises. The experiment led to numerous insolvencies.

16. The lengthy nature of procedures for compiling applications, according to those dealing with clients, constitutes an initial step in selecting applicants. The decision to extend credit takes several weeks and lengthens as it is passed up the levels of the hierarchy and thresholds for delegating lending decisions.

17. Anton P. confirmed this risk during a discussion in April 2011. After his departure from the banking sector, Anton P. was called upon to act as a witness in a legal action initiated by the bank that was his employer at the time of the on-site enquiry.

REFERENCES AND FURTHER READING

Barisitz, Stephan (2008) *Banking in Central and Eastern Europe 1980–2006. A Comprehensive Analysis of Banking Sector Transformation in the Former Soviet Union, Czechoslovakia, East Germany, Yugoslavia, Belarus, Bulgaria, Croatia, the Czech Republic, Hungary, Kazakhstan, Poland, Romania, the Russian Federation, Serbia and Montenegro, Slovakia, Ukraine and Uzbekistan.* London: Routledge (Routledge International Studies in Money and Banking).

Bonin, John, Iftekhar Hasan, and Paul Watchel (2008) *Helsinki, Bank of Finland Institute for Economies in Transition (BOFIT).* Discussion Paper, n° 12. Online at http://ssrn.com/abstract=1258830 or http://dx.doi.org/10.2139/ssrn.1258830, accessed on July 22, 2013.

Buyske, Gail (2007) *Banking on Small Business. Microfinance in Contemporary Russia*. Ithaca, NY: Cornell University Press.

Carruthers, Bruce G. and Barry Cohen (2010) "Noter le crédit, classification et cognition aux Etats-Unis," *Genèses* 79 (2): 48–73.

Clément-Pitiot, Hélène and Laurence Scialom (1995) "Réformer l'intermédiation financière en Russie: des options," *Revue économique* 46 (2): 433–455.

Delpeuch, Thierry (2008) "L'analyse des transferts internationaux de politiques publiques: un état de l'art," *Questions de recherche/Research in Question*, 27 (December). Online at http://www.sciencespo.fr/ceri/en/content/lanalyse-des-transferts-internationaux-de-politiques-publiques-un-etat-de-lart, accessed on July 22, 2013.

Dolgopyatova, Tatiana and Ichiro Ivasaki (2006) "Issledovanie rossijskix kompanij: pervye itogi sovmestnogo rossijsko- âponskogo proekta," Preprint WP1/2006/01 serija WP1. *Institucional'nye problemy rossijskoj èkonomiki* [Analysis of Russian Firms: First Conclusions of a Russian-Japanese Project," Working Paper Series 1. *Institutional Problems of the Russian Economy*], Moscow, Higher School of Economics. Online at https://www.hse.ru/data/2010/05/04/1216402620/WP1_2006_01.pdf, accessed on April 22, 2011.

Dufy, Caroline (2008) *Le Troc dans le marché. Pour une sociologie des échanges dans la Russie post-soviétique*. Paris: L'Harmattan.

Favarel-Garrigues, Gilles (2007) *La police des mœurs économiques. De l'URSS à la Russie (1965–1995)*. Paris: CNRS

Favarel-Garrigues, Gilles, Thierry Godefroy, and Pierre Lascoumes (2009) *Les sentinelles de l'argent sale. Les banques aux prises avec l'anti-blanchiment*. Paris: La Découverte.

Ferrary, Michel (1999) "Confiance et accumulation du capital social dans la régulation des activités de crédit," *Revue française de sociologie* 40 (3): 559–586.

Guseva, Alya (2008) *Into the Red. The Birth of the Credit Card Market in Postcommunist Russia*. Stanford, CA: Stanford University Press.

Guseva, Alya (2010) "Incertitude et complémentarité: le marché des cartes de crédit en Russie," *Genèses* 79 (2): 74–96.

Johnson, Juliet (2000) *A Fistful of Rubles. The Rise and Fall of the Russian Banking System*. Ithaca: Cornell University Press.

Laferté, Gilles (2010) "De l'interconnaissance sociale à l'identification économique: vers une histoire et une sociologie comparées de la transaction à crédit," *Genèses* 79 (2): 135–149.

Lascoumes, Pierre and Patrick Le Galès (eds) (2004) *Gouverner par les instruments*. Paris: Presses de Sciences-po.

Ledeneva, Alena (2002) "Underground Banking in Russia," *Journal of Money Laundering and Control* 5 (4): 268–279.

Leyshon, Andrew and Nigel Thrift (1997) "Spatial Financial Flows and the Growth of the Modern City," *International Social Science Journal* 49 (1): 41–53.

Leyshon, Andrew and Nigel Thrift (1999) "Lists Come Alive: Electronic Systems of Knowledge and the Rise of Credit-Scoring in Retail Banking," *Economy and Society* 28 (3): 434–466.

Mays, Elizabeth (ed.) (2001) *Handbook of Credit Scoring*. Chicago: Glenlake Publ. [Russian edition: (2008) *Rukovodstvo po kreditnomu skoringu*. Minsk: Grevcov Publisher].

Poon, Martha (2009) "From New Deal Institutions to Capital Markets: Commercial Consumer Risk Scores and the Making of Subprime Mortgage Finance", *CSI Working Papers Series* 014, Centre de sociologie de l'innovation (CSI), École des mines de Paris-CNRS. Online at http://www.csi.ensmp.fr/index.php?page=WP&lang, accessed on April 20, 2011.

Power, Michael (2004) "The Risk Management of Everything," *The Journal of Risk Finance* 5 (3): 58–65. Online at http://www.google.fr/url?sa=t&rct= j&q=&esrc=s&source=web&cd=1&ved=0CDYQFjAA&url=http%3A%2F%2 Fwww.demos.co.uk%2Ffiles%2Friskmanagementofeverything.pdf& ei=NQzuUaq1H4nK0QWDhICIDg&usg=AFQjCNEb0Q_n9DoBXNZOs7SM 64N2q9aDeA&bvm=bv.49478099,d.d2k, accessed on July 22, 2013.

5 "Coca-Cola Quit India"

Resisting Corporate Social Responsibility as a Global Management Strategy

Krista Bywater

The Coca-Cola Corporation[1] promotes itself as a responsible company while protesters from India and Colombia to the United States and Europe criticize its business practices. Coke, like many other transnational corporations (TNCs), has adopted corporate social responsibility (CSR) to protect its revenue and the reputation of its global goods and brand. Partnering with environmental groups, completing sustainability reports, and adopting international labor standards are some of the ways it exercises its corporate citizenship.[2] The company continues to expand its CSR agenda to address the social opposition it experienced when large-scale anti-Coke movements began in India in 2002, spread around the globe, and inspired vibrant transnational anti-Coca-Cola movements in the U.S. and Europe. The original protests against Coke's Indian subsidiaries started when people in the small village of Plachimada, Kerala, asserted that the company depleted and polluted its land and ground water (Bijoy 2006: 4333, Aiyer 2007: 644). Similar anti-Coke protests later arose around several other bottling plants in Mehndiganj, Uttar Pradesh; Kaladera, Rajasthan; Ballia, Bihar; and Sivaganga in Tamil Nadu.

While many scholars,[3] even those examining Coca-Cola's Indian operations (see Raman 2007 and 2010), observe that CSR is an important tactic in managing corporate legitimacy, few analyze all of the mechanisms through which the company's legitimacy is established and preserved. Sociological analysis, which to date is underrepresented in the field of CSR, can make valuable contributions, particularly in its approach to understanding "the dark side of legitimation" (Freudenburg and Alario 2007: 146). Freudenburg and Alario (2007: 153–163) state that scholars tend to focus on the obvious pillars of legitimacy (trust, tradition, expertise, prosperity, consensus, cultural capital, etc.) and overlook the equally important ways that legitimacy is maintained: 1) Through what is absent and 2) By diverting public attention to other topics. These misleading strategies constitute diversionary reframing—the practice of ". . . diverting attention away from any question about the existing distribution of privilege, not by brute force, but by changing the subject. . . ." (Freudenburg and Alario 2007: 146). Freudenburg and Alario (2007) examine the use of diversionary reframing within political contexts where it serves as a discursive practice that helps to uphold legitimacy by averting public attention away from disproportionalities in the allocation of costs and benefits of growth and development.

Diversionary reframing is a useful tool to analyze CSR because the concept helps to interrogate how inequities in the allotment of privileges and resources are masked through strategies of intentional misdirection. Freudenburg and Alario (2007) compare business proponents to magicians who conceal critical information while working in view of the audience using techniques of distraction and misdirection. In their analogy, public attention focuses on the magician's distraction—the politician's diversionary frame—and the sleight of hand needed to conduct the trick goes unnoticed establishing its validity. ". . . [E]ven the best eyes in the world are only capable of "seeing" in the direction in which they are pointed" (Freudenberg and Alario 2007: 153) and audiences shared inattention helps to establish the legitimacy of the trick. The diversion—the guise of legitimacy—enables actors to maintain inequality, power, and privileged access to resources (Freudenberg and Alario 2007: 153). This approach encourages scholars to ask: "what is our "shared inattention"?" (Davidson and Grant 2012: 75), and what diversionary frames are used to engender and sustain corporate legitimacy?

This chapter proposes that the politically contested nature of corporate legitimacy and CSR in the age of neo-liberalism can be further understood by employing Freudenburg and Alario's (2007) concept of diversionary reframing. Examining the ways that CSR promotes corporate legitimacy through diversionary reframing allows a more complete analysis of CSR as a global management strategy. Moreover, Coca-Cola's use of CSR to address the initial protests in India and the transnational anti-Coke movements in the U.S. are ideal cases to investigate the nuances and effectiveness of diversionary reframing within CSR. An examination of critical elements of Coca-Cola's CSR policy and program offers insight into the understudied aspects of how corporate legitimacy is preserved and enhanced through CSR discourse and policy.

Guided by Freudenburg and Alario's (2007) examination of the dark side of legitimacy, this chapter finds that CSR is used as a diversionary tactic to suppress social movements and limit the work of transnational activist networks in order to legitimize neoliberal economic relations and corporate globalization. The chapter begins by introducing the original Indian anti-Coca-Cola movement in the village of Plachimada where protesters demanded that "Coca-Cola Quit India." Then the origins and main principles of Coca-Cola's corporate social responsibility program are explicated to illustrate the publicly acknowledged functions of CSR. The next section analyzes how diversionary reframing is operationalized in Coca-Cola's CSR water stewardship program, which the company developed in response to the anti-Coke movements. Finally, to underscore the power of misdirection within CSR and its ability to suppress social movements, the chapter analyzes the anti-Coke student movement at the University of Michigan. The student movement began to support the anti-Coke protesters in India. Coca-Cola's use of CSR was particularly effective in quelling the transnational anti-Coke struggle at the University of Michigan and the case demonstrates the importance of interrogating the effectiveness of CSR as a global management strategy.

PLACHIMADA: INDIA'S PREMIER ANTI-COCA-COLA STRUGGLE

Reflecting on the plight of her small village Mylamma, a resident of Plachimada and a leader in the Anti-Coca-Cola Movement, stated:

> They came to our village with glittering offers; that our people would get ample job opportunities in the plant; the overall development of our village would be taken care of; the economic growth of our area would be strengthened etc., etc. We waited and waited . . . nothing miraculous happened. On the contrary, six months went by, slowly we started facing the reverse effects. Our precious water resource had been stolen. . . . Where would I get some fresh and pure drinking water anymore? How many kilometers should we have to walk to fetch a drop of water? Who will compensate the heavy loss incurred upon us by this giant cola plant?[4]

Mylamma and the *Coca-Cola Virudha Janakeeya Samara Samithy* (Anti-Coca-Cola People's Struggle Committee) symbolically began their protest against Coke on Earth Day, 2002 (Bijoy 2006: 4334). More than 1,500 protesters made a human chain around the firm's bottling plant in Plachimada, Kerala, interlocking their hands and wills to interrupt the company's transportation of products. Protesters demanded that Coca-Cola "Quit Plachimada, Quit India" because they believed the company's unsustainable business practices depleted and polluted the community's land and only source of water—the ground water (Bijoy 2006: 4333). Protesters asserted that all of the environmental problems occurred 6 months after Coca-Cola's bottling plant began its operations. Protesters also charged the company with selling its toxic waste—a sludge—to unsuspecting farmers as a fertilizer (Aiyer 2007: 644). The movement grew and strengthened over the next 2 years, and it additionally accused Coca-Cola of destroying people's livelihoods and privatizing the community ground water.

The Anti-Coca-Cola Movement started by Advasis and Dalits,[5] India's most marginalized groups, has spread throughout the country and gained support from some of India's leading activists including Vandana Shiva and Medha Patkar. In 2003, the BBC tested the water in Plachimada and discovered high levels of cadmium and lead in the ground water (Waite 2004). In addition, the Kerala State Pollution Control Board (KSPCB) found that although the total metal content in the water did not exceed legal limits, the levels were very high. The KSPCB instructed Coca-Cola to dispose of its waste according to India's hazardous waste guidelines and to provide residents with drinking water (KSPCB 2003). Subsequent movements against Coca-Cola have sprung up in Mehndiganj, Uttar Pradesh; Kaladera, Rajasthan; Ballia, Bihar; and Sivaganga in Tamil Nadu.[6] Locals living near Coke's bottling plants in these areas experienced similar ground water scarcity and pollution.

In 2003 and 2006, the movements against Coca-Cola gained national recognition when the Center for Science and Environment (CSE), a non-profit organization in Delhi, India, found high levels of pesticides in Coke and Pepsi's beverages (CSE 2003 and 2006).[7] These findings gave momentum to the struggle as middle-class consumers became concerned about the products' safety (Vedwan 2007). In addition to destroying the environment and the lives of people around bottling plants, the anti-Coke movement charged the company with selling pesticide-laden products (Aiyer 2007). Coke and Pepsi's sales dramatically declined,[8] and, due to concern for their own health, ministers in the central government banned the sale of Coke and Pepsi products in Delhi's parliament buildings. Many universities throughout India also stopped selling Coke's beverages as students worried about the health hazards and wished to support the Anti-Coca-Cola Struggle. What started as a local protest against unsustainable development became a national struggle against the company and India's neoliberal development policies.

The Coke plant in Plachimada is now closed and the company shut down its factory in Sivaganga due to water shortages and public opposition. Most notably, on March 22, 2010, World Water Day, a high-level committee formed by the Kerala state government found Coke liable for $48 million for the damage its plant caused in Plachimada, Kerala (Lakshman 2010). The committee determined that the Coca-Cola Company violated a number of key laws including the: Water (Prevention and Control of Pollution) Act from 1974; and the Environment (Protection) Act from 1986.[9] Upon the committee's recommendation, in 2011, the Kerala state government established an agency to handle the compensation process. Although the movement has obtained some success, 10 years after it began, residents living near factory still suffer from water shortages and pollution. Every other day women line their brightly colored water jugs on the roadside and await the water tanker sent by the state government. Protesters in Plachimada continue their anti-Coca-Cola struggles, and demand that, in addition to paying the $48 million in fines, Coke should be held criminally liable for its actions.

Protests against Coca-Cola's business practices are not limited to India. The Killer Coke Campaign accuses Coke of permitting poor working conditions at its subcontractors' bottling facilities and being complicit in paramilitaries' murder of several union members in Colombia (Gill 2009: 669–672). News reports of the Anti-Coca-Cola Movement in India and the Killer Coke Campaign in Colombia have led students at more than a dozen colleges and universities in the United States and Europe to force their organizations to cancel their contracts with the company. Students at Smith, Skidmore, and Oberlin Colleges as well as the University of Illinois are among those who have successfully demanded that Coke products not be sold on their campuses. Many more anti-Coca-Cola campaigns have taken place at institutions such as New York University and the University of Michigan. The case at the University of Michigan will be discussed later in the chapter.

The transnational movements against Coke continue at a time when there is growing recognition that the world is experiencing a global water crisis. Approximately 750 million people—almost a quarter of whom live in India—cannot access enough clean water. Yet access to potable water is essential for public health and sustainable development. Due to the increasing awareness of water scarcity and the popularity of the anti-Coke movement, Coca-Cola enhanced its CSR policy to help mitigate some of the damage to its reputation and global brand.

ITS SECRET FORMULA: COKE'S CORPORATE SOCIAL RESPONSIBILITY

There is ambiguity in the meaning and application of CSR across firms (Moon 2007: 296) but the definition usually cited presents CSR as "a concept whereby companies integrate social and environmental concerns in their business operations and in their interaction with their stakeholders on a voluntary basis" (Commission of the European Communities 2001: 8). From this definition and popular discussions, it is clear that CSR focuses on companies' self-regulation and promotes improving their social, environmental, and human rights records—their triple bottom line (Utting 2005: 375). CSR is a discourse as well as a set of managerial practices that usually exceed companies' legal obligations and consider firms' social, moral, and ethical obligations to society.

Since CSR relies on companies' voluntary self-regulation, the concept complements the neoliberal agenda to limit government intervention in business affairs and the marketplace. In the 1990s, many scholars and businesses revitalized and endorsed CSR policies that were introduced three decades earlier (Jenkins 2005: 526). This second major push for CSR arose as both governments and development agencies began to acknowledge that economic growth alone could not produce social and sustainable development (Stiglitz 2002). Transnational corporations, governments, and a wide variety of development organizations offered CSR as a means to curtail the destructive consequences of economic liberalization and privatization in order to preserve corporate legitimacy (Raman 2007: 103–106, Utting and Marques 2010: 2–3). "It is against this background that the development agencies have come to see CSR as a way for reconciling support for private enterprise and a market-based system with their central aim of reducing global poverty" (Jenkins 2005: 530). CSR offered a way to bridge the seemingly disparate objectives of corporate profits, social development, and environmental protection. Rather than seeing corporations as the source of social problems that include poverty, pollution, corruption, and human rights violations, proponents of CSR view multinational firms as potential facilitators of economic and social development (Blowfield 2005: 515). From this perspective, development is fostered by creating economic opportunities, growth, charitable projects, and by increasing revenues through taxes that can fund social services and build infrastructure. With the help of CSR, proponents believe economic growth and foreign investment can advance development in the Global South.

The push for CSR has not only come from development agencies but from within the business community. Peter Utting identifies the top-down promotion of CSR by corporations as "the movement of business" (2005: 378).[10] It seems reasonable that transnational corporations (TNCs) adopt CSR reforms to defend their reputations and consent to demands of oppositional movements against them, but why would companies lead the charge for increasing CSR measures? An overview of the main functions of Coke's CSR strategy helps to reveal its utility.

Operating in more than 200 countries and with revenues that exceed U.S. $35 billion annually, Coke is a high profile company subject to much scrutiny. Its global goods and brand benefit from people's trust in the quality and safety of its products and operations. CSR is a central component of the firm's business scheme. TNCs and in particular Coca-Cola must appease a variety of stakeholders who include investors, employees, consumers, and the communities in which they operate. Corporations use the discourse of CSR to satisfy groups, who often have competing interests, and gain their confidence. The company's former Chairman and CEO Neville Isdell recognized this in his speech when he accepted the 2006 Distinguished Award for Corporate Citizenship from the Committee for Economic Development (CED).

> Customers *trust* us to offer the highest level of service and attention to their needs. Shareowners *trust* that we will provide transparency in our accounting and excellence in our financial results. Corporate citizenship helps build and maintain trust with these and other stakeholders, including legislators, regulators and even—when we're *really* lucky—the news media. It earns us the benefit of the doubt when things go wrong, as they sometimes will in a system as big as ours. And when they do go wrong, I believe our corporate citizenship initiatives help us get back on our feet much more quickly than we would without them.
>
> (Isdell 2006)

Isdell recognized corporate citizenship as an important insurance policy as well as a defensive and proactive approach to mitigate outside regulation and public surveillance. Trust is an obvious pillar of legitimacy, and CSR is a key means through which confidence is fostered and facilitated. Coke's CSR initiatives are thus understood as ways to manage public perception and extend its social license to operate "when things go wrong" as they have according to protesters in India.

Coke's new Chairman and CEO, Muhtar Kent, who referred to himself as the company's chief sustainability officer, continues to stress the importance of Coke's CSR policies.[11] In his speech at the Globes Conference on Social Responsibility in 2009, Mr. Kent stated:

> The majority of global consumers claim that a company's social responsibility efforts carry nearly equal weight to price and brand quality when making a purchasing decision. Most consumers today feel that companies spend too much money on advertising and marketing and should put more resources behind social responsibility. The vast majority of consumers say that during a recession, they are more loyal to brands that are perceived as socially responsible.

From both CEOs' public statements, it is obvious that managing risks, profits, and reputation, and gaining a competitive edge are the chief reasons Coke pursues CSR initiatives.

Their formal declarations also suggest the "moral" and "business cases" for CSR. The moral case for CSR considers both the company's long-term survival (Goodpaster and Matthews 2003: 132) and its need to act according to economic, legal, ethical, and discretionary standards (Carroll 1979). The "business case" emphasizes how companies' profits are enhanced by CSR reforms (see Holliday et al. 2002, Epstein and Roy 2003, Wagner and Schaltegger 2006). According to this logic, companies can maintain or maximize profits while they improve their social, ethical, and environmental business practices. This reasoning is in line with neoliberal ideology that promotes the free market as the best means to foster economic growth, prosperity, and sustainable resource management. According to business arguments for CSR, economic growth is not understood to be antithetical to human and environmental well-being so that the common understanding is that CSR creates the opportunity for win-win business-society relations.

Within the "business case" arguments, companies can simultaneously: 1) Create employment opportunities and new consumers to buy their products (Lodge and Wilson 2006, Wilson and Wilson 2006), 2) Reduce pollution and costs by instituting reforms such as recycling, and 3) Conserve natural resources and increase efficiency and profits. Here, business and social objectives are not at odds; on the contrary, business activities are seen to improve social development and environmental management. Corporate citizenship is the magic formula that offers a way to recognize environmental concerns and human rights while enhancing a company's reputation and bottom line. Savvy CEOs like Muhtar Kent please the business community by underlining the business case for CSR and reassure activists by stressing its moral tenets.

The CSR strategy that Coca-Cola's leaders openly acknowledge—one that stresses building corporate legitimacy through trust and tradition—represents the typical ways that business proponents and scholars discuss the utility of CSR. Therefore, the obvious building blocks or pillars of legitimacy are publicly acknowledged, emphasized, and examined. In this traditional examination of legitimacy, scholars overlook the ways that legitimacy is maintained through what is not said and through the company's diversionary tactics. Analyzing Coke's CSR water stewardship program thus reveals the ways that CSR fosters corporate legitimacy through diversionary reframing.

THE MAGICIAN'S ASSISTANT: CSR
AS A DIVERSIONARY STRATEGY

Coca-Cola has spearheaded a number of programs to promote the company as an environmentally responsible firm that is concerned about water scarcity. Under Isdell's leadership, the company adopted the UN Global Compact's CEO Water Mandate. This global directive encourages firms to prioritize water resource management and work with governments, NGOs, UN agencies, and other stakeholders to address global water shortages. Coke designed its water stewardship program under this mandate to reduce its use of water resources and increase its operation's efficiency. The water stewardship program aims to reduce, recycle, and replenish the water used in its finished products (Wrights 2009: 4).

Coke's emphasis on the sustainability of its business practices, especially related to its water usage, began after the protests in India and with growing public knowledge of water shortages around the world. In the water stewardship section of its *2011/2012 Sustainability Report* (Coca-Cola Corporation 2012), the firm acknowledges that "(in) some parts of the world where water is acutely stressed, we have encountered opposition to our operations because of perceptions that we are using more than our fair share of water and depleting local water sources to the detriment of local farmers and residents. . . . We have been successful in securing the 'technical' and 'regulatory' licenses for using the water we need. But where we have sometimes been challenged is in securing the 'social license' for our operations among the communities that host us" (Coca-Cola Corporation 2012).[12] Coke's CSR water stewardship program is an attempt by the company to restore its social license to operate after the Indian anti-Coke movements gained local and transnational support. The following section evaluates some of the central components of the company's water stewardship program to illuminate how the conceptualization and implementation of CSR initiatives allows the company to gain legitimacy through diversionary reframing.

The Mantra of Eco-efficiency

Coke's water stewardship program is a central component of its sustainability initiatives and eco-efficiency is a guiding principle of the CSR water initiative. In its *2011/2012 Sustainability Report*, Coca-Cola states that the company has met its goal of increasing its water efficiency by 20 percent since 2004 (2012). The amount of water required to make one liter of a beverage has been reduced from 2.65 to 2.16 (Coca-Cola Corporation 2012). These numbers represent the average amount of water used to produce the company's more than 800 products around the world. Decreasing water usage, especially in nonessential beverage industries, is necessary to address problems of water scarcity. One can interpret Coke's environmental consciousness as a positive outcome of the business case for CSR because reducing the company's water usage improves its bottom line and puts less strain on water resources.

The company may be reducing the amount of water needed to make each product but its water usage continues to grow as it produces and sells more beverages. The company states that: "Greater efficiency in our water use does not mean making less product" (Coca-Cola Corporation 2012). Consequently, Coke's emphasis on improving its water efficiency by 20 percent and reducing the amount of water used to make each drink masks the increasing rate of its overall water usage. The company's use of water has increased from 2004 to 2012 from 278 billion to 293.3 billion liters (Coca-Cola Corporation 2012). The objective of water efficiency masks the larger issue that Coca-Cola will continue to exhaust more water resources as it expands its operations. In fact, Coke announced its plans to invest U.S. $5 billion before 2020 to develop its Indian operations. The expansion of its Indian operations is a vital component of its 2020 vision of doubling system revenues this decade. Based on its current CSR programs and growth trajectory, it is not clear how Coca-Cola will be able to achieve environmentally sustainable operations while seeking to double its business.

Profit making and expansion of production are inherently at odds with sustainability objectives in this case. The company's sustainability program demonstrates the limitation of the "business case for CSR" as the scenario is not a win-win situation for communities and firms. Under the current water stewardship program bottling plants will continue to use greater amounts of water. Water resources in areas where Coke's bottling plants continue to operate such as Mehndiganj and Kaladera will be further stressed. Here, CSR works as a diversionary tactic as initiatives focus on the company's efforts of efficiency and reducing the water used in each product. In this process, public attention is diverted from the company's overall increasing water usage and the conflict between corporate profits and environmental sustainability. Growth in production continues to outpace gains in water efficiency; this is obviously not the win-win scenario proposed by the business case for CSR.

Lund-Thomsen states that the business case "depoliticizes the role of TNCs in the [Global] South and ignores the gap which is often identified between the stated intentions of TNCs and their actual behavior in relation to poor communities" (2005: 4). In effect, Coke's CSR initiatives based on the business case might improve Coca-Cola's financial bottom line and its reputation, but they do little to address the problems it creates in water-scarce communities. Eco-efficiency is a useful CSR strategy because it misdirects public attention away from increasing resource usage necessary for corporate growth and focuses on efficiency as a win-win scenario for both the environment and companies.

The Myth of Water Neutrality

Another diversionary maneuver within Coke's water stewardship program is the emphasis of its objective of water neutrality—to replenish the same amount of water used to produce its products. In 2007, Coca-Cola announced at the WWF meeting on World Environment Day in Beijing that it would increase its water recycling and aim to become a water neutral company (Batson 2007: 10).[13] According to CEO Kent Muhtar, water neutrality "is good for business because it lowers our cost of production, it lowers our break-even points, it allows us to spend more money on our brands" (Environmental Leader 2010). To advance this goal, Coke partnered with the WWF in 2008 and donated U.S. $20 million to support water conservation projects in seven large river basins including the Rio Grande and Rio Bravo in the United States and Mexico, the Yangtze in China, and the Danube in Europe (Coca-Cola Corporation 2012). Focusing on its corporate giving and efforts to replenish ground water, the company also publicizes that it contributes to more than 320 community water projects in 86 countries (Coca-Cola Corporation 2012). "We estimate that this work has replenished about 31 percent of the water used in our finished beverages in 2010. Our goal is to replenish 100 percent by 2020" (Coca-Cola Corporation 2012). The goal of water neutrality and replenishing water resources appears to be part of a positive, progressive, and sustainable company program that simultaneously benefits businesses and communities. Yet water neutrality is another sleight of hand and form of diversionary reframing made possible by CSR programs.

The problem with the company's CSR strategy is that the initiatives do not address the inherent problems with Coca-Cola's unsustainable business practices in water-scarce regions. For Coca-Cola to become a water-neutral company, it would need to recycle and return the amount of water used in production to local watersheds and aquifers where the water was originally sourced. While water neutrality is a laudable idea, in reality supporting conservation of the Rio Grande does not replenish the ground water near Coke's bottling plant in Plachimada, India. Coke is not guaranteeing that any of its factories in India will be water neutral. If the company attains overall water neutrality or even just water neutrality in India as it claims it has, it would not lessen the impact of the company's operations on specific communities such as Mehndiganj. While the overall goal of supporting water replenishment is positive, the company proposes a vague goal of water neutrality rather than promising fully sustainable water practices at each of its factories. Again the intent of the CSR programs is to divert public attention away from Coke's water intensive business and redirect it to the companies "sustainability" initiatives.

Even if Coke stated that its aim was to make all of its Indian factories water neutral, the company would not be sanctioned if it did not meet this objective since the reforms are voluntary. Moreover, reports from the field and independent reviews of CSR projects (see Barkay 2011) vary greatly from the companies'—particularly Coca-Cola's—reports. With no or little outside oversight of CSR projects, companies can frame projects in the most positive light. By framing water scarcity as a global issue rather than addressing scarcity caused or exacerbated by Coke's operations, the company is again able to misdirect the attention from the impact of its operations. Coke's water neutrality is a meaningless goal if it does not address the sustainability of each of its bottling facilities.

Additionally, Coke's bottling plants in Mehndiganj and Plachimada sourced water from underground aquifers. These water resources are part of a complex water cycle and utilizing ground water affects the mineral content of the soil and the water and alters the water resources available for agricultural production and human survival. The company's approach to conservation treats water aquifers like empty containers that simply need to be refilled once depleted or emptied. The millions of gallons of water extracted by each of the company's bottling facilities can irreparably affect water and biological systems. Coke's notion of replenishing water resources fails to address the complexity of the water cycle and environmental systems. While the goal of water neutrality sounds desirable, it serves as a sleight of hand to distract the public's attention from its water-intensive business. For water-scarce regions like Mendiganj, Kaladera, and Plachimada, water use for human and agricultural needs should be prioritized above water for resource-intensive businesses that do not make products that are essential for people's livelihood.

SUPPRESSING SOCIAL MOVEMENTS WITH CSR

The harmful effects of CSR and diversionary reframing are especially evident when we exam how CSR can be utilized to suppress social movements that advocate for progressive social changes. Thousands of students in the United States and Europe have protested against Coke's business practices in India and Colombia. In particular, the struggles of students at the University of Michigan illustrate how CSR policies can be used to suppress dissent, prevent meaningful reforms, and legitimize and repair TNCs' reputations. Opposition against Coca-Cola began at the University of Michigan when students founded the Student Coalition to Cut the Coca-Cola Contract. Approximately 20 groups, which represented more than 5,000 students, formed the coalition. For more than 2 years, the group insisted that the university end its contracts with Coca-Cola. At the time, Coca-Cola's contracts with the university were worth almost $1.3 million (Peterson 2005: 1). In November 2004, the Students Organized for Labor and Economic

Equality (SOLE) submitted formal complaints to the university and citied Coke's depletion and pollution of ground water, dumping of toxic sludge, and selling of pesticide-laden products in India as well as labor violations at bottling factories in Colombia (Peterson 2005: 1).

As a result of the mounting protests, the University of Michigan's Vendor Code of Conduct Dispute Review Board (DRB) met with all interested parties including Coca-Cola, students, activists, and Indian and Colombian union leaders. It also held a public hearing on the matter in April 2005. After assessing the complaints, the DRB decided it needed more information, and it gave Coca-Cola the opportunity to investigate the complaints and correct the problems. The DRB required Coca-Cola to hire third-party independent auditors, who were acceptable to all parties, to investigate the charges in India and Colombia. The Dispute Review Board set several deadlines and required Coke to draft a corrective CSR action plan by the end of May 2006. In the meantime, the DRB recommended that the university should not begin or renew any contracts and that it should only agree to short-term, conditional extensions of existing contracts that would be reassessed "at each of the established deadlines to determine if Coca-Cola has made satisfactory progress toward demonstrating its compliance with the Vendor Code of Conduct." (Peterson 2005: 1)

Initially, it appeared as though the student movement had attained some success and that the protests of people in India resulted in a thriving transnational movement. In reality, the success of the student movement was short-lived as the university accepted Coke's proposal to have The Energy and Resources Institute (TERI), a Delhi-based research institute sponsored in part by Coca-Cola, to conduct the independent assessment of Coke's practices in India. As part of its diversionary reframing, Coke failed to highlight its relationship with TERI and the potential conflict of interest. To distance itself from TERI, Coke hired the Meridian Institute, a mediation firm, to act as a facilitator and manage the funding for the study. Hiring the Meridian Institute allowed Coca-Cola to state that it did not pay TERI to conduct the assessment although Coke indirectly funded the project. The student coalition and the India Resource Center, which serves as a transnational activist network linking the movement in India to struggles in the United States and Europe, did not believe TERI met the criterion of being a neutral or third-party auditor. Amit Srivastava, one of the main organizers at the India Resource Center, stated that choosing "TERI, which clearly has a mutually beneficial relationship with Coca-Cola, is neither fair, independent, or [sic] third party. By agreeing to Coca-Cola's choice of the group in India to develop the investigation, the University of Michigan is making a mockery of the concerns being raised by communities in India" (IRC 2006). The increasing funding of NGOs and organizations like TERI is part of Coca-Cola's CSR policy and in this instance the company utilized an organization that it had a pre-existing relationship with in order to manage the required "independent audit."

While in Delhi, I had the opportunity to speak with one of the leaders of TERI's Coca-Cola investigation. She dismissed the accusations that TERI was unable to produce an unbiased assessment of Coca-Cola because of its relationship with the company. A leader of TERI's Coca-Cola investigation stated:

> We have, on our website, put down under the frequently asked questions, this business and I think it clearly brings out that Coca Cola's support of TERI activities is probably a fraction of a percentage point. So I don't think in any way we are obliged, obligated to Coca-Cola for our existence or for our continued survival. TERI has relationships with almost every corporate, large corporate in the country. But that does not mean we have sold out to every one of them. . . . We have relationships with all multinational organizations—World Bank, UNDP, ADB, etc. Does that make us a stooge of these? . . . I don't think so.[14]

TERI's website lists Coca-Cola as one of its sponsors, but it does not disclose how much Coca-Cola donates or pays to support TERI's programs. In the statements above, TERI's representative suggests the institute is not unduly influenced by all of its sponsors. TERI like many NGOs, non-profits, and research institutes has numerous corporate and multinational partners. Companies through their CSR initiatives have developed relations with NGOs to enhance their credibility. There has been an increasing melding of corporations and organizations through financial sponsorship (Shamir 2008). Many organizations like TERI assert they are still capable of remaining independent and impartial despite their corporate partnerships and funding. Nonetheless, corporations' sponsorship, partnerships, and relationships with NGOs, non-profits, and research institutes exist because these are mutually beneficial associations.

The financial support and reputations of organizations become intertwined with those of their corporate sponsors, and as the boundaries blur, it is often not in organizations' best interest to sever ties with or support programs against companies' interests. For instance, in 2001 several years before conducting the assessment of Coca-Cola, TERI included Coke on its list of the most responsible companies in India. Coca-Cola has sponsored events with TERI including its annual Delhi Sustainable Development Summit and its 2003 Earth Day event at which the keynote speaker was Sunil Gupta, Vice President for Public Affairs and Communication at Hindustan Coca-Cola Limited. TERI also promotes Coca-Cola's sustainability efforts on its website and features an interview with Sunil Gupta about Coke's sustainability programs in India. With such close ties to Coca-Cola, TERI's reputation could be harmed if it publicized that the company it presents as a paragon of sustainable practices is in fact destroying the environment and people's livelihoods.

The University of Michigan accepted TERI's study despite the claims that TERI was not a neutral auditor and that Coca-Cola through its sponsorship limited the study's scope. TERI's investigation focused on the charges that

Coke's products were pesticide-laden and that the company produced hazardous waste at its Indian bottling plants. TERI tested the input and output water at six of Coca-Cola's 52 plants and found no pesticides (TERI 2008: 2).

One of the leaders of TERI's Coca-Cola investigation discussed the scope of TERI's project and stated:

INTERVIEWEE: I hope you're aware of the fact this [the study] is not addressing itself the problem of pesticide and Coca-Cola. That's a separate issue altogether.

KRISTA BYWATER: How so, what do you mean?

INTERVIEWEE: We are not looking at the product. We are looking at the inputs and the waste. We are not addressing ourselves to the product quality at all because there are a number of committees of the government of India dealing with that. . . . So we are only addressing ourselves to the water management policies and practices. It's a limited study to that extent.[15]

The scope of the study did not address student complaints about the contamination of Coke's beverages and instead focused on the input and output water. It is possible that the beverages contained high levels of pesticides, which might come from another ingredient or via contamination. Therefore, TERI's assessment did not directly address students' complaints about pesticides in Coca-Cola products or the exploitation of community ground water resources. Additionally, TERI only tested water at approximately 10 percent of Coca-Cola's bottling facilities in India. Given the limited nature of the study, contaminated water might be used at 90 percent of Coke's facilities, but the university was satisfied with the findings. The company was able to ensure that potentially incriminating information was absent. Its CSR program therefore enabled Coke to engage in diversionary reframing that dictated what was absent: 1) Coke's relationship with TERI and 2) The agenda of the third-party review.

From the comments above, statements by the University of Michigan, and the findings in TERI's report, it is obvious that Coca-Cola has not shown that its products are pesticide-free. The pesticide content was not assessed in TERI's investigation, because Coca-Cola limited the scope of the study; the products were not tested for pesticides and only a small number of facilities were assessed. Coca-Cola sidestepped the complaints by providing the university with results from the water used by six factories. One would imagine that a better way to determine the presence of pesticides in beverages would be to sample a number of beverages from numerous states in India and test the products for pesticides. This is what the Center for Science and Environment did when it tested Coke and Pepsi products and found high levels of pesticides in 2003 and again in 2006 (CSE 2003 and 2006). This is a clear example of Coca-Cola being able to set the agenda through the sleight of hand of its CSR study and limit the scope of the required third-party assessment.

In the final report produced for the University of Michigan, TERI recommended that Coca-Cola focused on improving its CSR policies by: conducting environmental assessments of watersheds before establishing plants, respecting farmers' rights to water, focusing on sustainable development, partnering with local governments to increase water conservation efforts, and, in some instances, helping the government supply residents with piped water (TERI 2008: 19–23). Ultimately, the University of Michigan was satisfied with the study and the CSR recommendations despite the problems addressed above and even though the research took much longer than expected. University faculty and staff reviewed the TERI report, and, in January of 2008, they recommended that the institution should continue to do business with Coca-Cola. Today, the university continues its contracts with Coca-Cola and is satisfied that Coca-Cola is not guilty of any of the charges in India.

The Student Coalition to Cut the Coca-Cola Contract spent a tremendous amount of time mobilizing students to boycott the Coca-Cola Corporation. The university also expended time and money to investigate the complaints against the company. In the end, all these efforts were undermined by the university's belief in Coca-Cola's promise to pursue its CSR policies. The university agreed to the principles of CSR, including the notion that companies can self-monitor and can be trusted to implement TERI's recommended reforms. It seems as if Coca-Cola's former CEO was right when he stated Coke's corporate citizenship initiatives "earn us the benefit of the doubt when things go wrong" (Isdell 2006). CSR enabled the Coca-Cola Corporation to limit the scope of the investigation and suppress the movement to ban its products from the University of Michigan. This case has had far-reaching effects as other colleges and universities rely on TERI's report and the position taken by the University of Michigan to make decisions for their campuses. The diversionary reframing within Coke's CSR policy helped the firm maintain its corporate legitimacy despite vibrant transnational movements opposing its operations.

CONCLUSION

Corporations, particularly ones that rely on brand recognition such as Coca-Cola, are vulnerable to social movements that question the safety of their products and sustainability of their operations. The social license to operate and corporate legitimacy are paramount within an increasingly competitive global market place. Through its CSR policy and initiatives, Coca-Cola has spent millions of dollars to enhance its public reputation and protect its brand. As part of its global management strategy, the company supports a variety of water programs and community development initiatives around the world to gain investor, employee, and consumer trust and confidence.

Through their study of "the dark side of legitimation," Freudenberg and Alario (2007) build on previous theories and posit that corporate legitimacy is dependent on more than establishing trust, tradition, expertise, consensus, and cultural capital. These scholars highlight the equally important ways that legitimacy is maintained with diversionary reframing. Using diversionary reframing to investigate Coca-Cola's operations reveals how the company uses CSR to carefully misdirect public attention away from its controversial behaviors and highlight its environmental and sustainability efforts.

By investigating the principles of Coke's CSR water stewardship program, this chapter examines how the company uses concepts such as eco-efficiency and water neutrality to conceal the firm's water-intensive and, at times, unsustainable operations. Likewise, the analysis of the student movement at the University of Michigan demonstrates how diversionary reframing enables CSR initiatives to help companies like Coca-Cola suppress social opposition. Much like the magician's distraction in the form of a sleight of hand, the company engages concerned citizens with flashy but insignificant CSR reforms without fundamentally addressing the sustainability or equity of its business practices. This chapter illustrates how actors can use CSR to secure corporate-led growth and legitimacy at the expense of communities and environmental conservation. Consequently, the examination of Coca-Cola's CSR policy challenges the stance of proponents[16] and even some critics[17] who, to varying degrees, acknowledge CSR as a useful means to limit the harmful effects of corporate maleficence and achieve progressive social change.

NOTES

1. Throughout the chapter I also refer to the Coca-Cola Corporation by its popular name—Coke.
2. I view CSR and related concepts of corporate social responsiveness, corporate citizenship, and corporate social performance as synonymous since much of the business community uses these terms interchangeably. Swanson and Niehoff (2001) and Waddock (2001) also argue that these terms share the same meaning (Banerjee 2008).
3. For examples of scholarship on the use of corporate social responsibility to establish, maintain, and expand corporate legitimacy within the age of neoliberalism see Utting (2007), Jenkins (2005), and Utting and Marques (2010).
4. The quote is cited in an anti-Coke campaign pamphlet entitled "Coca-Cola Quit Plachimada, Quit India." Mylamma, who was a powerful activist within the struggle, passed away in 2007.
5. Adviasis are tribal peoples who make up 1 percent of Kerala's population. They are among the least literate and remain largely excluded from politics. Dalits, formerly known as the Untouchables, are the lowest Hindu caste, and along with Adviasis, Dalits are among the most socially and economically disadvantaged groups in India.
6. The plants in Plachimada, Kaladera, and Mehndiganj are operated by Coca-Cola's wholly owned Indian subsidiary the Hindustan Coca-Cola Beverages Private Limited (HCCBL).
7. The Coca-Cola Corporation continues to dispute these claims.
8. August 13, 2003, the *Economic Times* reported that Coke's sales decreased between 30 and 40 percent in the wake of the pesticide allegations.

9. The laws violated also include the Indian Easement Act, 1882; the Factories Act, 1948; the Land Utilization Order, 1967; the Hazardous Waste (Management and Handling) Rules, 1989; the SC-ST (Prevention of Atrocities) Act 1989; the Indian Penal Code, and the Kerala Ground Water (Control & Regulation) Act, 2002.
10. Firms advocated for CSR at global conferences such as the Rio Earth Summit in 1992 (Clapp 2007) and the 2002 World Summit on Sustainable Development (WSSD) in Johannesburg (Hamann et al. 2003).
11. In May 2011, Beatriz Perez, Coca-Cola's Chief Marketing Officer for Coca-Cola North America, was appointed the company's Chief Sustainability Officer.
12. http://www.coca-colacompany.com/sustainabilityreport/world/water-stewardship.html#section-mitigating-riskfor-communities-and-for-our-system, accessed on July 5, 2013.
13. The idea of water neutrality is derived from the concept of carbon neutrality.
14. Interview conducted on May 10, 2007, in Delhi, India, with Chanchal Ahuj. To protect the identity of the interviewee a pseudonym is used here.
15. Interview conducted on May 10, 2007, in Delhi, India, with Chanchal Ahuj. To protect the identity of the interviewee a pseudonym is used here.
16. Proponents of CSR include Porter and van der Linde (1995), Figge et al. (2002), Holliday et al. (2002), Epstein and Roy (2003), Wagner and Schaltegger (2006).
17. For additional critiques of CSR in the Global South, see Blowfield and Frynas (2005), Jenkins (2005), Lund-Thomsen (2005), Newell and Frynas (2007), Preito-Carrón et al. (2006), and Soule (2009).

REFERENCES

Aiyer, Ananthakrishnan (2007) "The Allure of the Transnational: Notes on Some Aspects of the Political Economy of Water in India," *Cultural Anthropology* 22 (4): 640–658.
Banerjee, Subhabrata B. (2008) "Corporate Social Responsibility: The Good, the Bad and the Ugly," *Critical Sociology* 34 (1): 51–79.
Barkay, Tamar (2011) "When Business & Community Meet: A Case Study of Coca-Cola," *Critical Sociology* 39 (1): 1–17.
Batson, Andrew (2007) "Coke Aims to Improve water Recycling: Proposal Marks a Bid to Address Criticism in Developing Nations," *Wall Street Journal (Eastern Edition)* (June 6): 10.
Bijoy, C.R. (2006) "Kerala's Plachimada Struggles: A Narrative on Water and Governance Rights," *Economic and Political Weekly* (October): 4332–4339.
Blowfield, Michael (2005) "Corporate Social Responsibility: Reinventing the Meaning of Development," *International Affairs* 81 (3): 515–524.
Blowfield, Michael and Jedrzej G. Frynas (2005) "Setting New Agendas: Critical Perspectives on Corporate Social Responsibility in the Developing World," *International Affairs* 81 (3): 499–513.
Carroll, Archie B. (1979) "A Three Dimensional Conceptual Model of Corporate Performance," *The Academy of Management Review* 4 (4): 497–505.
Center for Science and the Environment (CSE) (2003) "Colanization's Dirty Dozen," *Down to Earth* (August 15): 10–15.
Center for Science and the Environment (CSE) (2006) "Soft Stand: Private Investment Rules Public Roost," *Down to Earth* (August 15): 29–36.
Clapp, Jennifer (2007) "Illegal GMO Releases and Corporate Responsibility: Questioning the Effectiveness of Voluntary Measures," *Ecological Economics* 66 (2–3): 348–358.

Coca-Cola Corporation. 2012. *2011/2012 Sustainability Review*. Online at http://www.coca-colacompany.com/sustainabilityreport/world/water-stewardship.html#section-mitigating-riskfor-communities-and-for-our-system, accessed on December 12, 2012.

Commission of the European Communities (2001) *Promoting a European Framework for Corporate Social Responsibility*. Green Paper. Brussels: European Commission.

Davidson, Debra J. and Don Grant (2012) "The Double Diversion: Mapping its Roots and Projecting its Future in Environmental Studies," *Journal of Environmental Studies and Sciences* 2 (1): 69–77.

Environmental Leader (2010) "Coke CEO Also Considers Himself Chief Sustainability Officer." Online at http://www.environmentalleader.com/2010/02/01/coke-ceo-also-considers-himself-chief-sustainability-officer/, accessed on April 28, 2013.

Epstein, Marc J. and Marie-Josée Roy (2003) "Making the Business Case for Sustainability Linking Social and Environmental Actions to Financial Performance," *The Journal of Corporate Citizenship* 9 (Spring): 79–96.

Figge, Frank, Tobias Hahn, Stefan Schaltegger, and Marcus Wagner (2002) "The Sustainability Balanced Scorecard-linking Sustainability to Management to Business Strategy," *Business Strategy and the Environment* 11 (4): 269–284.

Freudenburg, William R. and Margarita Alario (2007) "Weapons of Mass Distraction: Magicianship, Misdirection, and the Dark Side of Legitimation," *Sociological Forum* 22 (2): 146–73.

Gill, Lesley (2009) "The Limits of Solidarity: Labor and Transnational Organizing Against Coke," *American Ethnologist* 36 (4): 667–680.

Goodpaster, Kenneth and John Matthews (2003) "Can a Corporation Have a Conscience?" *Harvard Business Review on Corporate Social Responsibility* (January): 131–155.

Hamann, Ralph, Nicola Acutt, and Paul Kapelus (2003) "Responsibility verses United States Accountability? Interpreting the World Summit on Sustainable Development for a Synthesis Model of Corporate Citizenship," *Journal of Corporate Citizenship* 9 (1): 32–48.

Holliday, Chad, Stephan Schmidheiny, and Phillip Watts (2002) *Walking the Talk: The Business Case for Sustainable Development*. Sheffield: Greenleaf Publishing.

India Resource Center (IRC) (2006) "University of Michigan instates Coca-Cola Contract Prematurely: Allows Coca-Cola Funded Group to Design Investigation." Online at http://www.indiaresource.org/news/2006/1052.html, accessed on June 1, 2007.

Isdell, Neville (2006) Remarks at the Committee for Economic Development (CED) Corporate Citizenship Award presentation. The Coca Cola Company Press Center.

Jenkins, Rhys (2005) "Globalization, Corporate Social Responsibility and Poverty," *International Affairs* 81 (3): 525–540.

Kent, Muhtar (2009) Remarks at the Globes Conference on Social Responsibility. The Coca Cola Company Press Center.

Kerala State Pollution Control Board (KSPCB) (2003) "Hazardous Waste Discharge from the Factory," Memo. July 8. Reference # PCB/HO/HWM/CC-PLT/2003.

Lakshman, Narayan (2010) "Coca-Cola's Response Disappoints Plachimada Activists," *The Hindu*. Online at http://www.thehindu.com/opinion/op-ed/cocacolas-response-disappoints-plachimada-activists/article408788.ece, accessed on April 25, 2013.

Lodge, George and Craig Wilson (2006) *A Corporate Solution to Global Poverty: How Multinationals Can Help the Poor and Invigorate Their Own Legitimacy*. Princeton: Princeton University Press.

Lund-Thomsen, Peter (2005) "Corporate Accountability in South Africa: The Role of Community Mobilizing in Environmental Governance," *International Affairs* 81 (3): 619–633.

112 Krista Bywater

Moon, Jeremy (2007) "The Contribution of Corporate Social Responsibility to Sustainable Development," *Sustainable Development* 15 (5): 296–306.
Newell, Peter and Jedrzej G. Frynas (2007) "Beyond CSR? Business, Poverty and Social Justice: An Introduction," *Third World Quarterly* 28 (4): 669–681.
Peterson, Julie (2005) "CFO accepts recommendation for short-term extension of Coca-Cola contracts." Office of the Vice President for Communications. Online at http://www.ur.umich.edu/0405/Jun27_05/05.shtml, accessed on January 22, 2008.
Porter, Michael and Claas van der Linde (1995) "Green and Competitive: Ending the Stalemate," *Harvard Business Review* (September–October): 120–134.
Prieto-Carrón, Marina, Peter Lund-Thomsen, Anita Chan, Ana Muro, and Chandra Bhushan (2006) "Critical Perspectives on CSR and Development: What We Know, What We Don't Know, and What We Need to Know," *International Affairs* 82 (5): 977–987.
Raman, K. Ravi (2007) "Community—Coca-Cola Interface: Political-Anthropological Concerns on Corporate Social Responsibility," *Social Analysis* 51 (3): 103–120.
Raman, K. Ravi (2010) "Strange Bedfellows? Critiquing Corporate Social Responsibility," in Ravi Raman and Ronnie D. Lipschutz (eds) *Corporate Social Responsibility: Comparative Critiques*, pp. 1–24. New York: Palgrave Macmillan.
Shamir, Ronen (2008) "The Age of Responsibilization: On Market-Embedded Morality," *Economy and Society* 37 (1): 1–19.
Soule, Sarah (2009) *Contention and Corporate Social Responsibility.* Cambridge: Cambridge University Press.
Stiglitz, Joseph (2002) *Globalization and Its Discontents.* New York: W.W. Norton.
Swanson, Diane and Brian P. Niehoff (2001) "Business Citizenship Outside and Inside Organizations: An Emergent Synthesis of Corporate Responsibility and Employee Citizenship," in Jorg Andriof and Malcolm McIntosh (eds) *Perspectives on Corporate Citizenship*, pp. 104–116. Greenleaf: Sheffield.
TERI (2008) *Executive Summary of the Study on Independent Third Party Assessment of Coca-Cola Facilities in India.* India: TERI.
Utting, Peter (2005) "Corporate Responsibility and the Movement of Business," *Development in Practice* 15 (3/4): 375–388.
Utting, Peter (2007) "CSR and Equality," *Third World Quarterly* 28 (4): 697–712.
Utting, Peter and José Carlos Marques (2010) "Introduction: The Intellectual Crisis of CSR," in *CSR and Regulatory Governance: Towards Inclusive Development?*, pp. 1–2. New York: Palgrave Publishers.
Vedwan, Neeraj (2007) "Pesticides in Coca-Cola and Pepsi: Consumerism, Brand Image, and Public Interest in a Globalizing India," *Cultural Anthropology* 22 (4): 659–684.
Waddock, Sandra (2001) "Integrity and Mindfulness: Foundations of Corporate Citizenship," in Jorg Andriof and Malcolm McIntosh (eds) *Perspectives on Corporate Citizenship*, pp. 26–38. Greenleaf: Sheffield.
Wagner, Marcus and Stefan Schaltegger (2006) *Managing the Business Case for Sustainability: The Integration of Social Environmental and Economic Performance.* Sheffield: Greenleaf Publishing.
Waite, John (2004) "Face the Facts-Coca-Cola Update." Online at http://killercoke.org/bbccokeindia.php, accessed on August 21, 2013.
Wilson, Craig and Peter Wilson (2006) *Make Poverty Business: Increase Profits and Reduce Risks by Engaging with the Poor.* Sheffield: Greenleaf Publishing.
Wrights, Albert (2009) "Quantifying Water Access Benefits in Community Water Partnership Projects," Global Environment & Technology Foundation. Online at http://assets.coca-colacompany.com/85/67/795d1b2a447195bbb19ae7959d7b/replenish_benefits.pdf, accessed on August 21, 2013.

6 Ethnography of a Corporate Document

The Diversity and Social Cohesion Brochure of a French Corporation: The Ethnographic Journal of Tristan d'Inguimbert

Michel Villette

Rarely are the details of the preparations of a communications' operation published.[1] Similar surveys have studied the origins of an article (Lebrave 1984), the construction of scientific facts (Latour and Woolgar 1988), and the filming of a television broadcast (Siracusa 2001), but never, to my knowledge, the head office of a large international corporation.

In the case at hand, the collection of ethnographic material is the result of propitious circumstances. Tristan d'Inguimbert, having trained in ethnographic methodology, registered for a second year in a master's program at Ecole des Hautes Etudes en Sciences sociales (EHESS). Simultaneously, he found a job in a large corporation in the corporate Human Resources department where his main responsibility was that of copy-editor of the document whose conception is laid out in this chapter. This represents a case of a systematic collection of ethnographic material, an approach in English now labeled "covert research" but still long undertaken (Chapoulie 1984), including in France (Villette 1988b, 1994).

Tristan d'Inguimbert's journal, whose extracts follow,[2] provides complete, precise, and reliable ethnographic documentation. This information was collected in 2005 by participatory observation throughout the process of writing the brochure made by the corporate services of a major corporation herein referred to as "THE GROUP." This brochure, though initially devoted to the corporation's social responsibility, was finally, after much shilly shallying, titled "Diversity and Social Cohesion."

In analyzing the controversies that arise during preparatory meetings, the drafts, the deletions, the orders, judgments expressed by senior management, and the conflict between departments on what language to use, Tristan d'Inguimbert identifies the issues and defines the sphere of language constraints that weigh on the creation of such a document.

These observations illustrate the difficulties, the limits, the ambiguities, and even the paradoxes of this type of exercise. A brochure, supposedly destined for a wide audience, is created hastily in order to satisfy the imperatives of public relations *vis-à-vis* influential people on the recipient list for whom the text was written. Another paradox comes to light: having to publish the assessment of a policy that was only recently defined and has not yet been implemented. Moreover, numbers and graphs had to be produced, despite the difficulties of collecting even incomplete and unreliable information from the concerned departments.

One can thus argue that the idea was to weave a pretty fiction on glossy paper, fictions that sociological methods teach us precisely how to uncover. The arsenal of rhetorical and graphic artifices was used to produce ambiguity and fuzziness and to spare the contradictory interests at stake, to avoid a factual refutation, and prevent the involvement of the corporation.

Publishing such observations is not that simple. Certain deontological codes in social science research,[3] as well as certain political interest groups,[4] make an ethnographical inquiry undertaken by an employee concerning his or her own work, without prior written permission from upper management, difficult if not impossible. Yet such testimonies can be justified in the name of freedom of expression in a democracy but also in the name of scientific ideals. In order to better grasp the inner workings of major corporations, a sociological perspective cannot content itself with the public image controlled by the communications department and the confidentiality barriers that often go beyond the immediate necessities related to protecting technological, strategic, or commercial secrets.

By publishing this article 5 years after the events occurred and in an academic review like *Genèses*, we voice our desire to analyze rather than denounce. The respect for the anonymity of the place, the institutions, and people, while remaining as precise as possible in the description of the documents and interactions,[5] allows us to concentrate on the understanding of the social processes at work and to protect the corporation and the staff from the risk of ill-intentioned interpretations.

In order to structure his observations, Tristan d'Inguimbert sought inspiration in the works of the Institute of Texts and Modern Manuscripts (*Institut des textes et manuscrits modernes*) of the École Normale Supérieure and, in particular, the exegesis done by Jean-Louis Lebrave (1984) of an article by poet Heinrich Heine dedicated to the beginnings of the opera singer Sophie Löwe in Paris in *The Prophet* by Giacomo Meyerbeer. By studying crossed-out words, annotations in the margins, the deletions, and the additions, J. L. Lebrave reconstituted the constraints that Heine faced in writing the French and German versions of his article. He integrated into his work letters, including one written by Meyerbeer himself, referring to rumors on whether Sophie Löwe would be presented to the public as Meyerbeer's *protégé* or as a talented opera singer. The reputation of this young singer was at stake and was negotiated on either side of the Franco-German border. Little by little, we see the constitution of the field of social and linguistic forces in the framework of the article authored by the poet-journalist. One can conclude from this example that writing no longer appears to be a question of freedom but a sort of complicated navigation amidst pitfalls.

By reading the extracts of the ethnographic journal chosen here, we can follow the realization of the concretization of an institutional statement, from the initial decision to produce the brochure up until delivery to the recipients. However, it goes without saying, though these extracts try to faithfully reproduce the interactions, they give an account of observations and not of facts *stricto sensu*. They are the result of a twofold selection: first, the selective attention of the observer during the investigation and second, the editorial choices of the co-authors in the context of an academic article.

The journal does not simply illustrate a young professional's progressive exploration of a confusing work environment and his formation of a coherent image through a gradual, uncommon reflexivity, as the observer is simultaneously a recent manager and a student of social sciences. This document also gives useful indicators concerning the activity of the middle and upper management in a multinational corporation's headquarters and hints at the manner in which they experience their job on a daily basis. Finally, and above all, it provides information on the way in which large international corporations in France maintain relationships with governmental authorities and the executives of other major corporations.

In 2005, in the wake of a series of scandals concerning large multinationals, new management norms emerged. These norms have multiple names such as "business ethics," "corporate governance," "social responsibility," "diversity management," and "sustainable development" (Capron and Quairel-Lanoizelée 2004, Anquetil 2008, Bereni 2009). The case that concerns us specifically focuses on the thematic of "social responsibility" and in particular the diversity of employees, gender equality, and discrimination towards minorities.

Throughout 2004, the question of affirmative action in corporations consumed the media. In January, the *Institut Montaigne*, a think tank created and presided over by Claude Bébéar, published a report[6] on the subject that was taken up by the media. In the fall, the debate reappeared in from the angle of diversity. The same think tank published a note authored by a consultant from the Boston Consulting Group on the subject.[7] On October 22, 2004, the Institute brought together 35 executives to sign *The French Diversity Charter* (*Charte de la Diversité en Entreprise*), and the following month, Claude Bébéar presented to the Prime Minister a new report on the question.[8] It was followed by another report by Azouz Begag,[9] the future Secretary of State for Equality Opportunities, presented to Dominique de Villepin, Minister of the Interior at the time.

It's in this political and media context, according to the information collected by Tristan d'Inguimbert, that the Secretary of State for Youth Employment was invited to lunch at THE GROUP's headquarters at the end of November 2005. Amongst those present for this meeting were the CEO, his Chief of Staff, and the Corporate Director for Human Resources. Following this lunch and other informal contacts, it emerged that THE GROUP time lagged compared to other large corporations in their communications on such issues. The CEO of THE GROUP and his Director of HR hastened to create a brochure destined to express THE GROUP's commitment to diversity and social cohesion. The brochure was supposed to be distributed on January 14, 2006, in order to be synchronous with the government's announcement, parliamentary debates, and the media campaigns on diversity.

At this precise moment, Tristan d'Inguimbert's observations began as the young management intern was given the responsibility of copy editor of the document in question. Meeting after meeting, from telephone calls to the rewriting of successive drafts, the young manager and ethnographer gradually discovered the numerous pitfalls that strew the process of writing an institutional document. More precisely, he learned to identify the line between what might be flattering to showcase the social responsibility of THE GROUP and what could be said in order to avoid lawsuits and escape having the document interpreted as a commitment that THE GROUP did not want to make even though it was expected of them.

How should this testimony be interpreted?

Tristan d'Inguimbert's observation journal could be read as yet another confirmation of the thesis that large corporations are hypocrites (Brunsson 1991) hiding the reality of their actions behind rhetoric destined to dissimulate. This well-known hypothesis, born of the critical ideologies of Mannheim (1956) and Gramsci (1975), is reiterated by the website "The EnviroMedia Green Washing Index."[10] Here we can read that "Corporate Window Dressing" consists in misleading through words, images, and graphs; taking on vague commitments with unprovable results; exaggerating the relative importance of environmental (or social responsibility) policies in comparison to other policies within the corporation; and dissimulating important information that contradicts previous allegations. Obviously, the ethnographic observations presented here could corroborate and illustrate these general hypotheses.

With regards to institutional theories of the firm, this case could be viewed as an additional demonstration that large organizations are faced with numerous contradictory and ambiguous orders from varied interested parties and that, in response, they build ambiguous discourses in a quest for legitimacy. In turn, this quest could then lead to an eventual transformation of certain practices (Aron 1965, Boulding 1989, Aggeri et al. 2005), but it can also never result in the announced achievements (Acquier 2010).

When one considers sociological conflict theories, it can be argued that there is a power struggle to which the different departments of a corporate headquarters abandon themselves. These conflicts produce discourses largely disconnected from the operational reality within establishments. This is similar to the organizational theories of the firm and an illustration of the case of a loosely coupled organization, in which headquarters believe they know what they say and decide but, nevertheless, their discourse has little to do with the realities on the ground (Weick 1979, Minzberg 1994).

For my part, without excluding these multiple perspectives and possible readings, I would like to consider these ethnographic observations as the analysis of an event. The objective is to observe how, from a cluster of internal and external factors that are more or less independent from each other, a momentary order emerges. It was not programmed from the get go, neither necessarily very rational nor very efficient. This momentary order is the result of the interactions of a group of persons given orders to cooperate and to attain a desired result for a given deadline: publishing an informational brochure.

We can attempt to characterize this event in the following terms:

The executives of the largest corporations compare themselves and are mutually influenced on the question of who will appear to be the most socially responsible in the eyes of the general public and political leaders. Through this behavior, they disprove the liberal thesis presented by Milton Friedman (1970) according to which "There is one and only one social responsibility of business . . . to increase its profits." In short, one can say that the executives abstain from taking a public position in favor of this thesis. Instead they follow the classic recommendations of Niccolo Machiavelli, according to which, given that the only goal of the prince is to conquer and conserve his power by all means necessary, he must appear virtuous in all circumstances. As such, the executives of major corporations tend to promise and satisfy the allies needed in order to maintain a network necessary for good business (March 1962). Once, they have made these promises, they must find expedient ways to protect the organization against multiple and contradictory orders that could compromise organizational efficiency.

In current management norms, one of the ways frequently employed in order to make believe is mastering corporate discourse on its own activities. A large gap between institutional communications and daily operations is no longer abnormal: In fact, it is the norm. A good manager is supposed to tell pretty stories, and according to the current vulgate, nothing is less communicative than a realistic description such as the one proposed here. We witness the transition above and beyond the frontiers of the "society of the spectacle," beyond what authors such as Karl Weick (1979) theorized in the concept of "loose-coupling" and that more recent authors designated as "storytelling management," a technique purported to be the key to leadership (Denning 2000, Boudès 2002, Salmon 2006). These new doctrines plead for the ideal corporation identified by Villette (1988a: 142–156). They justify an increasing disconnect between the institutional policies proclaimed by corporate headquarters and the operational realities on the ground.

In the case studied in this chapter, we are confronted to a series of arrangements executed hastily in order to announce that the corporation was conforming to the precepts of a new doctrine that was both a political and media fad, even before it had been implemented.

LIST OF PERSONS APPEARING IN THE
ETHNOGRAPHIC JOURNAL

Persons external to THE GROUP in which the study took place:
President
Minister of Labor
Secretary of State for Youth Employment
Minister for Sustainable Development
Director of Human Resources for the group Pinault-Printemps-Redoute (PPR)
Claude Bébéar, President of the *Institut Montaigne* and former CEO of AXA
Freelance journalist hired to help in the writing of the document
Communications agency responsible for editing the leaflet
Recipients of the leaflet
Persons employed by THE GROUP in which the study took place (decreasing hierarchical order):
Chief Executive Officer of THE GROUP: CEO
Presidential secretariat
Managing Director: MD
Secretary General
Director of Sustainable Development
Financial Communications Manager
Jean-Daniel D. and Eric F.: Management Controllers
Deputy Managing-Director of Human Resources: DMDHR
Communications Officer, Human Resources Department: COHR
International Communications team, HR Department
Responsible delegated for sustainable development, HR Department: RDSD
Responsible for employment policy, HR Department: REP
Responsible for competencies approach, HR department, "Cédric N."
Managers in charge of accounting and social reporting, HR department: Ms G. and Ms B.
Director of Human Resources of one of the group's subsidiaries: DHR.
Head of a service (other than the DHR)
Ms X., co-worker that complained of an abusive use of her photo

THE DIARY OF TRISTAN D'INGUIMBERT, MANAGEMENT
INTERN AND ETHNOGRAPHER

Notes taken on December 8: "As I am walking in the hallway, my superior asks me to join her in her office. She is speaking with the responsible for employment policy. They are discussing a lunch they did not attend . . . ; after a few minutes, the REP turns to me: 'Come with me to my office. I am going to give you a file to copy. The Director of Human Resources (DHR) wants everything that is in that file and nothing else. It's easy, everything is in there, and the only thing left to do is to write it.'"

The DHR's request evolves over the next few days and gets particularly complicated.

Later, the same day (December 8): "The responsible of employment policy explains to us that the DHR came back 'stoked' from the meeting with the CEO and the Secretary of State. The Diversity and Social Cohesion brochure will position the CEO and the DHR on the subject of diversity. . . . THE GROUP will become exemplary on this issue. It's the DHR that is responsible for the subject, so she will be exemplary! (Laughs) Financing isn't a problem. The DHR will handle the expenses on her budget and is not sparing any costs. Given this good news, we can hire a freelance journalist.[11] . . . Two topics should be avoided: ageing-management (given the restructuring plans) and intercultural relations (in order to avoid the question of the recent merger with a large European corporation in the same sector). According to the head of employment policy, there are other constraints that exist that he does dare express, but he will clarify as necessary."

Extract of notes taken during a meeting on December 9:

REP: "He wants his own thing."

COHR: "If we talk about local residents and elected officials, what do we do about (the chief of staff that is also director of external relations)?"

REP: "I am not at all sure he wants the CEO interfering, at least not for now. . . . He wants his own brochure, sort of like the (former DHR at the time)."

COHR: "What do we do if (the former DHR) shows up?"

REP (SMILING): "I got the feeling it's not the goal in the least. There is no reason to go ask him anything at all!"

COHR: "So, if I am getting this right, even the document's format has to be the brochure for and by the DHR?"

REP: "Exactly. . . ."

Field notes taken on December 10th: "In the hallways of the HR department, a new version makes the rounds. At the end of the day, I manage to have a rapid discussion with the person responsible for the competencies approach who is supposed to hold the key to the enigma. He explains that he was present at a conference last Friday that brought together human resource professionals. During an informal conversation, the DHR of Pinault-Printemps-Redoute asked him: 'And you, what are you doing on diversity?' I told him that up until now nothing specific had been done and he responded: 'But it's super important, you have to do something! If you don't tell the Corporate DHR yourself, I will call him this week-end.' As a result, I think he called our DHR, and that's why we now have to produce a brochure in a hurry. . . ."

Notes taken during a meeting with the DDHR on December 21: "The DHR (one of the departments of the group): '... The goal of our DDHR is to position THE GROUP with regards to the government and its social cohesion plan, with respect to corporations that highlight diversity particularly with the new Charter, and finally to position the actions of HR within THE GROUP. The document has to be validated in 15 days and printed on January 14th.' The journalist pretends to think it's a joke, but the DHR sharply replies: 'It's because the DGDHR knows that the deadlines are so short that he is allowing us to work with a journalist.'

After having explained that she was the best person for the job, the journalist asks: 'I probably need to know where this is coming from?'

The DHR: 'It's simple. I went upstairs to talk to our DGDHR in order to suggest he sign Bébéar's diversity charter. We looked at whom we would be joining. He agreed in principle, but I came out with a report to hand in [laugh]. It's pretty new for us, since we really are not used to communicating on social issues.'

The journalist tries to negotiate a deadline. The DHR interrupts: 'I know, but let me remind you it would be really quite annoying if the DDHR didn't have his document on time. . . .'"

Field notes on December 30: "This morning, the communications officer brought together the operational actors on this project. The meeting went badly: all of the problems appeared at once. The communications agency proposed mock-ups, but a manager in the communications department does not want to validate them without having first received the graphics concept from another agency that is closed during the end of the year holidays. The journalist wants to know the number of words in order to write the texts. The graphic artist cannot suggest a definitive mock-up without having an idea of the length of the texts. The head of audio-visual services announced that he was leaving on vacation in two days, that his photographer had switched services and that he had yet to hire a new one. A number of developments are added to these technical elements. The outline goes from three to four sections. We don't know who will sign the editorial (the CEO, the DDHR, or the Secretary General). A manager suggests printing the brochure on recycled paper and having it assembled by the *Centre d'Aide par le Travail*.[12] His ecologically and socially responsible ideas will be rapidly abandoned as soon as he leaves on vacation. The idea of a 'virtuous circle of diversity' is discussed that would support the corporate strategy, but this idea is rapidly discarded given that it's difficult to illustrate and eventually perilous. New topics are added to the document: health and security in the workplace, the works of the GROUP's foundation, and its actions for the victims of the tsunami that occurred on December 26th, 2004."

Field notes on December 30th: "In order to get an extended deadline, the journalist tries to put off the conception of the mock-up until later, and proposes that the DDHR validate the texts before seeing the mock-up.

HR COMMUNICATIONS OFFICER: They can't validate the texts if they aren't in a mock-up! Remember, it's war between the former and new DGDHR!
THE JOURNALIST: But can't your DDHR go to the Executive Committee, show the mock-up and the texts, and say: 'We are excellent, this is it?'
HR COMMUNICATIONS OFFICER: No, they like to be able to give their opinions and make decisions, you know.
ANOTHER MANAGER ATTENDING THE MEETING: It's not for nothing that we call them the schoolyard leaders!
HR COMMUNICATIONS OFFICER: And I don't want to get bitten. . . ."

RHETORIC, LAYOUT, AND ICONOGRAPHY IN THE WRITER'S TEXT: SAY SOMETHING WITHOUT REALLY SAYING

Field notes: "While we were looking at the sustainable development report (from a CAC 40 company) for inspiration, the financial communications officer exclaimed: 'Now that's impressive! Look at how (a CAC 40 company) succeeded in turning round the problem. We talk about turnover, and they speak of 'the distribution of income to interested parties;' we mention operating results while they mention 'amounts kept in the company before reinvestment,' that's impressive!'

DIRECTOR OF SUSTAINABLE DEVELOPMENT: You know, in a few years, we will communicate like that as well.
FINANCIAL COMMUNICATIONS OFFICER: What they don't tell you, is how they obtained those results by putting pressure on the municipalities that they have occupied over the last 30 years. Still, isn't there a moral problem?
DIRECTOR OF SUSTAINABLE DEVELOPMENT: Yes, but that's the way we will get a good grade (laughs). . . ."

Ethnographer's observations: During a preparatory meeting, the DHR of one of the departments explains: "We can say that we have a certain excellence in human relations. Though, that's dangerous because we expose ourselves. Moreover, if we are already excellent, how can we progress? What will be the vectors of our progress?" This simple remark during a meeting explains one of the major characteristics of the final document. The document contains no commitment that could eventually create a future task for the corporation that is emitting it. One sole and very timid exception relates to the professional placement of handicapped persons. On this topic, THE GROUP is hardly worried about criticism. They have already gone beyond the legal requirements. On the other points, we resort to verbs that suggest commitment without totally signifying it. We say that the corporation is ready to "get involved," "contribute," "make it a priority," "favor," or "facilitate."
"THE GROUP is committed to facilitating the integration of young people in the workplace" (p. 25 of the booklet).

"The corporation is committed to favoring the development of professional opportunities" (39).

"THE GROUP contributes, within its means, to reducing unemployment of the employees in the sector" (30).

When the corporation hesitates to take charge of certain affirmations, it has other speakers take on the responsibility whether these are physical people (managers), another body (e.g., a foundation, an NGO), or any number of signatories to social dialogues that act as straw men. This rhetorical process, named poly-locution[13] by Jean-Louis Lebrave, consists of making others say what we don't want to say ourselves. Here are a few examples:

"19 companies mobilized to favor the professional placement of young local jobseekers" (29).

"All of the operational employees and managers, the entire human resources network are engaged in the diffusion and implementation of these measures" (11).

"The Foundation of THE GROUP has developed and supported since its creation in 1992, partnerships with associations and NGOs" (32).

"The proactive policy of THE GROUP makes integration through employment a priority" (24).

Finally, it's "the ISO 9001 certification" of the employment process and not directly the employer that "guarantees an equitable treatment of candidates and prevents hiring discriminations" (25).

COMPLETE LIST OF WORDS CROSSED OUT ON TWO PAGES OF THE LEAFLET'S PROOFS ON JANUARY 17, 2005

Nb: It is not possible to present the proofs here with the written corrections for reasons of confidentiality and legibility. We submit here instead a complete sample of the corrections from January 17, 2005, on two pages of the proof. These are sentences written by certain lower level writers (for example, the journalist or one of the HR managers) that were crossed out or modified by a reviewer whose position was higher up in the management hierarchy in the same department.

"THE GROUP that maintains the social cohesion of its human resources chose diversity as a major strategic priority." Sentence crossed out.

"(The DHR) participates simultaneously in the exemplary progress and signing of social contracts of THE GROUP: Agreement to progress together with the personnel; Collective agreement of the technical staff; Collective agreement of the commercial staff." Sentences crossed out.

"The agreement . . . foresees the preparation of a charter symbolizing the support of ethical concerns." Sentence crossed out.

"Placement and afterwards: employment sustainability." Subtitle in bold and at the top of the page crossed out and deleted.

(The integration policy of THE GROUP) "anticipated the foreseeable demographic evolutions, without being limited to replacing the retirements, it also created new jobs." This part of the sentence was deleted. "This plan of action and the ISO 190001 certification of the internal selection processes guarantee equal opportunity in the processing of career paths and mobility. The guarantee of being in charge of career opportunities (60 percent of management is the product of internal promotion) constitutes one of the foundations of social cohesion in THE GROUP." End of the paragraph deleted in one swipe.

Field notes, limited editorial committee meeting on January 18: "The journalist wrote: 'The aim of the conquest' makes THE GROUP a corporate leader, to build the best global alliance. The DDHR: 'Conquest? That's not good that will scare people!' And he crosses out the term that is replaced with 'our ambition.' Afterwards, the DDHR crosses out the end of a sentence on the dialogue with social partners: 'In a common vision for the future.' His deputy comments, smiling: 'We don't really have a common vision for the future. These are more layoffs!'"

Field note on January 19: "The delegate for sustainability: 'We cannot indicate salaries because those (of an important foreign subsidiary) are far more superior, and in France, you know, we have a tradition of aligning with the higher number. So if we highlight the fact that the employees of (the foreign subsidiary) are better paid, it will be catastrophic. . . . And in any case, it wouldn't make sense to indicate an average salary for THE GROUP. . . . On top of it, I am not even sure I can manage to get the information.'"

CALCULATED IMPRECISIONS

Field notes, leaving drinks for a retirement, 6:00 pm. "Around 50 people are there for the leaving drinks for Cédric N.'s retirement, responsible at the competencies approach for the DDHR. The speeches of his former colleagues follow that of the Director who evokes the difficult years spent with Cédric N. dedicated to the subsidiarization of certain of the company's activities. This experience allowed the director to appreciate Cédric N.'s qualities, and in particular his developed sense of precision. Then he adds: 'Being myself as well suited to being DHR as to wearing fishnet stockings, I took on Cédric N. as deputy, since I had already been able to appreciate the quality and precision of his work.' General laughter in the audience. He continues: 'The problem, at the time, I remember that Nicolas H. (current DHR for one of THE GROUP's departments) explained to me that in order to be a good DHR, one must always ask oneself after having written a note: Was I sufficiently imprecise?' Even more laughter.

A few minutes later, Antoine K., the deputy of the DDHR says some words:—'My dear Cédric, we have not worked together a lot, but I have heard so much about you! And I would add not always favorably. . . . Certain union leaders don't like you at all!' Still more laughter in the audience. Continuing in the same vain, he speaks of 'Cédric's legendary precision,' and finally admits that he cannot decide whether to be a good DHR you have to be 'scrupulously precise or scrupulously imprecise.'"

Ethnographer's comments: "A few elements of response appear in the booklet DIVERSITY AND SOCIAL COHESION. In fact, one of the important issues for THE GROUP in terms of social responsibility is to show that they are compensating for the negative externalities suffered by the residents near their sites (noise pollution for example) with job opportunities. It's in this perspective that a graph entitled 'Job Placement of Local Residents' appears on page 26 of the leaflet. It indicates that the portion of local residents admitted to the hiring tests of the group, its subsidiaries, partners, and subcontractors increased from 28 to 47 percent between 1999 and 2003. Only the imprecision of the notion of 'local resident' allows for such results. If we look at the statistical source used to build the graph, we see that the "local residents" in question are not those who directly suffered from the nuisance but the inhabitants of *Ile de France*, excluding inner Paris. Even with such a broad definition of the notion of local resident, displaying such an optimistic graph is the product of luck and pious omission. In fact, the data relative to 2004 is available at the offices of the DDHR but we "forgot" to mention it in the brochure. The portion of 'local residents' (in the broadest sense) hired went from 47 percent to 33 percent between 2003 and 2004."

SHOULD QUANTITATIVE ELEMENTS RESTORE CONFIDENCE?

Field notes: "At the request of the delegate responsible for sustainable development (RDSD), Ms G. and Ms B. receive us in their offices of the accounting and social reporting services of the DDHR. . . . The RDSD: 'I am coming to you because in last year's activity report we included a table with [she shows the table], because notation agencies like numbers and me too [general laughing]. We thought for a second, we would do it on subcontracting, but we quickly got rid of that idea [laughing]. So this table represents the group headcount in full time equivalency validated by the statutory auditor and that comes from you guys, I think. Afterwards, we have the data on social assessment, but it only concerns the establishments in France. This law does not specify the perimeter on which we must report, but everyone agrees that the larger the perimeter, the better. There are groups like Total that have software permitting them to report on the law's indicators for all of their subsidiaries. That's why I came to see you today. This year, we would like to report on the local personnel in our foreign establishments, but it doesn't seem very simple. And it doesn't make sense to give certain numbers, does it?'

Ms B.:   It definitely depends on what we want the numbers to say according to the perimeter. [She laughs.]

THE RDSD: Personally, I would like to know who, at the DDHR, gave these numbers to the statutory auditor?

Ms B.:   Those [she fingers the consolidated numbers at the group level], that's us, but more in relationship with accounting. . . . In fact, we just take Jean-Daniel's dashboard and then we just do an average.

THE RDSD: Oh yes, I saw him yesterday and he showed me his dashboard where he also has the premises. . . .

Ms G.:   It's complicated between Jean-Daniel and Eric. . . . Now when we put together budget scenarios, we walk on pins and needles because we never really know whether to ask Eric or Jean-Daniel. . . .

THE RDSD: But who consolidates the numbers with the subsidiaries?

Ms B.:   It must be. . . .

Ms G.:   Sure, but there is also M. . . . For the subsidiaries, we have a small network, since we had a training seminar with the management controllers, now we know them all. . . .

THE RDSD: But how do you explain the difference between the social assessment data calculated by Eric, and the data of the management controller?"

At the end, none of the debated quantitative data appeared in the brochure.

THE PROACTIVE APPROACH OF A SPONTANEOUSLY VIRTUOUS CORPORATION

Limited editing committee on January 18: "While reading the journalist's text on the charter on preventing harassment in the workplace, the DDHR crosses out the following sentences: 'Workplace harassment is an offense which risks criminal sanctions. If the internal bylaws of the corporation have been modified to take this into account, it is up to the General Direction to insure that the Charter and its legal obligations are respected.' He clarifies: 'I don't like this one bit!' And explains that a text explicitly recalling the legal framework (and the legal responsibility of the top executives) is not appropriate for a leaflet whose goal is to show the exemplary and spontaneous nature of the social policy of THE GROUP.

Personally delivered to the Minister of Labor, the President, and numerous ministers, the leaflet is written nonetheless as if the respect of the law was a minor element of the social responsibility policy. This posture is even more surprising given the recovery of diversity as an issue by major corporations and its transformation into a management decision. It can be viewed as a response to the current and future legislative evaluations as argued by Bereni (2009)."

THE GO AHEAD POLICY

Field notes on January 21: "During the last limited committee meeting, DDHR communicated his displeasure with the photos. He seemed annoyed when the communications officer tried to justify himself by invoking the bad quality of the photo bank: 'I don't want to hear that! Get a photographer and go (into an establishment) and get me pictures ASAP!' During an operational meeting, the responsible of audio-visual services explained that it was a particularly long process to obtain the necessary authorization to take pictures in the establishments. To overcome this constraint, the communications officer respectfully asked for the help of the DDHR secretary's office that obtained the necessary authorizations in 48 hours."

Field notes on February 17th: "Before leaving on vacation, the communications officer drops of the mock-up at the CEO's office in order to obtain the final validation of the President. The secretary tells us that she hopes for a response next Monday, but the following day, at the end of the day, an unannounced strike takes place at one of the sites of an establishment in THE GROUP. Disciplinary sanctions are taken against one of the striking employees and all of the media report on this unplanned strike. Worried, I imagine the CEO will never agree, since on the last two pages layout a photo taken in the establishment where the strike is taking place illustrates the topic 'Health, Security, and Solidarity.' I call the CEO's office Monday morning. A secretary responds: 'You know he is quite busy. . . .' I remind her of the urgency of the validation and she adds: 'I will try to get him to look at it tonight. He leaves for Washington tomorrow for two days and returns on Thursday for the *Comité Central d'Entreprise*.[14] He might be able to take a look during his flights.'

That Thursday, French riot police (CRS) are parked outside corporate headquarters, radios speak of an emergency committee meeting, and extra guards control ID badges. I start to worry that I will never get this final validation of my rather inappropriately named 'Diversity and Social Cohesion' leaflet.

At the end of the day, for the second time in this month, the Pope was hospitalized at the Gemelli clinic, after that, the medias forgot the strike so that I got a call in the evening from the CEO's office telling me the document was validated.

On March 1st, the last of the problems concerning the picture orders are dealt with and I give the go-ahead to print. We receive the first examples on March 8th and my boss, who is invited to breakfast at the Ministry of Labor in honor of Women's day, can deliver the brochure in person to a minister who is constantly boasting about his social cohesion program."

PUBLISHING THE DOCUMENT AND THE VIP LIST

In mid-March 2005, the "Diversity and Social Cohesion" brochure is finally made available to the media relation services and rapidly disseminated in particular to a VIP list of 84 people.

53 percent of these people report to the Presidency and the Ministries (including 8 ministers and Secretaries of State, 13 chiefs of staff and 15 special advisors).

17 percent belong to the prefectures and territorial collectivities in which THE GROUP has offices.

13 percent belong to the General Directions of other major corporations.

10 percent belong to organizations within the profession in which THE GROUP exercises its main activity.

7 percent are elected officials in the French National Assembly, Senate, and certain General Councils.

The concerned members of the General Direction and the corporate departments of THE GROUP personally address the brochure to their usual professional contacts. More specifically, as Figure 6.1 shows, seven of the 14 members of the Executive Committee of THE GROUP previously worked in French ministries. As documents of this sort are exchanged between colleagues, the person who previously worked for the French Presidency tends to send the document to the General Secretary of the President; the person who worked for the Ministry of Finance will send it to his contacts in the ministry; the DDHR will send it to his contacts in the ministries of Employment, Gender Equality, Health, Justice, etc. A step down in the hierarchy, the media relation service sends the brochure to its media contacts, as well as the communications officers in ministries, corporations, and professional organizations. Other managers and direc-tors of the group may also use the leaflet depending on their needs and the circumstances.

Too little and too late in the competitive market of discourse on a fash-ionable topic, the brochure had only a limited impact on the target audi-ence. "Much ado about nothing" could be argued. The document seemed to become both more important and more interesting when it came into the possession of those who were not the intended recipients.

Field notes on March 23: "Fifteen days after the publication of the bro-chure, the 'HR internal communications team' receives an e-mail from the head of a service regarding 'negative feedback' from a co-worker 'who is photographed without her knowledge in the brochure.'

Re: Problem with the use of the photos

'Hi,

Following the publication of your brochure 'Diversity and Social Cohe-sion', I would like to inform you on the very negative feedback I received from (Ms X.) whose picture is on one of the photos on page 18. . . . The photo was supposed to show a workplace, a teamwork situation in this service. It is not so much the use of the photo itself that is questioned, but its juxtapo-sition with a text concerning discrimination and victimization. . . . In this

Title	Education								Time in a ministry																		Date of entry into the corporation
	IEP	ENA	X	HEC	Other engineers	university	Others	1978	79	80	81	82	83	84	85	86	87	88	89	90	91	92	93	94	95	
CEO	x	x				x		■	■	■	■	■	■	■	■	■	■		89					■	■	1997
GD							■	■								■											1993
GD Finance		■									■	■	■	■	■	■	■	■	■	■	■	■					1998
GD communication										■	■	■	■	■	■	■	■	■	■	■	■	■	■	■	■	■	1998
GD RH						■														■							2003

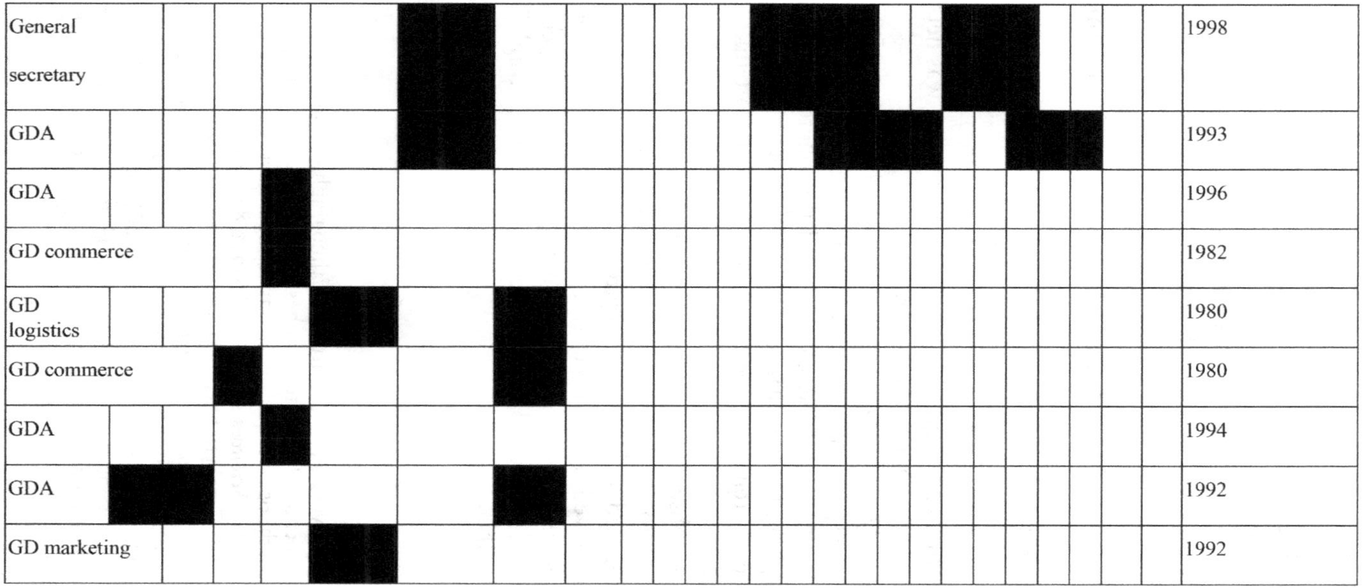

	Date
General secretary	1998
GDA	1993
GDA	1996
GD commerce	1982
GD logistics	1980
GD commerce	1980
GDA	1994
GDA	1992
GD marketing	1992

Figure 6.1 Education, Time Spent in Ministries, and Date of Entry in the Corporation of the 14 Principal Executives

case, the meaning that it takes on is solely linked to the presence of Ms X. and solely on the fact that she is a person of color. However, she thought that these images were to be used to represent workplace situations and were not to be used to instrumentalize her physical appearance even if it is done in a humanist or progressive spirit.

In agreement with Ms X., I reacted immediately and requested that these three photos that are present in the online photo bank be withdrawn as quickly as possible. I do not think Ms. X. wants to go any further with this. This message aimed simply at alerting you to this misstep. Regards.'

Response from the communications officer on March 23rd, 2005 at 6 pm

Re: Re: Problem with the use of the photos

'Sir,

I would first like to express my regrets to Ms. X. Our intention was neither to make her uncomfortable nor to injure her.

These pages do not simply evoke the risks of racial discrimination, even if the photo highlights more specifically this aspect, but also gender equality, preventing harassment in the workplace, etc. We used this photo in good faith. Its presence in the photo bank gave us a certain liberty in its use. Your reaction was the right one in removing the photos from the photo bank. I have noted your alert. . . .'"

The insistent and quasi-obsessional staging of people of color that the managers and executives who wrote the brochure considered as clever and that was purportedly supposed to show a socially responsible attitude takes on another sense once removed from the context of the politico-economic elites for whom and by whom it was conceived. Once it is seen by real people whose image has been instrumentalized, for them "socially responsible" becomes socially irresponsible.

NOTES

1. This text is the English version of the article "Ethnographie d'une écriture institutionnelle: la brochure Diversité et cohésion sociale d'une entreprise exemplaire. Journal ethnographique de Tristan d'Inguimbert présenté par Michel Villette," *Genèses, Sciences sociales et histoire* 85 (Dec.) 2011: 134–155. The authors thank Elizabeth Sheppard for her translation.
2. T. D'Inguimbert (2006) "La mise en scène de la responsabilité sociale d'une entreprise," Master Thesis in Sociology supervised by Michel Villette, Ecole des Hautes Etudes en Sciences Sociales, Paris. 2 vol., 201 pages.
3. See for example ASA Ethics Standards (2005) 13: § 04 (a): "Sociologists disseminate their research findings except where unanticipated circumstances or proprietary agreements with employers, contractors, or clients preclude such dissemination."
4. A proposed law relative to the protection of economic information was presented to the office of the National Assembly on January 12, 2011, by

Bernard Carayon and 124 other representatives. It suggested to insert in the Penal Code a new article written as follows: "Est puni d'une peine prévue par l'article 314–1 du Code Pénal le fait pour toute personne non autorisée par le détenteur ou par des dispositions législatives et réglementaires en vigueur, de s'approprier, de conserver, de reproduire ou de porter à la connaissance d'un tiers non autorisé une information à caractère économique protégée ou de tenter de s'approprier, de conserver, de reproduire ou de porter à la connaissance d'un tiers non autorisé une information à caractère économique protégée." The National Assembly rejected this proposal.

5. In the perspective of a historiographical use of this work, we will make available to those researchers interested in the name of the corporation concerned the necessary documentation after 2015.
6. Y. Sabeg and L. Méhaignerie (2004) *Les oubliés de l'égalité des chances.* Report of the *Institut Montaigne.*
7. L. Blivet (2004) *Ni quotas, ni indifférence: l'entreprise et l'égalité positive.* Report of the Institut Montaigne, October.
8. Claude Bébéar (2004) *Des entreprises aux couleurs de la France, Minorités visibles: relever le défi de l'accès à l'emploi et de l'intégration dans l'entreprise.* Report to the Prime Minister.
9. Azouz Begag (2004) *La République à ciel ouvert.* Report to the Minister of Interior. La Documentation française. November.
10. University of Oregon and EnviroMedia Social Marketing, EnviroMedia Greenwashing Index, http://www.greenwashingindex.com, accessed on December 2, 2009.
11. The journalist came recommended by the communications departments, which is supposed to master this type of production. However, they did not want to be directly implicated in order to better handle internal power games, and specifically the rivalry between the DDHR, the General Secretary, and the responsible for Sustainable Development.
12. These are workshops sponsored by the state to professionally reintegrate long-term unemployed.
13. Poly-locution exists when the author of a text attributes his words to others. It can be an efficient strategy to say something without taking responsibility for it.
14. The *comité d'entreprise* is a consultative body in French companies bringing together management and the representatives of employees. It is obligatory in any company of more than 50 employees according to the French labor code (article L2321–1).

REFERENCES

Acquier, Aurélien (2010) "Du développement durable au développement rentable : chronique de la marginalisation d'une démarche de développement durable dans une grand entreprise," *Gérer et Comprendre* 98 (12): 38–50.
Aggeri, Frank, Eric Pezet, Christophe Abrassart, and Aurélien Acquier (2005) *Organiser le développement durable. Expériences des entreprises pionnières et formation de règles d'action collective.* Paris: Vuibert.
American Sociological Association (2005) *Ethics Standards* 13: § 04 (a).
Anquetil, Alain (2008) *Qu'est-ce que l'éthique des affaires.* Paris: Vrin.
Aron, Raymond (1965) *Démocratie et totalitarisme.* Gallimard: Paris.
Bereni, Laure (2009) "Faire de la diversité une richesse pour l'entreprise, la transformation d'une contrainte juridique en catégorie manageriale," *Raisons Politiques* 35: 87–105.

Boudès, Thierry (2002) "Quand l'entreprise se raconte des histoires," *Expansion Management Review* 105: 25–31.

Boulding, Kenneth E. (1989) *Three Faces of Power*. New York: Sage.

Brunsson, Niels (1991) *The Organization of Hypocrisy: Talk, Decisions and Actions in Organizations*. Copenhagen: Copenhagen Business School Press.

Capron, Michel and Françoise Quairel-Lanoizelée (2004) *Mythes et réalités de l'entreprises responsable*. Paris: La Découverte.

Chapoulie, Jean-Michel (1984) "Everett C. Hugues et le développement du travail de terrain en sociologie," *Revue Française de Sociologie* 25 (4): 582–608.

Denning, Stephen (2000) *The Springboard: How Storytelling Ignites Action in Knowledge-era Organizations*. Boston: Butterworth-Heinemann.

Friedman, Milton (1970) "The Social Responsibility of Business is to Increase its Profits," *The New York Times Magazine*, September 13.

Gramsci, Antonio (1975) "Le concept d'idéologie," in François Ricci (ed.) *Gramsci dans le texte*, pp. 120–122. Paris: Editions Sociales.

Latour, Bruno and Steve Woolgar (1988) *La vie de laboratoire. La production des faits scientifiques*. Paris: La Découverte.

Lebrave, Jean-Louis (1984) "Le locuteur: la course au trésor—Étude de quelques contraintes d'écritures dans un fragment d'article de Heine," *Cahier Heine (3) Écriture et contraintes*, pp. 65–86. Paris: Éditions du CNRS.

Mannheim, Karl (1956) *Idéologie et utopie, une introduction à la sociologie de la connaissance*. Paris: Librairie Marcel Rivière et Cie.

March, James (1962) "The Business Firm as a Political Coalition," *Journal of Politics* 24 (4): 662–678.

Minzberg, Henry (1994) *The Rise and Fall of Strategic Planning*. The Free Press: New York.

Salmon, Christian (2006) "Une machine à fabriquer des histoires," *Le Monde Diplomatique* November, 18–19.

Siracusa, Jacques (2001) *Le JT, machine à décrire: sociologie du travail des reporters à la télévision*. Paris: De Boeck Université.

University of Oregon and EnviroMedia Social Marketing, *EnviroMedia Greenwashing Index*, Online at http://www.greenwashingindex.com, accessed on December 2, 2009.

Villette, Michel (1988a) *L'homme qui croyait au management*. Paris: Le Seuil.

Villette, Michel (1988b) "Qui veut publier la description ethnographique d'une entreprise?" in Martine Ségalen (ed.) *Anthropologie sociale et ethnologie de la France*, pp. 851–857. Louvain-la-Neuve: Peeters.

Villette, Michel (1994) *L'art du stage en entreprise*. 4th ed. Paris: La Découverte.

Weick, Karl (1979) *The Social Psychology of Organizing*. New York: McGraw Hill.

Part II

Resistance Movements to the Globalized Management Discourse

7 Resistance against New Working Practices in the Service Sector in Turkey

Esin Gülsen

In the last three decades, capitalism has undergone its most important trans-formation in history. Considering inherent dynamics of the capitalist system such as the decline of profit margins, crisis, and competition, one of the ele-ments of this transformation process, which has had an impact on almost all aspects of economic, social, and intellectual systems and has penetrated into social life since the 1970s, is characterized by the transformation of the labor process. In other words, the inherent tendency of capitalism to occasionally cause a crisis requires changes in the labor process and measures aimed at preventing resistance against changing and worsening working conditions. Thus, concealing the employers' objective of profit, with the workers' objec-tive of high salaries, becomes vital in the prevention of resistance. It seems as if the mainstream discourse on the working class in the social sciences has been the sentence that "Proletariat is dead!" as asserted by André Gorz with reference to the expansion of the service sector on a global scale and the fallback of the class struggle in the last decades. The mainstream discourse on the death of the working class has been accompanied by a discourse on an emerging "new middle class." This so-called new middle class has been presented as a group of skilled, well-educated professionals with prestigious jobs and careers. This category has claimed to control their tasks, to partici-pate in decision-making processes, and to work under conditions different from those of the working class. Within the context of this discourse that dominates the social sciences and business literature, some outcomes such as salary, educational level, and consumption styles have been presented as supporting evidence. For example, graduating from universities, earn-ing good incomes, working at clean offices in high plazas, and consuming according to patterns have been considered in differentiating the new middle class from the working class.

Marx underlined: "If there were no difference between essence and appearance, there would be no need for science" (Marx 1967: 817). The aforementioned group of people seems to work under comfortable con-ditions, to get relatively high salaries, and to dress and to consume well; however, when we focus closer on the labor process as a whole, it becomes obvious that a proletarianization process has happened despite this career discourse. Although it is very hard to analyze this process since it does not have a long history in Turkey, it seems that the changes experienced by the "new middle class" correspond to a new type of proletarianization. Distinctive characteristics of this process, such as routinization, deskilling, automation, loss of job security, decreased salaries, increased work load, mobbing, and so on, come to the forefront. Despite the fact that the new managerial discourse and practices seem successful, the so-called new middle class or white-collar employees in the service sector exhibit some signs of resistance against these practices in different forms. Even if it is not as frequent as among the classical working class, this group of employees organizes into trade unions, goes on strike, and slows down the pace of work. In addition to formal and collective resistance mechanisms, this group exhibits some informal and individual resistance forms that cannot be observed and controlled as easily as classical forms.

In the following part of this chapter, a brief summary of the literature on new resistance forms among employees is presented. Resistance practices in the service sector in Turkey based on experiences of call center employees and IBM Turkey employees are analyzed. Finally, new management practices and new forms of resistance in Turkey are displayed, referring to various examples from two different sectors.

NEW FORMS OF RESISTANCE: AN OVERVIEW OF THE LITERATURE

The recent management discourse, control and surveillance mechanisms, and resistance against these mechanisms by employees have been important topics of discussion in the social sciences in the last years. However, while much emphasis is placed on the consent of the worker or the ideological barrier, workers' ways of challenging new managerial regimes has not been adequately studied in the literature (cf. Fleming and Sewell 2002: 858). One of the problems with paying attention to management practices is the assumption that the Anglo-American management discourse shapes all activities of workers. However, "employees are not like lumps of clay to be readily molded into shape as part of a corporate program . . . of reengineering." (Knights and McCabe 1998: 186)

For the purpose of this study, the literature on new management practices and new resistance forms in call centers is of critical importance. While call center work is described by an author such as Daniel Bell as "knowledge work" and as a rewarding job with high levels of autonomy and employee satisfaction, Marxist theorists draw attention to changes in labor processes and new forms of control and exploitation applied to "mental labor" (Brophy 2010: 474). It is widely accepted that electronic surveillance has become the most important control mechanism in call centers, but it is a hot issue whether that kind of surveillance has rendered workers more or less powerless. Fernie and Metcaff have used the concept of "electronic panopticon" with reference to Foucault. They assert that the visibility of agents in call centers has created a perfect power scheme of supervisors who disregard the possibility of resistance and collective organization of these workers (Quoted by Taylor and Bain 1999: 103). However, Bain and Taylor (2000) have rejected the power attached to electronic panopticon and management underlined by Fernie and Metcaff with findings of a study conducted at Telcorp UK, a telecommunication company. These scholars argue that there are three dimensions where one can refute the thesis of the power of supervisors. The first one is that actual management processes are much more problematic such that one cannot simply create absolute control mechanisms. The second argument is that the performance of the electronic panopticon is not perfect. Finally, their case study shows the existence of collective resistance movements and organizations linked to trade unions (Bain and Taylor 2000: 11).

Knights and McCabe (1998) argue that there are always autonomous spaces that permit workers to escape and resist despite a high level of control. In a study conducted in a bank with employees charged with telephone banking, they found that there were "numerous means by which employees are able to retain or create some autonomous space" (Knights and McCabe 1998: 182) by making choices about how to perform work. As such, work has got its own rules: Managers may control a crucial part of the work but ways to escape from this control still exist. Knights and McCabe showed that a lot of workers employed by the call center of a bank had to receive calls for long hours. Since they also needed to rest, these workers sometimes stopped receiving calls and were just "mouthing" so their team leaders would think that they were still working. Furthermore, Knights and McCabe found that whether the work is performed with enthusiasm, detachment, or indifference is critical in understanding forms of resistance (Knights and McCabe 1998: 182).

One of the main problems with resistance movements against new management practices and discourses of workers is that the notion of resistance is linked to certain forms of actions such as those organized by labor unions (strikes). Any working environment where the management discourse states that employees and employers are members of one *happy* family and where traditional and overt forms of resistance are not observed may make people think that there is no resistance because of the fact that the managerial discourse and its practices are internalized by workers. Fleming and Sewell (2002) state that this would leave the impression as if "managerialism has finally succeeded in transforming the 'recalcitrant worker' into the supine, docile and biddable worker if the worker opposition is thought as a set of purely overt, organized and open economic practices" (Fleming and Sewell 2002: 859).

In fact, resistance can manifest itself in different forms such as individual or collective, open or hidden, passive or active, formal or informal resistance.

While resistance is usually thought of as a collective and formal action in the form of strikes organized by labor unions, there are many individual and informal forms of resistance. High turnover rates may even be considered as a form of individual resistance. Brophy (2010) writes about "ingenious techniques developed in order to slow down the pace of work, ranging from elementary forms of hacking call center technology to twenty-first century strains of industrial sabotage" (476) as informal strategies. Taylor and Bain (1999) mention that giving the impression of being engaged on calls while there is no actual interaction is an example of individual resistance in call centers. Further methods that employees use are deficits in technology such as exploring when the management listens to their calls (Taylor and Bain 1999: 112–113). A study that Man and Öz (2009) conducted in call centers of two banks in Turkey found that one way of controlling employees was that managers called employees as if they were customers. However, employees may detect this practice because their technical experience permits them to find out that the call is internal and not from a customer, so they may talk to the manager accordingly (Man and Öz 2009: 88).

An important concept introduced by Fleming and Sewell (2002) to understand individual and covert forms of resistance is "*Svejkism*," derived from the novel named *The Good Soldier, Svejik*, written by Jaroslav Hasek. New managerial practices have rendered open forms of resistance difficult, but this does not mean a demise of resistance, the novel argues. The authors use the concept of *svejkism* to define a covert form of resistance. They write: "(I)t is our contention that an underlying tactic of svejkism is 'disengagement' whereby the self is detached from the normative prescriptions of managerialism through irony and cynicism" (Fleming and Sewell 2002: 860). *Svejkism* does not present itself as a direct conflict but rather in forms such as scrimshanking and flannelling. Scrimshanking means to shirk duties and subvert unitary or common interests. Flannelling means the utilization of values of the organization in order to defeat those values: The flanneller "uses forms of respect to show disrespect and in such a way that the target [in the case of Svejk, Imperial Army officers and their lackeys, E.G.] will be contradicting himself if he takes offence and so will be made to look foolish. . . . That is the quintessence of flannelling and other forms of scrimshanking: using the proclaimed values of the organization to defeat those values" (quoted according to Bailey in Fleming and Sewell 2002: 866). The main feature of this form of resistance is the use of irony and cynicism in order to defeat the values and rules of organizations that are respected. For example, employees are expected to use standard text pieces when they talk to customers in many Turkish call centers. However, since employees are not robots and customers ask rather different questions, it is not possible to only use sentences from these standard texts. If workers respect the rules and only use sentences from these scripts, the actual dialogues would be more or less absurd. Applying the rules of the organization may thus disrupt work and may turn into a form of resistance. Fleming and Sewell explain the difference between the acts of the flanneller and the work-to-rule in its classical meaning in the following way: "(T)hrough an elaborate, even exaggerated, display of deference, enthusiasm, or conformity, the flanneller signals the exact opposite, displaying contempt for those very norms. It is this sense of exaggeration that distinguishes flannelling from what we know as the work-to-rule" (Fleming and Sewell 2002: 866).

In addition to emergent forms of individual resistance, open, formal, and collective organization forms are still increasing in importance so that it is possible to see this kind of resistance in call centers as well. One of the most successful examples of collective resistance in the service sector worth to mention is the 24-hour hunger strike by employees of a market research firm in New Zealand. Employees of this company organized several strikes and pickets through UNITE Union that had reunited some 11,000 members and had won collective agreements and salary increases (Brophy 2010: 470). Trade unions are considered an important tool of collective resistance in call centers. In addition to standard bargaining elements, they negotiate agreements on topics specific to call centers such as tea breaks, reward systems, or the non-monitoring of personal calls (Taylor and Bain 1999: 114). However, this is not the case everywhere in Turkey. As Mulholland states, while the existence of a trade union is important for a workplace, it may not go beyond its role limits in some cases. Trade unions cannot deal with all problems experienced at a workplace; other strategies of resistance and resolving of problems may be necessary. A study conducted in an Irish telesales company employing 300 workers showed that despite the existence of an official trade union that contained about one-third to one-half of the staff, many critical problems of employees were left untouched (Mulholland 2004: 713). While health and safety issues were covered by collective agreements, the trade union could not negotiate any agreement on such matters as work intensification, productivity, pay, or arbitrary management practices. These circumstances pushed workers to display informal resistance practices defined as "*Slammin' Scammin' Smokin' and Leavin',*" referring to sales sabotage, working according to given rules, work avoidance, absenteeism, and high turnover (Mulholland 2004: 713). We can find an example of this situation in the Burger King call center in Turkey that will be described below. In fact, workers were unionized; however, the trade union could not resolve many of the problems that workers had.

All of these examples show that the managerial discourse and its practices are not automatically internalized in enterprises even if they do not trigger open, formal, or collective forms of resistance. Intensification of control and surveillance may narrow the field of open resistance but it is probable that covert, individual, and informal forms of resistance continue to occur among employees. Thinking of resistance in only conventional terms may prevent the recognition of new challenges of work and new forms of opposition. Both new management practices and opposition against them should thus be considered as an elaborate and complex process that requires more attention in order to observe actual cases and possibilities.

NEW RESISTANCE PRACTICES IN THE TURKISH
SERVICE SECTOR

Organization and resistance at the workplace have always been identified with blue-collar workers, mainly factory workers. In parallel to the world-wide trend and as a reaction to worsening working conditions including increasing control and surveillance, unemployment, insecure and flexible jobs, alienation, and loss of control on the job, opposition movements of the white-collar, this new middle class, have become a current issue, especially since 2000. A group of people who have good careers and "clean" jobs, high education levels, and high purchasing power, white-collar employees include some professional groups such as teachers, physicians, lawyers, engineers, middle managers, and clerks. These actors were used to thinking that they had no reason to oppose management so that it was not necessary for them to organize and talk about their rights. However, a wave of white-collar actions of resisting and organizing has made management practices and resistance against them a matter of debate. This new wave started in the last years with the strike of media employees and journalists working at a Turkish TV and newspaper company belonging to the investment group Turkuvaz Media Group owned by Calik Holding, the unionization of software developers and computer engineers working at IBM Turkey, and Internet-based organization of call center employees. In this chapter, this organization and resistance strategies of IBM Turkey employees and call center employees will be presented and compared.

Computer engineers, software developers, and employees in the information technologies (IT) sector are regarded as part of the middle-upper class. They usually do not consider themselves being a part of the working class. In fact, compared to factory workers and call center workers, they are less exposed to routinization, automation, and deskilling practices. However, these well-dressed and well-paid employees cannot run away from the pressure caused by a management following different paths. For example, employees obtain a Blackberry as a company phone—in Turkey, most employees consider having a Blackberry as a status symbol since it is too expensive to buy for a wageworker—however, employers require them to work 24/7 in return for a laptop or Blackberry (Bora 2010: 54). According to results of a research conducted by iPass, a mobile service provider with 3,700 employees working in 110 different companies, 45 percent of employees keep their mobile phones near them even while sleeping and about 60 percent of them state that they are obliged to respond to their messages even in the bathroom.[1] To give an example from Turkey, Sani Şener, CEO of TAV Holding, a group of wide-scale construction companies, headquartered in Turkey, said: "I take back the BlackBerry of employees who do not answer any of my important e-mails within 15 minutes. I have done it for 4–5 times" (Doğu and Şit 2011).[2] Mobbing is another issue that shows that these skilled office workers are exposed to increasing pressure. In addition,

IT employees are confronted with problems such as the loss of job security and a decrease in salary. In recent years, emigration of IT specialists from India to Turkey has led to a decline of salaries in this sector. It seems as if in the near future, many Turkish companies plan to carry their information technology infrastructure to India through outsourcing. Employees in this sector may thus experience more serious problems rather soon. The working conditions of employees of IBM Turkey, a subsidiary of IBM Global, more than support this assumption as I argue below.

IBM Turkey employees unionized in 2007 on the primary position that their salaries had been frozen for the last five years. Decrease in standard of living, loss of job security, and violation of some rights of workers, such as paid annual leave, were further reasons. During this unionization process, the company started to dismiss unionized employees. First of all, the vice general manager, Can Özler, who was not unionized but was charged with "shutting his eyes to unionization," was dismissed. As a consequence of this dismissal, other employees thought that they did not have job security because the company could fire even a vice general manager without particular problems. The unionization process accelerated thereafter and 258 of 400 employees working at IBM Turkey became unionized. Although they had reached the required number to exercise collective bargaining so that the Ministry of Labor accepted their collective bargaining authorization application of June 11, 2008, company management decided to ignore this achievement and tried to prevent further unionization by dismissing unionized workers. Two further managers, Zafer Pınarcık and Cüneyt Türen, who had supported the already dismissed vice general manager, and three trade union representatives, Nedim Akay, Elvan Demircioğlu, and Berk Alev, were fired.[3] Although the management did not recognize the collective bargaining right of the trade union, the employees' resistance led to a salary raise of 25 percent after five years of frozen wages.

Unionization was not the only organizational strategy of IBM Turkey employees. They used Internet to take action, to disseminate their working conditions, and to force IBM Turkey to accept their demands. One of the employees stated their point of view about resistance in the following way: "We will not go to the street and say 'we are hungry'. We will do the thing that we know the best, we will use Internet" (http://www.sendika.org)[4]. Employees sent e-mails to the thousands of e-mail addresses they had and they created a group on Facebook. They were inspired by a cyberpicketing organized by Second Life (SL), a virtual platform run by IBM Italy employees. In this cyberpicketing, about 2,000 avatars from 30 countries shouted slogans at virtual islands of IBM, held banners, and succeeded in going in virtual meeting halls of the management. This cyberpicketing was selected one of the 10 most creative web projects and honored in a ceremony held at the French Senate in Paris in 2008. As a result of this virtual action, the management accepted demands of employees that were inspired by measures taken in IBM Italy. Due to the success of this activity, IBM Turkey employees contacted the UNI Global Union trade union that organized successful SL cyberpicketing. However, IBM Turkey employees did not organize such a cyberpicketing.

IBM Turkey employees have also created the "Plaza Activists Platform" with other employees working with large and prestigious companies in big *plazas* with high salaries but bad working conditions. Every week, they organized "plaza actions" at a place in Maslak, Istanbul, where the headquarters of IBM Turkey were located. People in Turkey thus saw for the first time a worker protest organized by employees working at "glorious" places. Other IBM employees founded an alternative association called "Information Sector Employees Association" aimed at coming together with employees from other companies operating in the information sector. However, due to problems experienced within the group, the association went bust. In January 2013, IBM employees were still unionized but they were no longer active in the Plaza Activists Platform. The platform maintains its activities at places where white-collar employees from mainly finance and insurance companies work. They organize anti-career days, mobbing seminaries, and meetings. One of the activists of the platform has explained their aim as follows: "Our aim is to make the so-called 'white-collar' employees, in other words the relatively 'aristocratic' part of the working class, recognize that they are not in such an aristocratic position and to raise unionization awareness among them to a certain degree" (Bora 2010: 49). The platform may be said to be in an embryonic form as the population it can reach is currently rather limited.

The other important sector where one can observe resistance movements are call centers. In Turkey, call centers have been established in the last decade. About 55,000 people are employed in these centers according to data from 2011. The sector is expected to employ 100,000 people over the next 5 years (Aktay 2011). Most of the call center workers are high school or university graduates. But they are not able to practice their professions due to high unemployment in Turkey. These professionals consider their call center work as being an initial step in their "career" hoping that they will occupy better jobs in the future. Nevertheless, they stay white-collar employees, have good working conditions in offices, and have good career prospects. However, their working conditions are not so different from those of an assembly-line worker. The work they do is routinized and automated. Moreover, they are becoming deskilled. Call center workers are exposed to a double-sided pressure. On the one hand, management drives them to increase sales and solve the problems of customers. On the other, customers drive them to bring solutions to their complaints by phone. In fact, working practices in call centers are good examples of Taylorist-Fordist labor processes in terms of routinization and automatization. In order to share their problems and suggest solutions to their own problems, call center workers in Turkey created a website with the name of "Call for Reality" in 2006. An association with the name "Association of Call Center Workers" was then created in 2008. The workers declare the goal of this website and their association as "unveiling the capitalist discourse on career" (Bora 2010: 58). One of the founders of the association explains the reason for these activities on the Internet as follows: "It was an obligation to organize via Internet because call center employees can access Internet easily and spend an important part of their working time in the Internet. The Internet use is a part of their culture" (Baştürk, Tartanoğlu, and Emirgil 2011: 159). These call center employees who founded the association affirm that the discourse on career has made their lives miserable: They feel like race-horses confronted with an evaluation of their performances. These employees try to introduce their association and website to their colleagues and resist working conditions that render their lives miserable. For the purpose of this study, two founders of the association and three call center employees were interviewed and the news on the website was studied.

The Association of Call Center Workers tries various ways to reach call center workers. This organization is different from a typical trade union organization. It does not have the hierarchical structure of trade unions and uses various informal resistance strategies that are not practiced by unions. This does not mean that founders of the association reject the importance of trade unions, but they think that the conventional trade union organization has difficulties adapting itself to new working conditions. Moreover, trade unions do not want to deal with call centers because the call center sector is not defined as an independent line of business in the Turkish Labor Act so that it is difficult to organize employees in call centers. The association is in contact with the trade union of BANK-SEN (Trade Union of Turkish Revolutionary Bank and Insurance Workers). However, this trade union does not have the right to organize collective bargaining in any workplace, so these contacts mainly serve a purpose of solidarity (Deniz K., İstanbul, former call center worker and one of the founders of the association, interviewed on October 2, 2011).

The most important strategy followed by the association are collective calling actions. When workers face problems in a particular call center, other call center workers and people supporting actions of the Association of Call Center Workers collectively call it. They talk to call center representatives, introduce themselves to their colleagues, try to stop services, and force the call center management to resolve the problem. One of these critical calling actions was related to a problem experienced by an employee working at the call center of a bank named Garanti Bank in 2010. She had a personal problem with a manager; she was exposed to systematic oppression by the management. She was isolated from other employees, was not allowed to talk to anybody, and was only allowed to sit down in the middle of the workplace without working because her password for entering the system was cancelled, and she was eventually forced to resign. She ended her labor contract due to insufferable mobbing but she sued against the bank. The suit has not yet been concluded but a collective action was made on the day of hearing of the suit. Many people called the call center of the bank on the same day and read the following text: "*Good evening, I am calling you on the demand of the Association of Call Center Workers. According to the information I obtained from the association, one worker who worked in your call center had a hearing of a suit ongoing with the bank where you work. . . . It seems that managers of your call center want to threaten you, prevent you to defend your rights and suppress you with this event and similar attitudes. We, who support labor rights, make this calling to remind you that you are not alone. . . . Please contact the Association of Call Center Workers for an organized working life where your rights are secured and you get in return for your labor*" (http://www.gercegecagrimerkezi.org).[5] One of the employees working at this call center says of the events of this day: "When the action started, I was working at my shift. I was worried when I took that call and I felt obliged to cut off the line with fear. However, everybody working at the call center started to talk about this call to each other after that and the center was suddenly locked up." (Baştürk et al. 2011: 167) This description shows that the action was a success.

In Turkey, working conditions at call centers have recently become an issue when four employees at Burger King Call Center decided to unionize and were discharged as a result. Burger King Call Center employs approximately 100 people. Burger King Call Center employees work for 11 hours a day in exchange for minimum wages. The only break during the long working day is a half-hour lunch break. Meals are limited to fast food such as hamburger and chips, which are known to lead to stomach diseases such as gastritis and ulcer. When any employee comes to the job a few minutes late, he/she is punished and has to stand on one foot. Considered being a *traditional* counter-strategy, some employees deployed a six-month secret effort to unionize. As soon as Burger King Call Center management dismissed four "pioneer workers" in order to prevent unionization, workers, as a *new* counter-strategy, organized a campaign on Facebook to support those who were dismissed. A Facebook group was also created. In June 2011, members of this group increased to 20,000 in one week. In addition, thousands of supporters called Burger King Call Center day and night and said: "*I support your struggle. I do not give order but I give support!*" which was the motto of the campaign. Thanks to this new form of reaction, the Burger King Call Center management was obliged to make successive statements. According to the workers who are still working there, the management felt itself under great pressure and started to introduce some improvements in working conditions. One of the employees stated that two columns written by a well-known columnist in a national newspaper on working conditions at the Burger King Call Center were successful in organizing a social media campaign so that about 20,000 calls were made to the call center (Ilhan P., İstanbul, former worker of Burger King Call Center, interviewed on October 5, 2011). The call center was locked up with incoming calls from supporters of the campaign, a fact that created a great enthusiasm among the employees. As a result, many employees decided to unionize and the management had to take steps back. Managers started to answer to calls together with employees. Furthermore, employees could take short breaks without any problem. However, this process did not proceed after that campaign due to the passivity of the trade union. For example, workers wanted to open a stand at a central location in Istanbul to make people aware of their problem. However, the trade union hindered it, claiming that they would not be able to get permission for that from local authorities. Workers opened a stand in front of the call center, but since it was not located at a central point in the city, they were not publicly visible. In short, the trade union prevented workers from taking radical actions. Nevertheless, some improvements were introduced due to this calling campaign such as unionization, but many problems are left unsolved. One may list a decrease of pressure on workers by managers as an improvement. However, some practices, such as giving fast food to workers, were not changed. Following this movement, the management started to organize social activities to improve the sense of belonging to the enterprise such as celebrating birthdays of employees. Managers try now to make employees work harder with a discourse that considers the reception of calls as a play and with the introduction of awards to be given to employees who receive the highest number of calls.

Yet unionization was not the unique resistance strategy for Burger King employees. "They try to play you off one against the other, but most of us try to keep relaxed about it," said one of interviewees working at a call center in the study conducted in Scotland by Taylor and Bain (1999: 113). This is similar to the information given by one of the interviewees I met for this study in Turkey. This employee, who was also one of the leaders of the unionization process, stated that the workers organized collectively against performance criteria applied at the workplace. In fact, the company management got the number of calls received by each employee at the end of each day. This statistical information allowed them to warn the employee who received the least number of calls. This meant that all employees were forced to work hard and compete against each other to not have the fewest calls. The employees thus decided to answer the same number of calls as much as possible, and if there was anybody accepting more calls compared to other employees, they warned him/her. Thus, the group did not allow any employee to feel alone. Moreover, they prevented the pressure introduced by performance criteria of the management (Erkan G., İstanbul, former worker of Burger King Call Center, interviewed on October 5, 2011). In fact, this form of organization, set up simultaneously by employees, would have been difficult to create by a formal organization like a trade union, since trade unions cannot foresee simultaneous and informal resistance strategies.

In some cases I found that individual resistance practices could also turn into collective actions. For example, when the management made the decision that employees who wanted to go to the restroom while working should raise their hands and get permission from team leaders, some employees resisted by not raising their hands, directly going to the restroom. When they had to defend their case they argued that it was their natural right, and they would not ask for permission by raising their hands like children. After a while, more employees started to not raise their hands so that this method disappeared rather soon. According to one of the employees, when the control of the management increased, a counter-reaction was immediately developed. Another employee working at the call center of a telecommunication company declared that employees always used some individual resistance strategies to oppose to pressures of the management in order to have some idle time. She stated: "I often changed the settings of my earphones. It took the team leader at least ten minutes to adjust settings so I could rest for these minutes" (Aysun L., İstanbul, call center worker, interviewed on October 6, 2011). She also asserted that some employees in the same call center who knew the computer system well changed some settings so that it seemed as though they were receiving calls when this was not the case. In this sense, Brophy, a British researcher, suggested some "elementary forms of hacking call center technology" as informal strategies (Brophy 2010: 476). These practices show that, despite the use of an advanced technology, employees can still find some insufficiencies that permit them to escape from or resist against the rules of their tasks.

CONCLUSION

An important argument of the literature on working conditions and resistance of white-collar employees or the new middle class is whether this group internalizes new management practices and what kind of resistance strategies they develop against these strategies. Since class struggle is linked to classical struggle and resistance mechanisms of blue-collar workers such as trade unionism and strikes, non-existent or low levels of overt and collective resistance forms among the white-collar employees have been considered as a lack of resistance in these groups. However, considering the rather recent literature on different forms of resistance and some published case studies from different sectors, it seems that employees do not simply internalize managerial practices and working rules. Instead they develop some formal, informal, individual, or collective resistance strategies against them. In Turkey, working conditions and resistance movements of the mentioned groups are rather recent research topics. In addition to individual and informal resistance strategies, there are some embryonic collective organizations functioning in a different way than classical trade unions and their resistance strategies. This chapter has described the form of these organizations and their functioning. The results show that these resistance strategies are still in their infancy. Doing research on them allows us to participate in an ongoing transformation process where a social dialogue begins to function that is different from the former class strategies of trade unionism.

NOTES

1. Doğu and Şit, http://www.radikal.com.tr/Radikal.aspx?aType=RadikalDetay V3&ArticleID=1052104&Date, accessed on January 13, 2013.
2. The quotations were translated from Turkish into English by the author of this chapter.
3. http://www.en.habervesaire.com, accessed on January 13, 2013.
4. http://www.sendika.org/2008/07/ibm-calisanlarindan-sanal-eylem-hazirligi/, accessed on January 13, 2013.
5. http://www.gercegecagrimerkezi.org/2010/11/4440333/, accessed on January 13, 2013.

REFERENCES

Aktay, Eylem (2011, 30 October) "Hattın ucunda eğitimliler var [There Are Educated People on the Line]," *Sabah, İş'te İnsan.* Online at http://web.archive.org/web/20111206235910/http://www.isteinsan.com.tr/isteinsan_gazete/hattin_ucunda_egitimliler_var.html, accessed on January 13, 2013.

Bain, Peter and Phil Taylor (2000) "Entrapped by the 'Electronic Panopticon'? Worker Resistance in the Call Centre," *New Technology, Work and Employment* 15 (1): 2–18.

Baştürk, Şenol, Tartanoğlu, Şafak, and Emirgil, Burak Faik (2011) "'Gerçeğe çağrı': Neo-liberal dönemde çağrı merkezi çalışanlarının enformel örgütlenme pratikleri ['Call to Reality': Informal Organization Practices of Call Center Employees in Neoliberal Period]," *Toplum ve Bilim* 121 (2): 152–173.

Bora, Tanıl (2010) "Plaza aktivistleri platformunun iki aktivistiyle söyleşi: "İşadamıgörünümlü memurlar, işçiler [Interview with two Activists of Plaza Activists Platform: "Businessman-looking Officers, Workers]," *Birikim* 259 (11): 49–55.

Brophy, Enda (2010) "The Subterranean Stream: Communicative Capitalism and Call Center Labour," *Theory and Politics in Organization* 10 (3/4): 470–483.

Doğu, Nuriye and Şit Ahmet Can (2011, 8 June) "İphone icat oldu, mesai bozuldu [Iphone Invented, Work Hours Destroyed]." Online at http://www.radikal.com.tr/Radikal.aspx?aType=RadikalDetayV3&ArticleID=1052104&Date=08.06.2011&CategoryID=80, accessed on January 13, 2012.

Fleming, Peter and Graham Sewell (2002) "Looking for the Good Soldier, Svejk: Alternative Modalities of Resistance in the Contemporary Workplace," *Sociology* 36 (4): 857–873.

en.habervesaire.com. (2009, April 14) "IBM, Sanal Grev, Örgütlenme, İşsizlik [IBM, Cyberpicketing, Organization, Unemployment]." Online at http:// en.habervesaire.com/haber/1383/, last accessed on January 13, 2013.

http://www.gercegecagrimerkezi.org. (Website of the Association of Call Center Workers). Last accessed on January 13, 2013.

http://www.sendika.org. (2008, July 3) "IBM çalışanlarından sanal eylem hazırlığı [Cyberpicketing preparation by IBM employees]." Online at http://www.sendika.org/2008/07/ibm-calisanlarindan-sanal-eylem-hazirligi/, last accessed on January 13, 2013.

Knights, David and Darren McCabe (1998) "What Happens When the Phone Goes Wild?: Staff, Stress and Spaces for Escape in a BRP Telephone Banking Work Regime," *Journal of Management Studies* 35 (2): 163–194.

Man, Fuat and Cihan Selek Öz (2009) "Göründüğü gibi olamamak ya da olduğu gibi görünememek: çağrı merkezlerinde duygusal emek [Not Being Able to Be Who

You Look Like or Not Being Able to Look Like Who You Are: Emotional Labour in Call Centers]," *Çalışma ve Toplum* 20 (1): 75–94.
Marx, Karl (1967) *Capital.* Vol. 3. New York: International Publishers.
Mulholland, Kate (2004) "Workplace Resistance in an Irish Call Center: Slammin', Scammin' Smokin' an' Leavin,'" *Work, Employment and Society* 18 (4): 709–724.
Taylor, Phil and Peter Bain (1999) "An Assembly Line in the Head': Work and Employee Relations in the Call Center," *Industrial Relations Journal* 30 (2): 101–117.

8 Precariousness and Resistance

A Case Study of a Supermarket and a Hypermarket in Argentina (2008–2011)

Julieta Longo

INTRODUCTION

Since 2003, Argentina's economic recovery has brought about significant changes in the labor market. The exponential economic growth reversed the trend of massive unemployment. The improvement of the job market was a key factor for the resurgence of the labor movement so that the workplace became a central topic and the trade unions regained power for collective bargaining (Etchemendy and Collier 2007). However, in keeping with the neoliberal years, the current economic model consolidates a fragmented labor market. The main constraint facing the labor market has to do with the high level of unregistered employment, informality and also the predominance of other working conditions, such as temporary employment and subcontracting (Pérez et al. 2010, Salvia and Vera 2011).

In the discussion on the expansion of globalization, increasing capital mobility and the fragmentation of the working class have brought about a "crisis" of the labor movement (Silver 2005); in this chapter I focus on the relationship between precariousness and conflict in the formal sector and, in particular, in retail stores.

The analysis is based on a case study in one of the largest retail companies in Argentina. The two questions I ask tackle the embeddedness of precariousness in these workplaces and the form conflicts take. In the concluding section, I analyze "mediations" between work situations and conflictive actions. The chapter suggests that fragmentation is not the only mechanism that renders difficult the organization and the possibility of developing workplace collective actions. The relationship between precariousness and conflict is not linear; as a result, it is necessary to analyze other mediations that operate in the labor-capital scheme.

THE CONCEPT OF PRECARIOUSNESS

While precarious forms of work can be found since the beginning of capitalism, the concept of "precariousness" was first used in Europe in the 1970s in order to warn about and condemn the development of forms of employment that were different from the "norm," i.e., of the protected, stable, and full-time jobs that characterized the "fordist employment" model (Busso and Bouffartigue 2010).

After the overproduction crisis in 1973, the answer of the capital was instability. This crisis came from a double limitation: on the one hand, from the rigidity of the Fordist model and, on the other, from the growing power of the labor movement (Vasapollo 2004, Antunes 2005). Thus, the reorganization of subordination mechanisms of the labor force, flexibility, and the precariousness of the labor market signified an intensification of the exploitation of the workforce and the disciplining of workers at workplaces (Harvey 1990).

In Argentina, as in other "peripheral" regions, precariousness is not a new phenomenon. Informal employment and various precarious situations characterized job conditions since the late 19th century, when Argentina joined in the world market (Busso 2006). However, the state-led Import Substitution Industrialization (ISI) was constructed on the basis of a growing power of workers and their organizations so that "stable employment" came to constitute a framework for workers' claims and actions. This situation changed with the last military dictatorship from 1976 to 1983 that focused on the disruption of organizations of workers through direct repression of shop stewards' committees (i.e., workplace organization) and the prohibition of trade union activity (Basualdo 2006). The shift from state-led ISI to more market-oriented economic models has led, on the one hand, to the shrinking and demobilizing of the labor movement (Etchemendy and Collier 2007) and, on the other, to a degradation of the labor market. It was after this "capitalist offensive" that the concept of "precariousness" gained weight, spread in Argentina's sociology, and was finally transformed during the 1990s into a concept that used to characterize changes in the labor market as a result of the introduction of neoliberal economic policies.[1]

Precarious work was understood in these early studies, following the main European definitions, as the one that moved away from the "typical" job to unstable employment (without a contract, fixed-term contracts, or temporary contracts) and without social rights (excluding pension rights, vacations, and leaves among others), a situation that gave no stability and security to workers (Galín 1986, Pok 1992).

PRECARIOUSNESS: AN ANOMALY OR A CHARACTERISTIC ELEMENT OF THE LABOR MARKET?

In the late 1990s, the spreading of unemployment and precariousness hindered the conceptualization of precariousness as an "exceptional" aspect. In this context, some authors, influenced by a neo-Durkheimian perspective, asked questions on the outcomes of precariousness and unemployment on *social integration* (Paugam 2000, Castel 2003). For these authors, the crisis of 1973 had opened up a deep crisis of "salaried society" by questioning the paradigm of homogeneous and stable employment.

According to this perspective, precariousness does not only influence stability but also job satisfaction (Paugam 2000). This dimension, which served Durkheim for his hypothesis on the "social division of labor," has to do with the possibility of recognizing the activity of workers and providing workers the possibility of "feeling useful" at work. When workers do not have a stable job or when their activity is not valued, their job becomes precarious. Precariousness results in a psychological and moral distress of workers that weakens social and labor bonds, and thus the basis of social integration. This trend has further implications outside the world of labor, such as generating disillusionment and political apathy.

From another perspective, associated to neo-Marxist studies, emphasis was given to the consequences of the *precariousness of power relationships* in workplaces. Bouffartigue and Béroud (2009) point out that labor stability is not itself a positive feature for workers. According to these authors, in the early 20th century, job rotation was an acquisition of workers, since it allowed them not to be tied to an employer and to change jobs in search of better wages. Both authors underline that it is necessary to look on the *control* that workers have of their work rather than the characteristics of the labor market. Therefore, the analysis of forms of resistance and organization becomes important. Considering the capital-labor relation as conflicting and dynamic, both authors suggest that it is necessary to look at the changes in resistance and the ways in which workers are opposed to management strategies in order to regain control in the workplace.

In this chapter, I will analyze the relationships between precariousness and conflict from the most recent perspective that underlines that precariousness is a form of power relationship between capital and labor, which, on the one hand, implies an *exacerbation of exploitation* through the intensification of work and, on the other, is an *extension of the domination* of capital over labor due to the reduced power of workers in their workplace. These are the two dimensions of precariousness that I analyze here, differentiating respectively between "precarious employment" and "precariousness of labor relations."[2]

PRECARIOUSNESS AT WORKPLACES: A CASE STUDY IN A RETAIL COMPANY

This research was carried out in the largest French retail company in Argentina, called hereinafter "CR." CR is the second-largest retailer in the world, and currently employs 410,000 workers.[3] In Argentina, the group opened its first hypermarket in 1982 and expanded its branches principally in the last 20 years. In the last decade, CR has increased its presence by merging small companies. Currently, 29 percent of retail sales take place in the country;[4] the company employs 20.000 workers[5] and is one of the 10 companies with the highest turnover in Argentina.[6]

The case study was realized in two local shops of the company between 2008 and 2011 as part of my Ph.D. thesis that analyzes labor disputes in precarious workplaces. I interviewed workers from different sectors. The first shop was a hypermarket located in the city of La Plata that had approximately 420 employees, where I led 17 semi-structured interviews. The second shop was a supermarket, located in the city of Buenos Aires that had about 100 workers, where I led 10 semi-structured interviews.[7]

Precarious Employment

Based on this case study, I can identify two policies that CR has implemented in its divisions that render employment precarious. On one hand, CR uses external flexibility in order to adjust the number of workers to the demand by subcontracting workers from temporary employment agencies, by outsourcing tasks, and by using part-time contracts. On the other, CR uses internal flexibility by a rotation of the working day around workplaces, the use of unpaid overtime, and the incorporation of tasks that are not included in the workers' contracts. The use of external and internal flexibility varies according to the sector and the size of the shop, mainly because the type of demand differs in supermarkets and hypermarkets.

In hypermarkets, there are a lot of workers hired from temporary employment agencies. By subcontracting, the firm adapts the workforce to large swings in demand. However, in supermarkets where the demand is more constant, there are few subcontracted workers (Emilia V., a 25-year-old cashier in Buenos Aires, interviewed on June 24, 2011). Part-time contracts and subcontracting are characteristics of the cashiers' sector. They are more frequent in the afternoon shift when cashiers are often young women. Furthermore, there are many sectors (replacement, advertisement, security, cleaning, and home delivery) where many workers are "external" (Eliana A., a 23-year-old promoter in La Plata, interviewed on October 25, 2008; Patricia G., a 29-year-old stock clerk in La Plata, interviewed on July 9, 2009; Damian P., a 26-year-old delivery worker in Buenos Aires interviewed on July 21, 2011). This means that these workers perform tasks in the CR's workspace, but they are employed by and depend on other companies. For example, stock clerks are normally hired by the brands they restock; security, cleaning, and advertisement staff are outsourced sectors where the laborers work for external companies. "Internal workers," i.e., those who work for CR, are concentrated in check-out lines and in hierarchical and administrative positions (supervisions, recounts, etc.). The various contracting forms are summarized in Table 8.1 below.

The existence of many employees and their different types of contracts at the same workplace produces a profound heterogeneity of wages among

Table 8.1   Contracting Forms in Supermarkets
and Hypermarkets

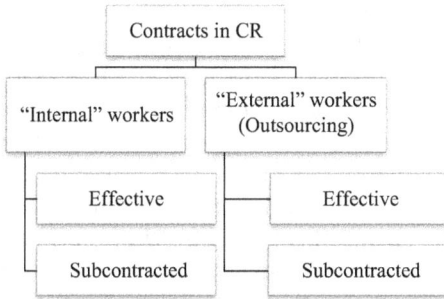

```
                    ┌─────────────────┐
                    │ Contracts in CR │
                    └─────────────────┘
          ┌──────────────────┬──────────────────┐
   ┌────────────────┐   ┌──────────────────┐
   │"Internal" workers│   │ "External" workers│
   │                 │   │  (Outsourcing)    │
   └────────────────┘   └──────────────────┘
     ┌──────────┐           ┌──────────┐
     │ Effective │           │ Effective │
     └──────────┘           └──────────┘
     ┌──────────────┐       ┌──────────────┐
     │ Subcontracted │       │ Subcontracted │
     └──────────────┘       └──────────────┘
```

Source: Scheme based on the author's interviews.

workers. In 2011, an outsourced stock clerk from a food or beverage company earned about 6,000 pesos (1,400 U.S. dollars)[8] while a worker who performed the same task but who was subcontracted earned half that amount. On the other hand, part-time workers were paid less than 2,000 pesos (500 U.S. dollars); delivery workers earned even less than 1,500 pesos (350 U.S. dollars) per month.

The working day varies according to the sector. The cashiers' sector is the most flexible in these terms, because the staff rotates weekly on the basis of free days and working days (Ana M., a 22-year-old cashier in La Plata, interviewed on September 24, 2008). However, in supermarkets, working hours are more constant than in hypermarkets (Emilia V., a 25-year-old cashier in Buenos Aires, interviewed on June 24, 2011). In the case of stock clerks, working hours may vary according to season, promotions, or any event that affects the renewal of the shelves (Omar C., a 25-year-old stock clerk in La Plata, interviewed on October 21, 2008).

On the other hand, the working day of all workers can also be changed on an "informal" base. When there are few customers in the supermarket or hypermarket, supervisors allow workers to leave earlier but these hours are compensated by days when more workers are needed. In this way, overtime performed by employees is suppressed and, according to "the company's policy," is not paid (Mara V., a 25-year-old cashier in La Plata, interviewed on October 12, 2008).

Workplace variation is specific for "external" workers, especially stock clerks and promoters. Some workers have to restock in various supermarkets and hypermarkets of the region during their working day, according to a weekly schedule that indicates where to do their work (Patricia G., a 29-year-old stock clerk in La Plata, interviewed on July 9, 2009). Promoters, meanwhile, also change their workplace each day since their workplace and the number of days they work depend on the type of promotion and agency they work for (Eliana A., a 23-year-old promoter in La Plata, interviewed on October 25, 2008).

Finally, the tasks performed by each worker, although they are scheduled in collective bargaining, depend on the company's need. Stock clerks sometimes are responsible for receiving, tracking, and storing the goods, place the Point-of-Purchase (POP) material, clean and keep the deposit, check prices, and ensure minimum stocks in storage (Patricia G., a 29-year-old stock clerk in La Plata, interviewed on July 9, 2009). Promoters, in some cases, are also responsible for restocking, ordering the shopping cars, or making "returns" (Eliana A., 23-year-old promoter in La Plata, interviewed on October 25, 2008). According to cashiers, they are "the jokers" of the supermarket. In addition to their tasks, they are in charge of returning goods, restock, clean the checkout, check if prices are updated, and compare these prices with their competitors (Ema M., a 23-year-old cashier in La Plata, interviewed on October 31, 2008; Julia S., a 33-year-old cashier in Buenos Aires, interviewed on July 27, 2011).

What has just been described is a clear example of the profound heterogeneity of contracts, working conditions, and salaries among workers of retail companies. In the following section, I will analyze how this workforce heterogeneity within the same workplace has differentiated workers into "internal," "external," "effective," "hired," and "outsourced" staff.

Precarious Labor Relations

The heterogeneity of working situations at the same workplace has had numerous consequences on the strength of workers. First, this heterogeneity generates a new hierarchy of workers. These rankings are constructed according to wages, types of contracts, and working conditions. They range from "internal" to "external." In this order, subcontracted and temporary workers are the last link in the chain. These hierarchies and distinctions attempt to define the conflict between workers and directors as a competition among workers who are employed by different companies and "brands":

> When I came to CR "by the agency," other workers called me "mule" or "slave." Mule or slave means the same: workers who made the "hard-working," who were the "last link in the chain." A hierarchy exists among employees: the "internal," the "external," and the "mule" or worker' agency.
>
> (Hector P., a 29-year-old recount worker in La Plata, interviewed on September 14, 2009).

Furthermore, the existence of many employers, as the result of outsourcing and subcontracting, reduces the rights of workers by multiplying hierarchical levels they must respond to (Neffa 2008). The labor force is also threatened by uncertainty. As already noted, subcontracting allows the company to adapt the number of workers to the demand. But, at the same time, this is a mechanism asking workers to stay in a long probationary period that explains the large amount of time they are employed by temporary agencies.

This is the first experience of insecurity: When workers are subcontracted, they can be fired. Moreover, the fact that there are many subcontracted workers generates instability among them. There are always new workers who are waiting for jobs. As Mara V. said: "You know that there are twenty people behind you, who want your job" (a 25-year-old cashier in La Plata, interviewed on October 12, 2008).

These outcomes, linked to the heterogeneity of working situations, undermine the identification of workers, complicate hierarchical relationships, and individualize the employment relationship.

WORKPLACE CONFLICTS

The discussion of the thesis of the "crisis of (the) labor movement" (Silver 2005) is tackled in this section. One of its basic arguments is that the fragmentation of the working class weakened the labor movement. In other words, "traditional unionism" that emerged from "fordism" is no longer adapted to the current heterogeneous world of labor.

During the 1990s, this thesis was exemplified in Argentina by the emergence of a new trade union: the Central of Argentine Workers (CTA). The CTA, in opposition to traditional labor unions, particularly represented by the General Confederation of Labor (CGT), started as a *social movement union* that was supposed to unify the different interests of the heterogeneous working class (Serdar 2010).

However, the labor union resurgence that took place in Argentina after 2003 was characterized by the maintenance of a fragmented working class under conditions of informalization and unregistered jobs and was led by CGT-traditional unions (Etchemendy and Collier 2007, Serdar 2010). This situation was analyzed by Etchemendy and Collier (2007) and was defined as "segmented neo-corporativism." It was segmented "given the size of the informal sector, (that) encompasses only about 40 percent of the working class (i.e., economically active population [EAP]) or 60 percent of wage earners" (Etchemendy and Collier 2007: 365).

Even if the main segmentation line can be found among registered and unregistered jobs, there are other segmentations among registered workers (see section 3). In this chapter, I analyze the relationship between precariousness and workplace conflict among registered workers. In my fieldwork, the union that represented the majority of workers was the Commercial Employees' Union (SEC). The SEC is a traditional and corporative union, belonging to the General Confederation of Labor (CGT). The following discussion attempts to identify resistances in these fragmented workplaces, where traditional labor unions are hegemonic. The analysis will show that the fragmentation of workers is not the only factor that makes difficult the emergence of collective action. In this sense, I propose other factors (called "mediations") that operate in the labor-capital relationship.

From Common Demands to Resistance and Direct Actions

There is an extensive discussion regarding the question why conflict is manifested in workplaces (Edwards and Scullion 1982, Atzeni 2010). Qualitative studies allow accessing not only open conflicts with traditional forms of struggle (strikes and demonstrations) but also less institutionalized conflicts (such as individual resistances, collective sabotage, and boycotts).

The first step in analyzing conflicts in supermarkets is to identify the existence of *common demands*. I have identified four common demands. The main complaint has to do with labor timetables. On the one hand, the questioning arises in connection with the weekly rotation of working hours and, on the other, in connection with the existence of "unsocial" timetables[9]: The work in supermarkets and hypermarkets is more intense when most people rest, i.e., on weekends and holidays (Ema M., a 23-year-old cashier in La Plata, interviewed on October 30, 2008; Ana M., a 22-year-old cashier in La Plata, interviewed on September 24, 2008; Hector P., a 29-year-old recount worker in La Plata, interviewed on September 14, 2009). In fact, the variations of working days hinder the organization of the leisure time of workers and influence their possibilities of performing other activities and devoting time to their family and social life.

The second claim concerns the stress in the relationship between workers and managers, as well as among workers and customers (Mara V., a 25-year-old cashier in La Plata, interviewed on October 12, 2008; Ana M., a 23-year-old cashier in La Plata, interviewed on September 1, 2009; Emilia V., a 25-year-old cashier in Buenos Aires, interviewed on June 24, 2011).

The third claim affects specific demands made by some workers, such as the case of hired workers who demand job stability (Eliana A., a 25-year-old promoter in La Plata, interviewed on October 25, 2008; Damian P., a 26-year-old delivery worker in Buenos Aires, interviewed on July 21, 2011). Finally, there are demands related to work intensity and poor working conditions (Hector P., a 30-year-old recount worker, interviewed in La Plata, on September 10, 2010; Mariano L., a 27-year-old recount worker in La Plata, interviewed on September 18, 2009).

Common demands concern "conflicts of interest" at workplaces (Edwards and Scullion 1982) that are expressed in open conflicts. Furthermore, there are more individual and less institutionalized practices: These conflicts can be called *resistances*. However, which actions are defined as resistances? Following Edwards and Scullion (1982), actions have no meanings in themselves. Actions get a sense in a social relationship. It is therefore necessary to consider the meaning of an action for workers and managers in a particular labor process. Here, I consider "resistances" to practices that are directed against the company and that the company identifies as disruptive because they alter the "normal" labor process.

In the supermarkets and hypermarkets analyzed here, there is a first group of resistances, made up by many single and scattered practices. These actions primarily arise from the dissatisfaction of workers and their inability to change their working conditions. I include in this type actions that challenge the profitability of a shop (such as theft and the breakage of stock), absenteeism,[10] and turnover. These practices are a topic of constant dispute between the company and its workers. They have different meanings depending on the respective situations. For example, turnover can be a management practice since the high level of employee turnover reduces conflicts. This situation gives employers a temporary perception of their workforce and weakens the strength of workers (Longo 2012). Yet sometimes, workers can re-signify this practice. The high turnover and the existence of multiple employers allow some workers to come back to the company after being laid off, reemployed by another employer. In fact, this practice reduces the power of managers:

> Sometimes they dismiss an employee, and then s/he comes back to the supermarket with a better job, for example, hired by another company or agency. And we know that it does not contribute anything, but we like it . . . because we know that the boss is angry . . . and we laugh at him, because the boss laid off a worker, who later returned to work.
> (Mariano L., a 27-year-old recount worker in La Plata, interviewed on September 18, 2009)

A second type of resistance challenges the corporate hegemony at the workplace. I could find two practices. First, the implementation of lawsuits against the company exists mainly due to interruptions, disciplinary measures, dismissals, and illness. Through these practices, workers may manage to avoid the implementation of new control systems.[11] The second practice consists of disregarding disciplinary measures and warnings imposed on the workers. These actions question the authority and legitimacy of the management.

Finally, there are actions that are explicitly directed to regain control over the labor process by questioning work intensity. These practices are diverse and range from working at a slower pace, refusing to work overtime, coming in late, and making employers respect breaks and working schedules to refusing to perform tasks that are not included in collective agreements:

> I'm late every day; it's a sign that I want to go . . . and I'm not interested to fulfill . . . if you arrive early every day you get a prize, you get $50 . . . but for me it is better to have breakfast and rest in my house for 10 minutes, and come late.
> (Mariano L., a 27-year-old recount worker in La Plata, interviewed on September 18, 2009)

Table 8.2 Types of Resistance in Supermarkets and Hypermarkets

	Ways of attacking profitability
Resistance unfocused	Absenteeism
	Turnover
Resistance in order to challenge the business hegemony	Judgments against the company
	Refusal to accept penalties
Resistance in order to seek change in the control over the labor process	Delimitation of the working day
	Restriction of tasks

Source: Compilation based on the author's interviews

In this sense, Paula C. (a 42-year-old stock clerk in Buenos Aires, interviewed on June 24, 2011) said that her salary was reduced because she did not work overtime, but she preferred that because she "prefers tranquility." In Table 8.2, I summarize these types of resistance.

However, despite common demands and resistances, collective actions were scarce and lasted for a short period of time (less than an hour) in both shops. Some measures were taken due to specific claims arising from the branches. In one case, in a Buenos Aires supermarket, the reason was the non-payment of workers' overtime and, in the other, a demand for the improvement of the heating system in a La Plata hypermarket. Both involved a strike. But after a short time period, the company reacted positively to the demands of the workers. Other measures consisted of protest demonstrations decided by a labor union at levels that were larger than the workplace. Examples of these actions were the demonstrations included in a campaign to transform Sunday in a non-working day. Other activities took place amidst collective bargaining or intra-trade union disputes (Hector P., a 29-year-old recount worker in La Plata, interviewed on September 14, 2009; Julia S., a 33-year-old cashier in Buenos Aires, interviewed on July 27, 2011; Lucas M., a 27-year-old production worker in La Plata, interviewed on October 15, 2010).

These features may help us understand the reasons of the low occurrence of collective actions and the belief of workers that collective actions are not a viable strategy to solve their claims. Most of these workers expressed a negative view of "conflicts" and considered the best way to solve problems being "dialogues" with managers.

"Mediations" at the Workplace

In this section, I will introduce three essential mediations that do not consider the relationships between precariousness and conflict as a linear one. These mediations explain, on the one hand, why Argentinean retail workers have a negative view of conflict and, on the other, how conflicts are canalized.

Trade union characteristics are fundamental to understanding why "common demands" do not have a voice in collective actions that seek to modify working conditions. The SEC is part of the Argentinean Federation of Commerce and Service Employees (FAECYS), one of the oldest trade unions and the largest in the country, which has more than 1 million members. Since 1980, it has been led by Armando Cavalieri. It was during the 1990s that one of the unions, which mostly supported the flexible labor policies of neoliberalism, abandoned typical union claims and devoted itself to the "provision of services" to members. Martuccelli and Svampa (1997) considered the SEC a paradigmatic example of the "service union" that based its organization on three principles: the culture of negotiation, service delivery, and training. A final feature of the SEC has been the existence of limited internal democracy, expressed in few requests of meetings and assemblies with the workers (Abal Medina 2011). After the resurgence of conflicts in 2003, the union remained within the CGT but stayed in opposition to the ruling leadership of Hugo Moyano.[12] In this new context, SEC kept its "service union" strategy but added its participation in collective bargaining without important labor conflicts.

In the shops where I carried out the case study, delegates belonged to two different positions of political unions. In the hypermarket, delegates were officials (near to Armando Cavalieri); in the supermarket, the delegates were opponents (near to Hugo Moyano). However, workers shared a similar opinion on the typical delegate.

The workers say, for instance, that a delegate's main task is to redistribute among its members the benefits obtained by the union, such as holiday discounts, summer camp, recreational club facilities, diapers for pregnant women, and cultural discounts.[13]

> We have a relationship to the union through the delegate. Well, usually, the delegate is here to give diapers to girls who are pregnant and all the administrative paperwork. This is the task of the delegate.
> (Damian D., a 26-year-old cashier in Buenos Aires,
> interviewed on July 21, 2011)

A second function of the union is to mediate between the company and the employee. Delegates belong to a second hierarchy within the company (workers → delegates → managers). Workers should thus contact the delegates when the "traditional" hierarchy does not solve problems (workers → managers). As pointed out by a worker "a delegate from the supermarket is not a representative of the workers, s/he is a mediator between the company and the workers" (Hector P., a 29-year-old recount worker in La Plata, interviewed on September 14, 2009). He/she should solve individual problems of workers with dialogues. The trade union should thus transmit a "new culture of union" in line with the transformation of trade unionism in the 1990s, prioritizing negotiation over conflict:

> [The union intervenes] in each problem. For example, if you get "bad holidays," because, every second year, you do have "good vacation," thus, holidays between December and April. Well, if you do not get them *the delegate is going to talk to your boss*. . . . The problem of the timetables is similar. Delegates talk a lot to the managers.
>
> (Mara V., a 25-year-old cashier in La Plata, interviewed on October 12, 2008)

A second type of mediation concerns an informal practice that enables the company to "negotiate" between managers and workers. Several interviewees pointed out that this is the principal approach of workers in order to solve their individual conflicts and maintain a pleasant working environment:

> You have to make sure for yourself that there is no misunderstanding. I have been in the customer service for a year. I am the person who provides the changes between workers and allows them to take a break, and . . . and . . . and it's like everything, everything is negotiated. You have to try not to offend anyone . . . try, if you can, to give them their breaks in pairs so they can drink something and make the working day more enjoyable. After a pleasant break, people will work more. . . . If you do not let them go to the bathroom, for instance, you will not be able to negotiate later.
>
> (Emilia V., a 25-year-old cashier, Buenos Aires, interviewed on June 24, 2010)

This informality of the relationships in the company allows negotiating workers' rights around the unequal "terms" of supervisor and employee as the workers seem to have a permanent "debt" to the company. However, this as a positive feature for workers allowing them to face difficulties arising from constant changes of schedules and the existence of "unsocial" working hours.

Finally, a third mediation concerns the career of workers and the labor market situation in Argentina. Most workers have had short-term but intense job periods marked afterwards by unemployment and precariousness. Their work experience usually begins at a very young age: They work in bars, restaurants, and deliveries, take care of kids, work in family homes, or carry out a variety of "little jobs."[14] These precarious jobs are usually performed in small businesses and shops: These workers have neither rights nor job stability. They face frequent periods of unemployment. Two examples can describe this type of a worker's career. Lucas is 27 years old and he has worked in the hypermarket where the case study took place since he was 21 years old. This job was his first registered job. Previously, he worked intermittently in the construction industry and did other little jobs that alternated with periods of unemployment (Lucas M., a 27-year-old production worker in La Plata, interviewed on October 15, 2010). Another case: Mara is 25 years old and begins her third year in CR and her first registered job. Previously, she worked in the care sector for children, cleaned houses, taught as a substitute in primary schools, and worked in the customer service of small shops (Mara V., a 25-year-old cashier in La Plata, interviewed on October 12, 2008).

Thus, working in a supermarket signifies in these cases an improvement of working conditions in comparison to those of previous activities. This new job provides access to a large company and the first registered job.[15] In this sense, employees appreciate the current job in comparison to a situation of unemployment and poor working conditions they had known in the labor market. This assessment is reinforced by the labor market situation since jobs that workers consider being "potential jobs" in case of losing their current job, seem to be even worse:

> "I'm just looking for something else. But . . . I would like to have a job from Monday to Friday, as my brother. However, I do not want to be in a small shop seven days a week to earn less. No, no, this cannot convince me. Here, I have a registered job and I know what I earn each month. . . ."
>
> (Ana M., a 23-year-old cashier in La Plata, interviewed on September 1, 2009)

While in the 1990s, unemployment functioned as a powerful tool for disciplining workers; in the 2000s, unregistered work performs a similar function. Under these conditions, one can understand the following sentence: "Many people say: why would I leave this job if I have a monthly salary?" (Mariano L., a 27-year-old recount worker in La Plata, interviewed on September 18, 2009). In a context of high levels of unregistered employment, having a secure job is much appreciated. The common belief is that it is important to take care of your work and meet the requirements requested by supervisors and managers in order to avoid conflicts.

CONCLUSION

The changes that have affected the Argentine labor market in the last decades have restructured power relations at workplaces. In this chapter, I have analyzed the relationship between precariousness and workplace conflict.

After reviewing the main discussions around the concept of precariousness, I have analyzed how precariousness can be understood as an exacerbation

ANNEX:

Table 8.3 Characteristics of Interviewed Workers

Name*	Age	Sector	Contract type	Seniority (in years)	Time subcontracted	Interview year	Place interview
Ana M.	22	Check out	Internal effective	1	6 months	2008 and 2009	La Plata
Ema M.	23	Check out	Internal effective	2	4 months	2008 and 2009	La Plata
Mara V.	25	Check out	Internal effective	3	4 months	2008	La Plata
Franco C.	24	Electro	Internal effective	4	2 years	2008	La Plata
Omar C.	25	Bazzar	Internal subcontracting	1	1 year	2008	La Plata
Hector P.	29	Recounts	Internal effective	8	3 years	2009 and 2010	La Plata
Mariano L.	27	Recounts	Internal effective	5	1 year	2009	La Plata
Lucas M.	27	Production	Internal effective	6	2 years	2010	La Plata
Patricia G.	29	Grocery	External outsourcing	8	8 years	2010	La Plata
Eliana A.	23	Promoter	External outsourcing	1	1 year	2008	La Plata
Rosa B.	37	Sector chief	Internal effective	17	0	2010	La Plata
Mariana M.	39	Sector chief	Internal effective	10	0	2010	La Plata
Pedro M.	42	Sector chief	Internal effective	12	0	2010	La Plata
Federico P.	40	Sector chief	Internal effective	12	0	2010	La Plata
Damián P.	26	Delivery	External subcontracting	4	4 years	2011	Buenos Aires
Matías L.	24	Delivery	External subcontracting	1	1 year	2011	Buenos Aires
Jorge A.	22	Delivery	External subcontracting	1	1 year	2011	Buenos Aires
Emiliano D.	19	Delivery	External subcontracting	2	2 years	2011	Buenos Aires
Emilia V.	25	Check out	Internal effective	2	8 months	2011	Buenos Aires
María C.	40	Grocery	Internal effective	15	0	2011	Buenos Aires
Paula C.	42	Grocery	Internal effective	12	0	2011	Buenos Aires
Carlos R.	27	Check out	Internal effective	5	1 year	2011	Buenos Aires
Damian D.	26	Check out	Internal effective	4	1 year	2011	Buenos Aires
Julia S.	33	Check out	Internal effective	10	0	2011	Buenos Aires

* The workers' names have been changed to help preserve anonymity.

of "exploitation" because of the intensification of work and an extension of the domination of capital over labor, ending in a growing precariousness of labor relations. In this sense, I have analyzed the specific character of precariousness in supermarkets and hypermarkets in Argentina based on a case study of a transnational retail enterprise. I have shown how the profound heterogeneity of contracts, working conditions, and salaries among workers of retail companies generates the *heterogeneity of working situations*. At the same time, this heterogeneity undermines the identification of workers, complicates hierarchical relationships, and individualizes the employment relationship. In other words, heterogeneity *fragments the labor force*.

In the section "Workplace conflict," I analyzed the forms workplace conflicts take. While common demands exist they are not expressed in collective actions that try to change the labor situation. The consecutive discontent is expressed in individual resistances where workers can temporarily crack the corporate hegemony by various actions. However, the company has reacted to individual resistances in these workplaces.

Finally, I have shown how the gap between common demands and the lack of collective actions can be explained by the existence of "mediations" that focus on the negative opinion of conflicts: the characteristics of organizations, the existence of informal management practices, the characteristics of careers of workers, and the labor market situation in Argentina. The absence of many open conflicts in these spaces can be explained by the "mediations" that channel the discontent of workers. The analysis of these "mediations" enabled me to display the complex relationship between precariousness and conflict, shedding light on other factors that, along with a high level of fragmentation, hinder the development of collective actions at precarious workplaces.

Acknowledgments: I am grateful to Ulrike Schuerkens for her valuable comments and suggestions on a previous version of this chapter. I would also like to thank all these workers who selflessly gave me their time making possible this research. The present study is part of my Ph.D. thesis under the supervision of Dr. Mariana Busso, to whom I am very grateful. Financial support was provided by the *Consejo Nacional de Investigaciones Científicas y Técnicas* (CONICET), Argentina.

NOTES

1. In Argentina, neoliberal economic policies included the privatization of public companies, fiscal incentives for transnational capital investment, and a reform of the labor law system legitimizing flexibility in both the workplace and the labor market (Atzeni 2010).
2. In another paper (Longo 2012), I consider a third dimension of precariousness ("precarious work") associated with a neo-Durkheimian perspective. In this chapter, due to space and the complexity of this dimension in Argentina's labor force, this aspect will not be included.
3. CR Group official website: http://www.carrefour.com/, accessed on October 24, 2012.

4. Página 12 (2008) "Qué es el monopsonio", *Página/12 website*, May 5, 2008. Online at http://www.pagina12.com.ar/diario/economia/subnotas/2-32709-2008-05-11.html, accessed on October 24, 2012.
5. CR Group official website in Argentina: http://www.carrefour.com.ar/, accessed on October 24, 2012.
6. http://www.prensaeconomica.com.ar/index.php?modo=rankings_1000, accessed on October 24, 2012.
7. The sample was made following the method named "theoretical sampling." It was realized by taking into account the principal differences between workers, i.e., sector and type of contract (Glasser and Strauss 1967), cf. the characteristics of the interviewed workers (Annex 1, Table 8.3).
8. Approximate wages for November 2011 based on the information found at http://www.faecys.org.ar/ESCALASALARIALJUNIO2011-ABRIL2012.pdf, accessed on January 14, 2013.
9. "Unsocial" hour is the work schedule that hinders the development of social activities such as weekend work or night work. According to Baudelot and Gollac (2011), "unsocial" hours are a psychosocial risk factor.
10. Within the company that is 7 percent, according to public statements by the director of human resources group in Argentina Recursos Humanos (2010) "7 Gerentes y Directores de RRHH comentan sus proyectos para 2010", *Los Recursos Humanos website*, August 3, 2010. Online at http://www.losrecursoshumanos.com/contenidos/7223-7-gerentes-y-directores-de-rrhh-comentan-sus-proyectos-para-2010.html, accessed on October 24, 2012.
11. "My colleagues have had to organize groups, not 10 or 15 . . . more than 30 cashiers! Who looks for a private lawyer! Because the union told them that they could not change anything. . . . And with this lawyer and through legal letters with their claims, the cashiers got for example a recognition of seniority that appeared an impossible thing for the trade union" (Hector P., a 29-year-old recount worker in La Plata, interviewed on September 14, 2009).
12. Clarín (2012) "Con aval 'gordo', Caló liderará la CGT Balcarce", *Clarín website*, September 24. 2012. Online at http://www.clarin.com/politica/gordo-Calo-liderara-CGT-Balcarce_0_779922018.html, accessed on October 24, 2012.
13. See the official website: http://www.sec.org.ar/ and http://www.seclaplata.org.ar/inicio.html.
14. The little jobs (called *changas* in Argentina) are temporary jobs, which are held for a short period of time and are generally very unstable and without any kind of labor laws.
15. Unregistered employment is actually the main problem of the labor market in Argentina. This varies according to activities; the rates are very high in construction, gastronomy, and cleaning, activities that have grown since 2003. According to data released on October 16, 2012, by the Institute of Statistics and Census ("INDEC"), 34.5 percent of the workers are not formally registered. According to some authors, this problem is a "legal problem" so that it seems necessary to add more inspections and discuss with unions, workers, business chambers, and justice. Other authors suggest that the persistence of high rates of unregistered workers is a "structural problem" and the unregistered laborers contribute indirectly to an over-accumulation of large capital (see Pérez et al. 2010).

REFERENCES

Abal Medina, Paula (2011) "Estatutos Sindicales, la Fuente Olvidada. El caso de las estructuras sindicales de empleados de comercio," *Trabajo y Sociedad* 15 (17): 213–227.

Antunes, Ricardo (2005) *Los sentidos del trabajo.* Buenos Aires: Herramienta.

Atzeni, Mauricio (2010) *Workplace conflict. Mobilization and solidarity in Argentina.* London: Palgrave Macmillan.

Basualdo, Victoria (2006) "Complicidad patronal-militar en la última dictadura argentina: Los casos de Acindar, Astarsa, Dálmine Siderca, Ford, Ledesma y Mercedes Benz," *Revista Engranajes (FETIA-CTA)* 5 (March 2006). Online at http://www.nodo50.org/exilioargentino/2006/2006_Mayo/i_complicidad_patronal.htm, accessed on October 29, 2012.

Baudelot, Christian and Michel Gollac (eds) (2011) *¿Trabajar para ser feliz? La felicidad y el trabajo en Francia.* Buenos Aires: Miño y Dávila/CEIL/Trabajo y Sociedad.

Bouffartigue, Paul and Sophie Béroud (2009) *Quand le travail se précarise, quelles résistances collectives?* Paris: La dispute/SNEDIT.

Busso, Mariana (2006) "El trabajo informal en Argentina: la novedad de un fenómeno histórico" in Julio C. Neffa and Pablo Pérez (eds) *Macroeconomía, mercado de trabajo y grupos vulnerables. Desafíos para el diseño de políticas públicas,* 139–158. Buenos Aires: Asociación Trabajo y Sociedad / CEIL-PIETTE del CONICET.

Busso, Mariana and Paul Bouffartigue (2010) "¿Más allá de la 'precariedad' y la 'informalidad'? Aportes para el debate desde una perspectiva comparada," in Andrea Del Bono and Germán Quaranta (eds) *Convivir con la incertidumbre. Aproximaciones a la flexibilización y precarización del trabajo en la Argentina,* 201–220. Buenos Aires: Ciccus/CEIL-PIETTE.

Castel, Robert (2003) *From Manual Workers to Wage Laborers: Transformation of the Social Question.* New Brunswick, NJ: Transaction Publishers.

Clarín (2012) "Con aval 'gordo', Caló liderará la CGT Balcarce", *Clarín website,* Sep 24. 2012. Online at http://www.clarin.com/politica/gordo-Calo-liderara-CGT-Balcarce_0_779922018.html, accessed on October 24, 2012.

Edwards, K. Paul and Hugh Scullion (1982) *The Social Organization of Industrial Conflict. Control and Resistance in the Workplace.* Oxford, UK: Basil Blackwell.

Etchemendy, Sebastián and Ruth Collier (2007) "Down But Not Out: The Recovery of a Downsized Labor Movement in Argentina (2002–2006)," *Politics and Society* 35 (3): 363–401.

Galín, Pablo (1986) "Asalariados, precarización y condiciones de trabajo," *Nueva Sociedad* (85, September/October 1986): 30–38. Online at http://wwww.nuso.org, accessed on November 5, 2012.

Glasser, Barney G. and Anselm L. Strauss (1967) *The Discovery of Grounded Theory: Strategies for Qualitative Research.* Chicago, IL: Aldine.

Harvey, David (1990) *The Condition of Postmodernity: An Enquiry into the Origins of Cultural Change.* Cambridge, MA: Blackwell Publishers.

Longo, Julieta (2012) "Las fronteras de la precariedad: Percepciones y sentidos del trabajo de los jóvenes trabajadores precarios de hipermercados," *Trabajo y Sociedad* 16 (19): 375–392. Online at http://www.unse.edu.ar/trabajoysociedad, accessed on October 29, 2012.

Martuccelli, Danilo and Maristella Svampa (1997) *La Plaza Vacía: Las transformaciones del peronismo.* Buenos Aires: Editorial Losada.

Neffa, Julio (ed) (2008) *La informalidad, la precariedad laboral y el empleo no registrado en la Provincia de Buenos Aires.* Buenos Aires: Ministerio de Trabajo de la Provincia de Buenos Aires / Centro de Estudios e Investigaciones Laborales (CEIL).

Página 12 (2008) "Qué es el monopsonio", *Página/12 website,* May 5, 2008. Online at http://www.pagina12.com.ar/diario/economia/subnotas/2-32709-2008-05-11.html, accessed on October 24, 2012.

Página 12 (2012) "Vamos a defender este modelo económico y social", *Página/12 website* [online], April 10, 2012. Online at http://www.pagina12.com.ar/diario/elpais/1-204866-2012-10-04.html, accessed on October 24, 2012.

Paugam, Serge (2000) *Le salarié de la précarité: Les nouvelles formes de l'intégration professionnelle*. Paris: Presses Universitaires de France.

Pérez, Pablo, Pablo Chena, and Facundo Barrea (2010) "La informalidad como estrategia del capital. Una aproximación macro, inter e intra sectorial," in Mariana Busso and Pablo Pérez (eds) *La corrosión del trabajo. Estudios sobre informalidad y precariedad laboral*, 171–202. Buenos Aires: Miño y Dávila Editores y CEIL-PIETTE (CONICET).

Pok, Cyntia (1992) *Precariedad laboral: personificaciones sociales en la frontera de la estructura del empleo*. Buenos Aires: Centro de Estudios e Investigaciones Laborales (CEIL). Online at http://www.ceil-piette.gov.ar/docpub/documentos/docceil/dc29pok.pdf, accessed on October 27, 2012.

Recursos Humanos (2010) "7 Gerentes y Directores de RRHH comentan sus proyectos para 2010", *Los Recursos Humanos website*, August 3, 2010. Online at http://www.losrecursoshumanos.com/contenidos/7223-7-gerentes-y-directores-de-rrhh-comentan-sus-proyectos-para-2010.html, accessed on October 24, 2012.

Salvia, Agustín and Julieta Vera (2011) "Cambios en el sistema económico, productivo y laboral durante fases de distintas reglas macroeconómicas." Paper presented at the *10° Congress ASET (Asociación Argentina de Especialistas en Estudios del Trabajo), Facultad de Ciencias Económicas*, UBA. Buenos Aires, Argentina.

Serdar, Ayse (2010) "Limits to the Revitalization of Labor: Social Movement Unionism in Argentina" in Ulrike Schuerkens (ed.) *Globalization and Transformations of Social Inequality*, 151–174. New York: Routledge.

Silver, Beverly (2005) *Fuerzas del trabajo. Los movimientos obreros y la globalización desde 1870*. Madrid: Akal.

Vasapollo, Luciano (2004) "Trabajo precario y nuevas pobrezas en la fase de la competencia global," *Laberinto* 15 (November 1, 2004): 14–29. Online at http://laberinto.uma.es/, accessed on January 19, 2013.

9 When Resistance Crosses over the Workplace in a Context of Precarious Labor

A Study of the Invisible World of Agribusiness in the Limarí Valley, Chile

Tamara Heran

INTRODUCTION: MAKING OTHER ACTIVITIES OF RESISTANCE VISIBLE

Workers' acts of resistance are frequently linked to social organizations or movements so that they are conceived as collective acts. However, if a collective is to be established, contextual conditions have to be accepted, such as the freedom of organizations or the recognition of collective rights. When management frameworks hamper labor organizations and do not recognize certain collective bodies, there is a problem. In cases of high flexibility and precariousness when informality, poor quality of contracts, and job insecurity are present, this may apply. What chances do workers have under these circumstances to resist management practices considered being abusive? What opportunities do they have to express grievances at the workplace under highly precarious working conditions?

This chapter analyzes different forms of resistance that emerge in work contexts with complex organizations and social manifestations based on the study of seasonal agricultural workers, called *temporeros* and *temporeras* working in the export agribusiness in Chile. As part of the implementation of rural development policies since the mid-1970s that have given rise to large agribusiness export groups, these jobs have become an opportunity for hundreds of thousands of rural and urban people. *Temporeros* and *temporeras* are involved in harvesting and packing agricultural products that are shipped around the world. This mainly feminine work is carried out seasonally under precarious and informal conditions (cf. Arteaga 2000, Riquelme 2000, Valdés 1992 and 1995, Venegas 1992). The particular job characteristics and the situation of these seasonal workers have hindered organizational efforts and social mobilization around traditional mechanisms of resistance. However, one can observe the emergence of other forms of collective and individual resistances, both in the field of work—that we call active resistance—and in the private sphere—that we call passive resistance. These are forms of resistance that are not always apparent or acknowledged but they try to counter what the workers consider unfair or incorrect practices.

In order to tackle the challenge and make visible less frequent and atypical forms of resistance, we use the concept of the "invisible world" (Max-Neef 1993) that tries to understand changes and social transformations brought up by development. The dominant paradigm of development has neglected an "invisible world" that goes beyond the merely practical and economic results. Daily lives, individual and collective strategies, identities, and popular memory belong to this "invisible world." Social relations that occur in these economic, social, and cultural worlds and changes engendered by development efforts can then be understood.

Chile is an example of these hidden aspects of development and globalization. Aggressive economic plans established at the end of the 1970s, and promoting development and progress thanks to an export model based on the paradigm of comparative advantages, have led to important transformations in various sectors. On the one hand, these transformations have improved economic indicators to the point that Chile has become a development model integrated in international trade. Its recent admittance to the OECD is an example. Chile was the first South American country that joined this international organization. Nevertheless, different social indicators display high levels of inequalities in areas such as health, education, income, and gender.[1] In the labor sector, flexible policies have brought up new ways of working characterized by precariousness, insecurity, informality, and instability.

In rural areas, these interventions have been particularly important. With the industrialization of agricultural production schemes whose produce are largely destined for the export market, new actors and new ways of working have emerged. Seasonal agricultural work, for example, has provided job opportunities for men and women and a new way of life. At certain times of the year, Chileans, and more recently Peruvians and Bolivians as well, move under precarious conditions around the country for a salary. These opportunities have considerably changed social relationships, identities, and local cultures outside of the work place (cf. Arteaga 2000, Gómez and Echeñique 1988, Riquelme 2000, Valdés 1992 and 1995, Venegas 1992).

In this new space of flexibility, precariousness, and social change at the workplace, resistance activities had to be adapted and reinvented. This chapter aims to demonstrate and discuss certain forms and acts of resistance that can appear in a highly adverse and repressive context. Following Hollander and Einwohner's analysis (2004), I define the concept of resistance by individual and collective behaviors and actions that seek to counter situations considered being oppressive, abusive, unequal, or unfair by some people. Thus, individuals or collectives can undertake active (intentional) and passive (involuntary) behaviors or actions in order to ease this oppression that may or may not be recognized by the "oppressors." Given the context of my research, resistance movements analyzed here go beyond resistance based on organizations (such as unions) and social manifestations (such as strikes or work stoppages) and address forms of resistance that do not involve protests or organizations (cf. Scott 1987) and that are more characteristic of the invisible world I study.

To address this issue, my research is based on cultural anthropology and follows the method of ethnographic investigation (cf. Beaud and Weber 1998). Additional techniques were used to approach unofficial and unrecorded information. My strategy was based on content analysis of official and unofficial materials (censuses, annual reports, proceedings, contracts, lists, etc.) produced by different actors involved in my research topic (institutions, services, programs, companies, group leaders, unions, local researchers, and churches, among others). Furthermore, this chapter is based on an empirical study including participant observation and interviews (more than 35 non-directive interviews and 95 guided interviews) of the main participants in agricultural work (laborers, employers, labor subcontractors, local representatives of institutions and government agencies, and non-governmental actors such as universities, unions, and organizations of the churches, among others).

My fieldwork focused on the Province of Limarí (see Figure 9.1), a choice based on the specialization of the region in agricultural exports, mainly fruits such as grapes, avocados, and citrus. Limarí is a province where the two main economic activities are mining and the agricultural export industry, the latter generating most of the jobs. This province, named after the Limarí River Valley, where it is located, has a semi-arid climate and optimal water resources with a large irrigation infrastructure. Thus, the Valley has become an ideal region for the development of agriculture. It is the leading agricultural province in Coquimbo Region and an important national region.

First, the framework of the emergence of seasonal agricultural labor in Chile and the invisible world, as a background for its analysis, will be presented. Second, before analyzing resistance, I will take a moment to examine seasonal agricultural labor today, with the aim of presenting flexibility, seasonality, and precariousness of work configurations. For this, I will present the empirical data based on a gender approach that will permit me to explain the current status of seasonal agricultural labor, particularly regarding its working conditions. Then I will show the particular mechanisms of resistance that the seasonal workers use to deal with what they consider being abuses and injustices. These mechanisms are presented according to the following categories: collective and individual, active and passive resistance. These categories permit us to address uncommon or more invisible forms of resistance. Finally, some reflections on social transformations and possible forms of resistance in a context of globalization and development will be presented.

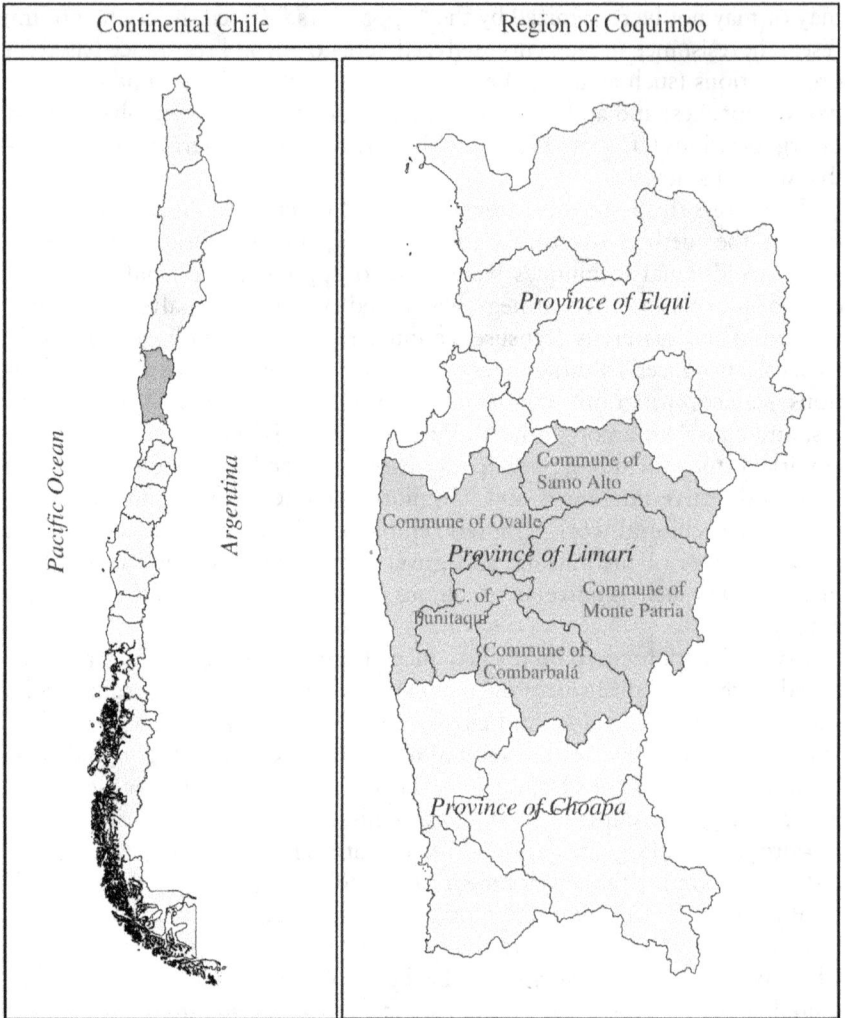

Continental Chile	Region of Coquimbo

Figure 9.1   Administrative Map of Chile, Region of Coquimbo, Province of Limarí

THE EMERGENCE OF SEASONAL AGRICULTURAL WORK IN CHILE AND ITS INVISIBLE WORLD

Recent Changes in the Agricultural Sector

Before 1980, the rural workforce generally consisted of peasants. Whether as *inquilinos* or tenant farmers, small farmers, or workers on large farms, the peasantry was the main rural labor force of the country. From the 1980s onwards, with the advent and success of agricultural export companies and the failure of traditional small and mid-sized peasant farmers, various transformations have influenced the physical, social, and cultural landscapes of rural areas (cf. Gómez 1982, Gómez and Echeñique 1988, Valdés and Araujo 1999). In this new agrarian system, the appearance of seasonal agricultural workers or *temporeros* and *temporeras* as new social actors (Gómez 2000) became a response to the new order of rural labor.

The transformation of peasants into salaried agro-export laborers seems to be what many authors call the "proletarianization" of the agricultural workforce (cf. Salazar 1989, Valdés 1992): These social actors are men and women without property who depend on their income from a salaried manual activity in a rural landscape formerly known for its rural landlords. This change that seems normal for today's urban societies has irrevocably transformed agricultural labor and the rural world. On one hand, by denying access to land ownership and assistance to small-scale agriculture, this process meant the exclusion of the peasants' modes of production. On the other, it meant the abandonment of a development project and rural livelihood by transforming individual actors and families into paid employees in agribusiness, one of the few job opportunities available in rural areas (cf. Gómez 1982, Gómez and Echeñique 1988, Valdés and Araujo 1999).

For all these reasons, seasonal agricultural work has become the only remaining *chance* for work and livelihood in the rural world, particularly for farmers who, dispossessed of their job opportunities in agriculture, have had to move to this new source of employment. The export agriculture development strategy in rural areas has thus brought up new forms of work as well as new ways of living. These new forms of production and work have included numerous social transformations, opening up an entire invisible world particular for seasonal agricultural work.

The Concept of Invisible World

In order to address the issue of seasonal agricultural work and consider its complexity, the notion of the invisible world will here be used. Not only the visible and invisible presence at work (cf. Bidet and Schoeni 2011, Dolbeau 2011, Jarty 2011) but also activities, practices, relationships, the intrinsic dynamics involved in mobility, the continuous search for paid work, the organization of domestic activities, and gender relations constitute this complex invisible world. Moreover, this notion goes beyond the informal sector, understood as comprising income-generating activities that take place outside institutional norms.

The notion of the invisible world also transcends economic and quantitative problems. It links economic, social, and cultural systems covering complex situations as in the case of seasonal agricultural work. It involves the relationships of mixed economic, social, and cultural systems, productions, and reproductions, increasing not only connections within but also the origin and recurrence of social problems. As shown by Yves Schwartz (2004), to enter the invisible world implies measuring continuities, circulations, and transfers in all directions, between formal, informal, domestic, and commercial forms.

The concept of the invisible world proposed by Manfred Max-Neef (1993) will be used here. It refers to the existence and production of relationships between economic, social, and cultural practices in a development context. The invisible world contains different, socio-cultural expressions and dynamical relationships between diverse actors, including those who were often forgotten and marginalized. This approach tries thus to make visible what was invisible in conventional economics. This concept attempts to recover a world where experiences, practices, and the social life-world, previously quite ignored by the conventional analysis of development, are now recognized and highlighted. In this invisible world, representations, practices, and traditions that broadly integrate culture, economy, and society are interlocked.

The Invisible World of Seasonal Agricultural Work in Chile

This approach permits us to analyze the inherent peculiarities of seasonal agricultural work, such as temporality, precariousness, informality, mobility, occupational diseases, and working conditions as well as individual and collective histories, salary processes and strategies, new identities, relationships, labor intermediation, and social and cultural transformations in general. Empirical studies and official statistics conducted in the 1980s and early 1990s revealed several aspects of this invisible world, including temporality, precarious work, and the feminization of seasonal agricultural work.

Seasonal agricultural work depends on the conditions of its production, which in turn vary with natural conditions, such as climate and the vegetation cycles of different agricultural crops. These are conditions that can hardly be controlled and that require a great deal of flexibility. Thus, the quantity of laborers and agricultural production differs throughout the year and leads to fluctuating demands. These work conditions confine intensive work to a few months per year. That is why agricultural work is largely seasonal, as I have shown in Table 9.1.[2]

Precarious work is a second aspect that is characteristic for seasonal agricultural work. Various studies have shown a lack of formality in seasonal agricultural work and in particular in informal labor contracts. The weak data available have shown that half of the seasonal work is done without contracts

Table 9.1   Permanent and Seasonal Agricultural Workforce, 1964–1965 to 2006–2007

Workforce	1964–65	1975–76	1986–87	1996–97	2006–07
Permanent	208,000	161,000	120,000	521,000	188,000
Seasonal	147,000	198,000	300,000	276,000	402,000

Established by the author. Source: National Statistics Institute (INE) Agricultural Censuses, except for the 1986–1987 season (estimation of Gómez and Echeñique 1988). The data on the seasonal workforce concern the period of the highest activity in these years (February to April).

(Venegas 1992 and 1995). According to the 1998 National Survey of Socioeconomic Indicators (CASEN), only 36 percent of seasonal workers had signed an employment contract, a figure that shows a deteriorating situation. The same survey revealed that 67.3 percent of seasonal agricultural workers did not pay social security taxes and, therefore, were not entitled to social welfare measures (Riquelme 2000). In fact, this is a problem that is caused by gaps in the Chilean Labor Code on seasonal agricultural work (cf. Venegas 1992 and 1995, Riquelme 2000). But this is also the result of farm employers' efforts to escape legal obligations and that of temporary workers trying to obtain the highest possible amount of money (Díaz 1994, Venegas 1992 and 1995).

Irregular salaries paid for seasonal agricultural work, both in amounts as well as in the forms of payment, are the counter-part of this informality. Different studies have shown that wages are paid in two ways: according to the working day, which may (or may not) include extra work hours; and by piecework, according to each worker's productivity and efficiency (cf. Arteaga 2000, Venegas 1992). Thus, salaries can greatly vary outside their temporary conditions. Venegas (1992) showed that seasonal wages were on average 24 percent higher than the wages of permanent workers. However, these data do not consider the number of working hours, work conditions, or other aspects that may benefit permanent workers. Indeed, the working days of seasonal workers are characterized by surpassing the scheduled working day, mainly with tasks performed in the fruit packing centers (Arteaga 2000, Venegas 1992).

A final aspect is related to women's participation in seasonal agricultural work. While the overall amount of seasonal work is difficult to quantify, women's participation in these tasks has been even more difficult to uncover. However, a significant increase in demands for the female labor-force paralleling the expansion of modern agriculture has been detected in several studies. This request for women is due to the rise in both well-known and new activities, such as field processing and packaging that are associated with feminine qualities of delicacy and attention to detail, attitudes developed thanks to a gender differentiated socialization process (Valdés 1988). However, farm modernization also needs to rely on cheap labor. Thus, women and young people have become good alternatives for a competent and advantageous workforce that contributes to the growth of this sector.

The incorporation of women in seasonal agricultural work (as illustrated in Figure 9.2) has shown very high levels, surpassing even traditional rates of female participation in the agricultural labor market (Valdés 1992). In the early 1990, Venegas (1992) found that female temporary workers represented 52 percent of the total seasonal agricultural labor-force. This percentage could even go up to 62 percent for some crops, as in the case of the table grape production (Venegas 1995). The high participation of women in seasonal agricultural labor, recognized by different authors, has revealed the feminization of this sector (Riquelme 2000, Valdés 1988 and 1998, Valdés and Araujo 1999) and a female proletarianization (Valdés 1995).

Figure 9.2   *Temporeras* Harvesting Table Grapes.
Source: Photos Originating from Tamara Heran's Fieldwork, January 2009, Caren

Various studies conducted in earlier decades made known some aspects of this invisible world of seasonal agricultural work. The very specific characteristics of seasonal agricultural labor have penetrated the strict domain of work, transforming the lives of thousands of men and women who have found a salary opportunity in modern agriculture.

FLEXIBILITY AND PRECARIOUSNESS IN AGRICULTURAL LABOR TODAY: THE SETTING FOR OTHER ACTS OF RESISTANCE

Seasonal Labor?

Thirty years after the creation of a seasonal farm labor market linked to the export of fruits and vegetables, transformations and continuities can be remarked in this invisible world of seasonal agricultural work. This activity involves today more people than in the 1980s. According to the Agricultural Census of 2007 (Instituto Nacional de Estadísticas de Chile [INE] 2008), one of the most reliable sources, the number of seasonal workers exceeds 400,000 during the months of Chile's spring and summer (November to April), when harvesting and packing activities are intense, while in the months of autumn and winter (May to October), this number varies from 150,000 to 200,000, as shown in Figure 9.3.

The demand for labor varies and depends on the agricultural production scheme: Most activities are concentrated on the months dedicated to harvesting and packing. Nevertheless, the data provide evidence that there is a demand for temporary labor throughout the year. Even in the month known for its feeblest activity, the demand for seasonal labor is similar to the numbers of the permanent workforce. In fact, according to my research in Limarí Province, the monthly period of working has become longer for seasonal workers. The diversification of agricultural production that includes various products such as citrus, avocados, nuts, or olives, in addition to the principal

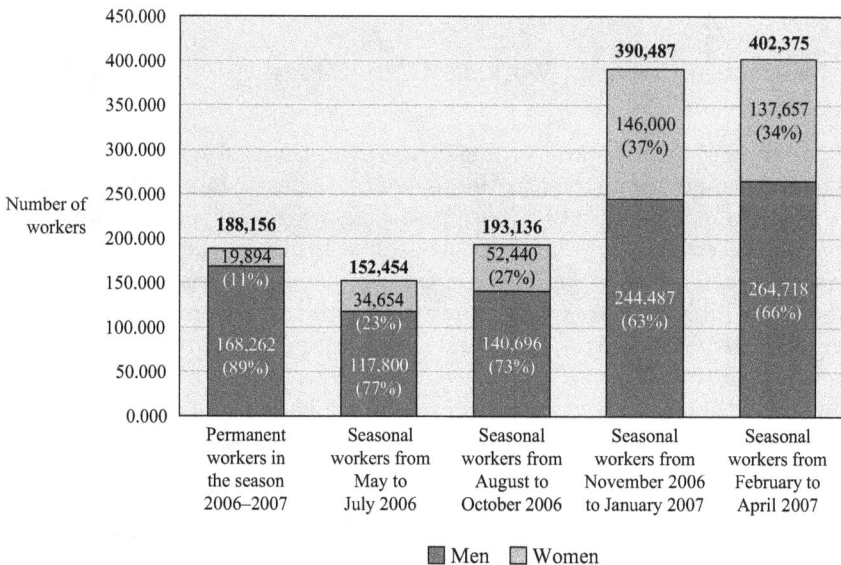

Figure 9.3 Seasonal Agricultural Ratio, by Sex, in Chile 2006–2007.
Prepared by the Author. Source: Agricultural Census 2007

Table 9.2   Duration of Agricultural Seasonal Work for the Period 2007–2008

	Total	Men	Women
Average months worked in 2007–2008	6.8	6.6	7.0
Seasonals who worked from 0 to 3 months	34%	39%	29%
Seasonals who worked from 4 to 6 months	10%	5%	15%
Seasonals who worked from 7 to 9 months	12%	10%	15%
Seasonals who worked from 10 to 12 months	44%	46%	41%

Prepared by the author. Source: Interviews with seasonal agricultural workers (2008–2009).

harvesting of table grapes, has extended farming activities according to the interviewed farmers. Thus, while the average seasonal work period was limited previously to 4 months a year, its duration is today close to 7 months. It is slightly higher for women than for men, as shown in Table 9.2.

This analysis allows to identify three types of seasonal agricultural workers: seasonal-*seasonal* workers who work at the most for 3 months a year (about a third of the seasonal workers) that coincide with the time of the most important agricultural activity; the seasonal-*average* workers who work for 6 months as seasonal workers (approximately one fifth of the temporary workers); and seasonal-*permanent* workers who work in this job (almost half of the total) the largest part of the year. This latter category confirms the existence of a seasonal type that has been recognized by several studies: the permanent seasonal worker (cf. Arteaga 2000, Riquelme 2000, Venegas 1992 and 1995). But if about 6 months of the seasonal agricultural working year are seasonal, why does this work continue to be temporary?

Management Practices, Working Relationships, and Precarious Work

The nature of their working arrangements gives seasonal agricultural workers their temporary character. Although working hours are being extended in order to include most of the year, working arrangements are temporary, even if the employer is the same. Thus, a seasonal worker can have several contracts per agricultural year, including with the same company, as shown in Table 9.3. According to my survey, the average number of working arrangements per season is slightly higher for men than for women (2.5 against 2.2). It was a man who stated in my fieldwork that he had the largest number of agreements in an agricultural year (20 working arrangements).

According to my fieldwork, 73 percent of working agreements registered during the 2007–2008 agricultural year were established with a formal employment contract. This is a rather high figure that can be explained by the campaign of the Labor Ministry intended to regulate seasonal work mainly for women, as shown in Table 9.3. However, several seasonal workers noticed that there are valueless contracts. Having an employment

Table 9.3 Work Agreements for Seasonal Agricultural Workers (2007–2008)

	Total	Men	Women
Number of working agreements (average)	2.35	2.51	2.20
Work agreements with labor contract	73%	64%	81%
Work agreements managed by agricultural companies	43%	35%	50%
Work agreements managed by labor sub-contractors	57%	65%	50%
Work arrangements paid by piecework	76%	83%	70%
Work arrangements paid by working day or fixed amount	15%	11%	19%
Work arrangements characterized by mixed payments	8%	6%	10%

Prepared by the author. Source: Interviews with seasonal agricultural workers (2008–2009).

contract does not necessarily mean that there is, for example, social welfare coverage. I could see on some receipts for payments that were prepared in accordance with social laws applying to seasonal workers, that pension, sickness, or unemployment insurance were not paid by employers. Seasonal workers link this problem to the presence of subcontractors for agricultural labor, negotiators who establish contracts and wage payments of seasonal workers. Today, the existence of a subcontractor who manages more than half of the work arrangements, as shown in Table 9.3, has contributed to the particular precarious character of labor agreements.

> *The non-payment of taxes, there isn't a contract, they don't argue with the law. You go and they don't respect your rights. . . .*
> Roberto B., a 44-year-old *Temporero*,
> on December 17, 2008, Ovalle[3]

> *The informality of work, if I get sick, if I stop (working), I don't receive any pay. . . .*
> Marcelo V., a 22-year-old *Temporero*,
> on January 8, 2009, Ovalle

The presence of employment contracts does not mean that there is any control of the working conditions or the duration of the working day. Even if Chilean law requires a periodic record of working days in order to control overtime, these records are often inexact and sometimes nonexistent. Working days often exceed the 10-hour regulations[4], particularly in the fruit packing plants (as shown in Figure 9.4) where the working day can last more than 12 hours. According to my fieldwork, seasonal workers have to sign time controls for attendance with fake times to get the records "in order." Overtime is not paid as extra hours, but as piecework, and is thus the way most of the hours worked by seasonal agricultural workers are classified.

Another element that contributes to the current precariousness of agricultural work is the method of payment. In my study, more than three quarters of work agreements were paid by piecework, as shown in Table 9.3. For

Figure 9.4   Seasonal Workers at a Table Grape Packing Plant.
Source: Photos Taken during Tamara Heran's Fieldwork in April 2009, Camarico

men, this part is even higher while some 25 percent of women are paid daily or with a fixed amount that is often close to the minimum wage. The payment for piecework varies and depends on the abilities and efforts of seasonal workers who must work hard to increase their salaries. This form of compensation is very harsh: It means that seasonal workers must show a permanent self-exigency to successfully achieve higher wages.

> *Yes, yes, of course, a seasonal worker is someone who doesn't have an unlimited contract. They* (employers, T.H.) *cut short your work all the time, each season. You never know if they will give you a new contract, there is a lot of uncertainty. . . . I work twelve months a year in the company, ten of them are managed by the company, and two by the* contratista (agricultural labor subcontractor), *so that they can give me a temporary contract each time.*
>
> Alberto A., a 37-year-old *Temporero,*
> on April 2, 2009, Camarico

> *Yes,* (I'm a *temporera*) *because I work seasonally, although I'm still in the same company, we are all* temporeros *here.*
>
> Camila S., a 30-year-old *Temporera,*
> on April 2, 2009, Camarico

(Working) *for piece-work is always harder, you exploit yourself. . . . It's boring and dangerous. Sometimes you're on the hillsides. . . . You fight for the boxes* (units for storing the harvest), *for the rows of grapes. . . .*
Damian D., a 22-year-old *Temporero*,
on December 3, 2008, Ovalle

According to my fieldwork, unlike previous studies that showed that incomes of seasonal workers are close to the minimum wage or insufficient (Coutard, Livenais, and Reyes 2003, Riquelme 2000, Venegas 1992), the seasonal workers' wages in Limarí Province are high. As shown in Table 9.4, the average wage for a seasonal worker is $227,000 Chilean pesos, or U.S. $465, while the minimum wage at the time of this study was $159,000 Chilean pesos, or U.S. $325.

In my study, the average salary of male seasonal workers is slightly higher than that of female workers. At the same time, wages below the minimum wage are more frequent for women. This wage difference between men and women can be explained by two facts. First, my sample includes elderly women who are retired and choose to work a few days per month to supplement the family budget. Second, it contains female beginners with no experience who receive lower wages. However, for more than half of both men and women, the revenue segment from $200,000 to $260,000 Chilean pesos (U.S. $410 to U.S. $530) is the most common one. Thus, for most seasonal agricultural workers wages are above the minimum salary. For two of the highest income segments, a small difference in favor of men could be found. However, the highest salary was identified being that of a woman aged 22, who worked as a seasonal worker during the Chilean summer (late December, January, and February): She worked as a packer (packaging of fruit) and attended university during the rest of the academic year. But she remarked that these high salaries do not hold throughout the year: *The wages they pay* (employers to seasonal workers) *correspond to the minimum the rest of the year. . . . It's this time of the year when we are paid more.*[5]

In short, seasonal agricultural work has displayed and continues to display significant job flexibility and precariousness. The duration of work throughout the year, the types and the quality of contracts, labor intermediation and

Table 9.4   Seasonal Workers' Salary in the Province of Limarí

	All	Men	Women
Average salary (amount in Chilean pesos)	227,000	237,000	216,000
< $159,000	9%	3%	15%
≥ $159,000 and < $200,000	26%	28%	25%
≥ $200,000 and< $260,000	43%	43%	43%
≥ $260,000 and< $320,000	14%	18%	10%
≥ $320,000	9%	10%	8%

Established by the author. Source: Interviews with seasonal agricultural workers (2008–2009).

the presence of subcontractors, and forms of remuneration and salaries are some of the elements that characterize this work. These elements are possible thanks to a regulatory framework that supports job flexibility and that regulates (or omits) different aspects of seasonal agricultural work, such as organizing and unionizing suggested by the International Labor Organization, as discussed below.

Limitations to Organizational and Social Manifestations on the Job by Seasonal Workers

The first and main issue on regulations of seasonal agricultural work is its definition. Although 50 percent of seasonal *temporeros* and *temporeras* work around 10 to 12 months a year, it is not the duration of work that is temporary but the contractual situations or working arrangements. However, the Chilean Labor Code still considers these workers as seasonal agricultural laborers.[6] The problem raised by this inclusion is that the employment status contains a series of definitions and special "seasonal" rules. Let us review some of them.

The types of contracts established by law and regarding *temporeros* and *temporeras* are the "Contract for work or job" (*Contrato por obra o por faena*) and the "Contract for transitory work or job" (*Contrato por obra o por faena transitoria*). While both refer to temporary jobs, the difference is that the first refers to the completion of a specific material or intellectual work limited to a certain duration, while the second is limited to jobs that, by their characteristics, are momentary or temporary; these are facts that must be demonstrated in each case (Dirección del Trabajo 2004). Thus, *temporeros* and *temporeras* can sign (although they do not know this) both types of contracts, depending on each case. But their signature implies further rules.

With regard to unionization and according to the law, temporary workers can join temporary or transitory trade unions. However, this does not mean that this occurs regularly as we shall see below. The difficulty of bringing different people together in temporary jobs, the mobility of people working temporarily, and the poor social image that unionization has hinder the unionization of *temporeros* and *temporeras*. Furthermore, belonging to a union does not necessarily give the ability to bargain collectively.

In fact, collective bargaining is a labor right that seasonal agricultural workers have rarely obtained. However, this depends on the type of contract. According to the definition of the Chilean Labor Code, collective bargaining means the process by which one or more employers are related to one or more trade unions and/or workers reunited for this purpose who do not necessarily belong to a labor union. This definition permits us to define common working conditions and remunerations (Dirección del Trabajo 2011, Libro IV). Despite this definition, the Labor Code further states that "workers under apprenticeship contracts and those contracted exclusively to work in a specific, transitory or seasonal job" (Department of Labor 2011 Book IV: 145) shall not bargain collectively. Thus, seasonal workers with a "contract for a transitory work or a job," including numerous *temporeros* and *temporeras*, have no collective bargaining rights under this regulatory framework. Thus, depending on the types of contract enumerated above, seasonal agricultural workers can be entitled to bargain collectively if they sign a "Contract for work or job."

In sum, the labor legislation on *temporeros* and *temporeras* affects their organization and demonstrations on the job, while reducing their formal spaces of collective resistance. If we add the high turnover and the mobility of seasonal agricultural workers, the chances for any kind of resistance are further reduced. However, as shown below, despite these obstacles, seasonal agricultural workers have managed to open up new spaces of resistance, both at work and in the domestic sphere.

ACTIVE AND PASSIVE RESISTANCE OF SEASONAL AGRICULTURAL WORKERS

Temporeros and *Temporeras*' Collective Acts of Resistance at Work

Collective acts of resistance are probably the most studied and recorded types of resistance. Workers' collective resistance requires specific context conditions that allow its establishment, for example, a particular work environment, a grassroots organization, relations between workers and employers, and a policy framework that endorses it. When these elements are not given, the emergence of collective resistance is more difficult, as in the case of *temporeros* and *temporeras*. As discussed above, job flexibility (temporality, contract quality, labor intermediation, payment and compensation, among others), and job precariousness, together with a regulatory framework that hinders social organization and expression in the workplace, has hampered the collective resistance of *temporeros* and *temporeras*.

However, despite all these obstacles, seasonal agricultural workers in the Limarí Valley have established some collective resistance movements. First, they have formed a union of seasonal agricultural workers called *Sintemor*.[7] This union was created in August 2007, and had by the end of 2008 approximately 200 members, according to information provided by its then-president. These are not many members when one considers that in the Province of Limarí, according to the latest Census of Agriculture 2007, there are about 16,000 *temporeros* and *temporeras* during the busiest months. According to the president of *Sintemor*, this is because seasonal agricultural workers do not want to become involved in the union for fear they may lose their jobs. This is indeed what happened to this office holder after a protest. This possibility coupled with the need to have a job is what leads *temporeros* and *temporeras* not to claim their legal rights.

Table 9.5   Union Membership Rate in the Province of Limarí

	Seasonal agricultural workers stating union membership	Seasonal agricultural workers stating no union membership
Total (N = 82)	7%	93%
Men (N = 41)	15%	85%
Women (N = 41)	0%	100%

Realized by the author. Source: Interviews with seasonal agricultural workers (2008–2009).

This low participation of *temporeros* and *temporeras* in unions is also reflected in the guided interviews I realized, as shown in Table 9.5. According to my sample, the union membership rate amounts to only 7 percent of all seasonal agricultural workers and is only significant for men, not for women. In fact, none of the women interviewed stated that they belonged to a union.

Among the union demands discussed in meetings and assemblies were wage increases and improvements in working conditions. Concerning the first topic, union *temporeros* and *temporeras* claimed that the success of export agriculture in recent years has not been matched by an increase in the salaries they received. Related to working conditions, among others, the union notes the violation of labor laws and labor contracts, the non-payment of social security taxes, the lack of safe and adequate transportation, insufficient food, and a poor hygienic infrastructure.

When one considers the turnover and job alternation, the problem is that these claims have been played down by employers, who say *temporeros* and *temporeras* receive decent wages and have suitable working conditions. The Job Inspection Service that oversees regulations and working conditions cannot alone respond to these numerous demands. And the Provincial Government, while it acknowledges the demands of *temporeros* and *temporeras*, has pointed out that this situation has to be resolved by private companies and their employees, as indicated in the local media.[8] In this context, one can ask the question which possibilities the seasonal workers' unions have found to make their voice heard.

Massive strikes, road and highway blockades, and mass marches have been collective resistance movements that could be found. As noted by one union official: "For us, the only way to mobilize is to stop production. . . What we have achieved is that workers have marched for their rights, what we want is an improvement in working conditions, and the only thing we need is that the Labor Code is applied and inspections are carried out on the farms."[9] So, in early 2008, after many meetings and assemblies, *Sintemor* union workers called not only union workers to protest but also temporary workers in the Province. These protests consisted in not going to work on February 6, 2008—in the middle of the area's fruit harvesting season, blocking the roads that gave access to farms, and marching through the capital city of the Province.

While not many people participated in these protests (according to local media there were only some hundred protesters), many agricultural employers decided not to work that day while others decided to change their work schedules. However, tripartite discussions were established to defend and analyze the labor demands of these *temporeros* and *temporeras* and greater oversight from the local Labor Inspection was promised.

In short, there are not many possibilities to organize collective resistance movements of seasonal agricultural workers when one considers the temporary characteristics of work, contract conditions (especially irregular contracts, absence of contracts, and improper access to social security), and the Chilean regulatory framework on temporary work. Therefore, I will consider in what follows other forms of resistance that can be established at individual and intermediate levels at the workplace.

Temporeros and *Temporeras'* Individual and Collective Acts of Resistance at Work

Another resistance mechanism identified in my fieldwork is of a mixed nature, i.e., it was found at individual and small collective levels. This resistance involved labor stoppages. A certain activity carried out on the job is halted or work is even stopped for the working day at a particular point because of disagreements. According to workers, due to the method of payment—which is generally by piecework so that the employer sets the price of each "piece" of work—there is often disagreement between employers and seasonal workers. And as employers unilaterally fix the amount of the payment, one of the mechanisms found to resist this imposition is to stop working.

As already observed, this stoppage can sometimes be individual and sometimes it involves small groups of workers, for example, one team. Workers stop the activities they are charged with and wait in order to negotiate the price of the piecework. Employers quickly notice this stoppage (whether it is the contractor or the agribusiness), so they are sometimes ready to negotiate because they need these workers. One should remember that farms are often far from populated centers, so a quick replacement is not viable.

> *In many cases, if it is not right for you then you don't follow them, but the opinion of everyone on the team is taken.*
> Martín V., a 22-year-old *Temporero*,
> on January 8, 2009, Ovalle

> *You stop if it's bad, if the pay was not what was said. But if you complain too much, then the contractor fires you.*
> Cristián C., a 54-year-old *Temporero*,
> on January 7, 2009, Ovalle

However, at the same time, workers are afraid of losing their jobs, so this type of resistance generates a lot of distrust. Despite job precariousness, many interviewees said they preferred not to complain because they fear losing their job opportunity. I suppose that this is one of the essential reasons why collective acts of resistance are not very important among *temporeros* and *temporeras* and why one can see some forms of resistance at the individual level, as described below.

Temporeros and *Temporeras'* Individual Acts of Resistance at Work

I could identify different individual resistance strategies implemented by temporary workers. Two of them are analyzed here: abandonment and absenteeism. According to my research, abandonment means to resign and remove oneself from one's current job commitment, a behavior that may occur the same working day or from one working day to another.

As I have seen in my fieldwork, different reasons can lead seasonal workers to abandon their jobs. First, as noted above, there may be disagreement with the payment for the piecework, as in the case of stoppages. If the payment is not considered fair, abandonment may occur even the same working day. Second, these dropouts can be associated with more attractive job opportunities that arise at the same moment. If the payment offered by this new opportunity is better than the former one, workers just give up their jobs. This is possible because of the flexibility of labor contracts or, in some cases, the absence of formal contracts. Poor working conditions, such as mistreatment, meager nutrition, or infrastructure problems are further causes of abandonment, as shown below.

> *Because it's better elsewhere, if it's bad* [the payment] *you change. If by midday I have earned four or five* lucas [one thousand Chilean pesos] *I leave, even though the half-day worked is not paid. There's no commitment. . . .*
>
> Roberto B., a 44-year-old *Temporero*,
> on December 17, 2008, Ovalle

> *When it's bad, they don't pay well, if next door they pay more, you leave.*
>
> Romina G., a 59-year-old *Temporera*,
> on January 28, 2009, Monte Patria

> *If it's bad* [the piecework arrangement] *I get my things and I leave, at noon. We tell the boss, we say that we have something to do.*
>
> Nirma V., a 38-year-old *Temporera*,
> on February 13, 2009, Rapel

Absenteeism is another form of individual resistance, but unlike abandonment, employers do not perceive it as a form of resistance. In interviews with employers, I heard that one of the problems they face is absenteeism. This phenomenon occurs primarily on Mondays, at the start of the working week when *temporeros* and *temporeras* fail to show up. For employers, even being Chileans in all the cases observed, this absenteeism is considered being a cultural problem characteristic of the "lazy" Chilean, his/her "lack of commitment," or alcohol problems. Therefore, employers explain that quite a lot of workers fail to appear on Mondays.

However, when one returns to the type and the quality of the contracts of temporary workers, and in particular the type of payment they receive for piecework, the working situation of *temporeros* and *temporeras* is quite simple: If they do not work, they do not receive any money; if they work, they get paid. Therefore, absenteeism is a voluntary decision that they may take and they accept these conditions.

Up to this point, I have analyzed some forms of collective and individual resistance at the workplace or acts of resistance that directly affect working conditions. These are forms of resistance that are understandable for workers. Nevertheless, I have identified other forms of resistance that cross over the job itself and concern gender relations and the domestic sphere.

Temporeras' Passive Acts of Resistance in Gender Relations at the Workplace

Until now, I have analyzed acts of resistance in seasonal agricultural work by considering gendered data. How about gender relations and representations? Chile is a country with important challenges regarding gender equality. Women remain disadvantaged in different fields, such as salary, labor force participation, political leadership participation, and domestic responsibilities (PNUD 2010). However, one can find a different situation in terms of gender equality and women resistance in seasonal agricultural work. I have observed acts of resistance in gender relations and representations at the workplace as well as in the domestic sphere. In interviews with women I found that most of them acknowledge some progress in gender equality at the workplace as well as in the domestic and family environment, even though there are always some women left who do not remark this improvement.

At the workplace, gender equality is visible in the man to woman ratio. Studies have shown that since the 1990s, the Chilean labor market has been characterized by seasonal agricultural feminization and female proletarianization (cf. Riquelme 2000, Valdés 1988 and 1995, Venegas 1995). Unlike the national female workforce that corresponded to just 36 percent of the workforce in 2002 (INE 2003), a high participation of women in agricultural work could be found (52 percent in the 1990s) (Valdés 1995, Venegas 1995). More recently, according to the 2007 Agricultural Census, the ratio of seasonal men and women workers is in favor of men as shown in Figure 9.3. In the 3 months from November to January when harvesting and packing is substantial, female participation in the workforce reached

37 percent nationwide. But it represented 45 percent in the Province of Limarí and 48 percent in the municipality of Monte Patria where the maximum of seasonal agricultural work in Limarí Province can be found. This more or less equitable work participation was observed in the field so that the representatives of agricultural companies reported that men and women worked under rather equal conditions.

> *Just about, yes,* (we work) *equally. Some very heavy tasks* (are for) *men, but it's almost the same proportion.*
>
> Ismael G., administrator of a large company,
> on January 28, 2009, Ovalle

> (Men and women do) *the same jobs, there are more women than men in the companies. When harvesting, there are more men; in the packing sector, there are more women, but it's mixed. There are men who do the packaging selection* (tasks previously restricted to women). . . .
>
> Andrés B., administrator of a large company,
> on March 3, 2009, Chañaral Alto

This equal participation could also be observed in the organization of jobs realized by men and women. Apart from rare exceptions for a heavy load, regulated by the Chilean Labor Code,[10] seasonal workers and employers recognize that men and women do the same jobs and have the same abilities to perform various tasks. This recent equality is far from the feminization of certain tasks that occurred in the 1980s and 1990s, for instance, in the selection and packing of fruit for export. Currently, both, men and women clean, pick, and pack fruit, harvest, or pallet.

> *They do the same thing, the heavy work such as the almond harvesting. Grapes and citrus are the same, the same number or more* (women) *sometimes. Even in irrigation, storage, and maintenance.* . . .
>
> Leandro R., administrator of a large company,
> on March 19, 2009, Camarico

> *The same, I believe, there are men in the selection of fruit, women in the palletizing . . . this is the same thing, about the same.*
>
> Laura C., a 45-year-old, *Temporera,*
> on December 17, 2008, El Palqui

> *They have already realized that women can do as much as men. We are on equal terms.*
>
> Romina N., a 30-year-old *Temporera,*
> on April 2, 2009, Camarico

Temporeras' Passive Acts of Resistance and Gender Equality in the Domestic Arena

Outside of the workplace, acts of resistance can be found in the domestic area, in particular, if one considers women's double workload (Venegas 1992) as seasonal workers and at home. According to my survey, men and women as members of a family share today domestic duties. As shown in Table 9.6, if there are 29 percent of women with a double workload, 15 percent report sharing household chores with other members of the family group, and 54 percent report that these chores are not carried out by them, but by other members of the family group.

Thus, it is often the mother or another female relative (daughter or sister) who takes care of domestic responsibilities instead of *temporera* women. According to these results, it seems that men (spouse, brother, and son) help out with these duties a little more each day, according to several *temporeras* women. This fact is for women an important step towards gender equality.

> *My friend* (partner) *is the one who does the cooking. . . . But if it's meat, I'm the one who cooks at night.*
>
> Angela C., a 58-year-old *Temporera*,
> on January 21, 2009, Cerrillos de Rapel

> *Everyone takes care of his or her things at home* (domestic work), *it's shared.*
>
> Erica V., a 28-year-old *Temporera*,
> on March 11, 2009, Chañaral Alto

In sum, passive acts of resistance—as it has been shown, equal capacities and tasks performed by woman and men, and the increased involvement of other family members including men in domestic work paralleled by an important female integration into wage labor—have affected gender relations and women's position in the local society. Before 1980, women had rarely paid jobs and were fully occupied by household chores; during the 1980s and 1990s, they were recruited to perform tasks linked to

Table 9.6   Performance of Domestic Duties in Seasonal Women's Homes

Person who takes care of domestic affairs	%
Temporera women only	29
Temporera women and another member of the family	15
Member of the family (not *temporera* women)	54
Other person	2

Established by the author. Source: Interviews with seasonal agricultural workers (2008–2009).

qualities considered being exclusively feminine; today the situation is different. The incorporation of women in wage employment in the 1980s and 1990s has triggered acts of resistance in gender relations and transformations at the workplace as well as in the domestic sphere. The enhancement of seasonal agricultural work and the recognition of qualities and skills of women as workers let appear a significant change in the participation of men and women in agricultural wage labor. But these transformations have also affected gender relations and the representation of women at home.

CONCLUSION: LABOR RESISTANCE BEYOND THE WORKPLACE: A ROAD TO EQUALITY AND SOCIAL JUSTICE?

The development of the agro-export industry, recognized as a top economic performer and a model of integration into international trade relations, has brought up many social transformations, revealing an invisible world inherent to seasonal agricultural labor. Linked to this invisible world, I have done research on different types of collective and individual resistances that have emerged in particular situations. Thus and despite adversity, workers have sought ways to fight for what they consider being a fair treatment. Seasonal agricultural work has become an opportunity for workers, but can this example of economic development also stand for social development in rural areas? Which sort of resistance does this model of economic development give to workers? And what resistance opportunities do workers have in a highly flexible and precarious economic context?

The current job management model limits the rights of workers to fight for social justice in the agribusiness. The respective answers depend on what is meant by social justice. We should remember that the concepts of equal opportunity, welfare, social justice, and democracy are based on given local traditions. Today, discourses and strategies seek to legitimize these precepts. Nevertheless, several scientific and political approaches compete in defining these concepts, in particular the notion of social justice. Different views on the distribution of rights and duties of members of a given society exist. These approaches permit to characterize moral and political philosophies on the building of social projects.

John Rawls (1997) proposed, for instance, that justice should form the basic structure of a given society defined by freedom, rationality, and equality. And Amartya Sen (2003) tried to go further, proposing the "capabilities" approach. This approach specifies not only an equality of means but also an equality of effective opportunities that people could have to perform various actions. Thus, this approach sees the notion of development as a process looking for the extension of personal choices, strengthening the capacities of people, and leading to an expansion of human freedom. It involves the capacity and the freedom of human beings to choose different life styles. It is an approach that seems to be far from the current situation of seasonal agricultural work and its resistance movements when one considers the flexibility and precariousness of this work and, in particular, its conceptualization and regulatory framework.

Collective or individual, active or passive resistance movements are ready to fight for something that is assessed as unfair or abusive. In this sense, resistance movements are established to achieve more justice. But, at the same time, resistance movements require some "capability" to be constituted. If the socioeconomic context and the regulatory framework are not favorable, and are, on the contrary, restrictive and repressive, resistance movements will have more difficulties being established. In the case of seasonal agricultural work, one can say that the capacities to build resistance movements are restricted so that the search for freedom and social justice is limited.

When one looks at workers' acts of resistance beyond the workplace, it should be asked if the findings of my fieldwork relate to new capabilities that may permit resistance. The struggle for gender equality at the workplace and in the domestic area is not new. But despite historical obstacles to gender equality and labor precariousness, social spaces where these workers can express resistance, ask for equality, and try to obtain more social justice seem to open up. *Temporeras* women have conquered ground in terms of gender equality and the pursuit of social justice. However, it cannot be said that this type of resistance is a sure and easy way to the pursuit of further equality and social justice.

The question seems to be that existing projects aiming at more equality and social justice need to be adapted to the situation of the temporary agricultural worker and his/her invisible world, together with, and not subordinate to, the economic and development successes of this activity. Going beyond resistance, the study of seasonal agriculture and its invisible world can show the necessity to review labor flexibility and precariousness in development and social justice strategies.

NOTES

1. For example, the Gini coefficient shows a considerable inequality of income distribution (55.0) (Ministerio de Planificación y Cooperación [MIDEPLAN], 2010).
2. It should be noted here that the quantitative data for the years 1980 and 1990 could not be carefully established from national censuses because of a lack of exact measurements (Riquelme 2000).
3. In this article, the author has translated the quotations. In order to respect the respondents' anonymity, the first names reported in the article are fictitious.
4. In Chile, the normal working day consists of 8 hours per day that can be extended to 10 hours, with a maximum of 2 extra hours per day (Ministerio de Trabajo y Previsión Social, Subsecretaría del Trabajo 2008).
5. Rosario A., a 22-year-old *Temporera*, on January 27, 2009, Rapel.
6. "Seasonal agricultural workers are all those who perform temporary or seasonal work in cultivation, commercial or industrial activities deriving from agriculture and in sawmills and timber harvesting plants and related industries" (Dirección del Trabajo 2011: 48).

190   *Tamara Heran*

7. The meaning of the union name is interesting: *Sin Temor* means fearless in English.
8. See for example, local newspapers like *El Día* or *El Ovallino* for the months of January and February 2008.
9. See Galleguillos (2008).
10. Individuals under 18 years and women are not allowed to manually load, pull, or push loads heavier than 20 kg. (Ministerio de Trabajo y Previsión Social Subsecretaría del Trabajo 2008).

REFERENCES

Arteaga, Catalina (2000) *Modernización agraria y construcción de identidades. Identidad social, identidad laboral y proyectos de vida de temporeras/os frutícolas en Chile. El Palqui 1969–1977.* México D.F.: Plaza y Valdés, Facultad Latinoamericana de Ciencias Sociales (FLACSO), Centro de Estudios para el Desarrollo de la Mujer (CEDEM).
Beaud, Stéphane and Florence Weber (1998) *Guide de l'enquête de terrain. Produire et analyser des données ethnographiques.* Paris: La Découverte, Guide Repères.
Bidet, Alexandra and Dominique Schoeni (2011) "Décrire les présences au travail, analyser la structuration de la vie sociale, "*Ethnographiques.org* 23 (December). Online at http://www.ethnographiques.org/2011/Bidet,Schoeni, accessed on November 13, 2012.
Coutard, Pascale, Patrick Livenais, and Héctor Reyes (2003) "Las consecuencias del modelo de desarrollo agro-industrial de exportación en Huatulame," in Patrick Livenais and Ximena Aranda (eds) *Dinámicas de los sistemas agrarios en Chile árido: la Región de Coquimbo*, pp. 465–476. Santiago de Chile: LOM Ediciones Ltda.
Díaz, Estrella (1994) *Impactos del modelo exportador en los trabajadores y el medioambiente; análisis de los sectores agrícola y pesquero.* Santiago de Chile: Universidad ARCIS.
Dirección del Trabajo (2004) *ORD. N° 2389/100.* Santiago de Chile: Dirección del Trabajo. Online at http://www.dt.gob.cl/1601/w3-article-66558.html, accessed on November 13, 2012.
Dirección del Trabajo (2011) *Código del Trabajo.* Santiago de Chile: Dirección del Trabajo. Online at http://www.dt.gob.cl/legislacion/1611/articles-59096_recurso_1.pdf, accessed on November 13, 2012.
Dolbeau, Monique (2011) "Visibilité et invisibilité du travail dans la maréchalerie," *Ethnographiques.org* 23 (December). Online at http://www.ethnographiques.org/Visibilite-et-invisibilite-du, accessed on November 13, 2012.
Galleguillos, Patricio (2008) "Temporeros consiguen mesa de diálogo con autoridades y empresarios". *Diario El Día*, February 8, p. 8.
Gómez, Sergio (1982) *Instituciones y procesos agrarios en Chile.* Santiago de Chile: Facultad Latinoamericana de Ciencias Sociales (FLACSO), Consejo Latinoamericano de Ciencias Sociales (CLACSO).
Gómez, Sergio (2000) "Organizaciones rurales en América Latina (marco para su análisis)," *Revista Austral de Ciencias Sociales* 4: 27–54.
Gómez, Sergio and Jorge Echeñique (1988) *La agricultura chilena: las dos caras de la modernización.* Santiago de Chile: Facultad Latinoamericana de Ciencias Sociales (FLACSO).
Hollander, Jocelyn and Rachel Einwohner (2004) "Conceptualizing Resistance," *Sociological Forum* 19 (4): 533–554.
Instituto Nacional de Estadísticas de Chile (INE) (2003) *CENSO 2002. Síntesis de resultados.* Santiago de Chile: Empresa Periodística La Nación S.A.

Instituto Nacional de Estadísticas de Chile (INE) (2008) *Resultados Censo Agropecuario 2007*. Santiago de Chile: Author. Online at http://www.censoagropecuario. cl/index2.html, accessed on April 27, 2014.

Jarty, Julie (2011) "Le travail invisible des enseignants 'hors les murs'," *Ethnographiques.org* 23 (December). Online at http://www.ethnographiques.org/ 2011/Jarty, accessed on November 13, 2012.

Max-Neef, Manfred (1993) *Desarrollo a escala humana*. Montevideo: Editorial Nordan-Comunidad.

Ministerio de Planificación y Cooperación (MIDEPLAN) (2010) *Distribución del ingreso. Encuesta Casen 2009*. Santiago de Chile: MIDEPLAN. Online at http://www.mideplan.gob.cl/casen2009/distribucion_ingreso_casen_2009.pdf, accessed on November 13, 2012.

Ministerio del Trabajo y Previsión Social, Subsecretaría del Trabajo (2008) *Código del Trabajo*. Santiago de Chile: Galas Ediciones.

Programa de las Naciones Unidas para el Desarrollo (PNUD) (2010) *Desarrollo Humano en Chile 2010. Género: los desafíos de la igualdad*. Santiago de Chile: PNUD.

Rawls, John (1997) *Théorie de la justice*. Paris: Éditions du Seuil.

Riquelme, Verónica (2000) "Temporeros agrícolas: desafíos permanentes," *Tema Laboral* 15 (Dirección del Trabajo, Gobierno de Chile). Online at http://www. dt.gob.cl/1601/articles-60349_Tema_Laboral_Temporeros_agricolas_Desafios_ permanentes.pdf, accessed on November 13, 2012.

Salazar, Gabriel (1989) *Labradores, peones y proletarios. Formación y crisis de la sociedad chilena del siglo XIX*. Santiago de Chile: Ediciones Sur, Colección Estudios Históricos.

Schwartz, Yves (2004) "La conceptualisation du travail, le visible et l'invisible," *L'Homme et la société* 152–153: 47–77.

Scott, James (1987) "Resistance without Protest and Without Organization: Peasant Opposition to the Islamic Zakat and the Christian Tithe," *Comparative Studies in Society and History* 29 (3): 417–452.

Sen, Amartya (2003) *Un nouveau modèle économique. Développement, justice, liberté*. Paris: Odile Jacob.

Valdés, Ximena (1988) "La feminización del mercado de trabajo agrícola en Chile central," in Ana María Arteaga, Cecilia Cardemil, Ximena Díaz, Mariluz Dussuel, Thelma Galvez, Eugenia Hola, Marcela Latorre, Lilian Letelier, Dánica Malic, Sonia Montecino, Sergio Morales, Giselle Munizaga, Adriana Muñoz, Josefina Rossetti, Elena Serrano, Rosalba Todaro, Ximena Valdés, and Angélica Wilson (eds) *Mundo mujer: continuidad y cambio*, pp. 388–430. Santiago de Chile: Ediciones CEM.

Valdés, Ximena (1992) *Mujer, trabajo y medioambiente, los nudos de la modernización en Chile*. Santiago de Chile: Ediciones CEDEM.

Valdés, Ximena (1995) "Relaciones de género y transformaciones agrarias: la hacienda y la pequeña propiedad en Chile central," in Ximena Valdés, Ana María Arteaga, and Carolina Arteaga (eds) *Mujeres, relaciones de género en la agricultura*, pp. 95–117. Santiago de Chile: Ediciones CEDEM.

Valdés, Ximena and Kathya Araujo (1999) *Vida privada. Modernización agraria y modernidad*. Santiago de Chile: Ediciones CEDEM.

Venegas, Sylvia (1992) *Una gota al día. . . . Un chorro al año. . . . El impacto social de la expansión frutícola*. Santiago de Chile: LOM Ediciones.

Venegas, Sylvia (1995) "Las temporeras de la fruta en Chile," in Ximena Valdés, Ana María Arteaga, and Carolina Arteaga (eds) *Mujeres, relaciones de género en la agricultura*, pp. 119–155. Santiago de Chile: Ediciones CEDEM.

10 Marikana's Meaning for Crisis Management

An Instance of South Africa's Resource Curse

Patrick Bond

INTRODUCTION

The future of multinational corporate management from the standpoint of social and environmental responsibility and community investment is grim, given how the World Bank's International Finance Corporation (IFC) regularly bragged about the "developmental success" of the South African operations of a major mining firm, Lonmin. In reality, 5 years after committing U.S. $200 million to Lonmin, the firm's Marikana platinum mine quickly became one of the most notorious recent cases of economic-labor-social-ecological-gender relations in the world's extractive industries. The 2012 Marikana Massacre was preceded by IFC financing—a U.S. $15 million equity stake and U.S. $150 million loan commitment in 2007 due to be fully repaid by 2014—and the introduction of IFC "best case" practices ranging from economic development to racially progressive procurement and community involvement to gender work relations (IFC 2006).

The IFC was not the only agency to laud Lonmin's Marikana management. In 2008, the South African commercial bank most actively greenwashing its record of minerals and coal investment, Nedbank, awarded Lonmin and the World Bank its top prize in the socio-economic category of the Green Mining Awards (Daily Business News 2008). By 2010, Lonmin's *Sustainable Development Report* was ranked "excellent" by Ernst and Young. The World Bank was especially delighted with Lonmin's "gender equity" work (Burger and Sepora 2009). Moreover, according to its 2012 *Sustainable Development Report*, Lonmin

> has established community resettlement policies which comply with the World Bank Operation Directives on Resettlement of Indigenous Peoples and Cultural Property. There were no resettlements of communities and no grievances lodged relating to resettlements. In terms of the Restitution of Land Rights Act 22 of 1994, the Company is in the process of addressing several land claims lodged against it before 2011. The resolution of these claims is being managed within the legislative framework of the regional Land Claims Commission and Land Claims Court.
>
> (Lonmin 2012)

This justification for mining on stolen land ignores the long historic context of pre-1913 land dispossession, as well as the relegation of the platinum-rich area just west of Marikana to "Bantustan" status (as the tyrannical "Bophuthatswana" dictatorship) from 1961 until 1994. Another important and related bit of historical context, ignored in all IFC literature promoting Lonmin, is the company's roots—from 1909 until 1999—as "Lonrho," the London and Rhodesian Mining and Land Company Limited. Lonrho gained a very poor reputation for its role in Africa, especially in the years 1962–93 when Roland Walter Fuhrhop ("Tiny Rowland") managed it, for as Brian Cloughly explained:

> A British prime minister, Edward Heath, observed in 1973 that a businessman, a truly horrible savage called "Tiny" Rowland, represented "the unpleasant and unacceptable face of capitalism." The description was fitting because Rowland was a perambulating piece of filth who had indulged in bribery, tax-dodging, and the general range of ingenious whizz-kid schemes designed to make viciously unscrupulous people rich and keep them that way.
>
> (Cloughly 2008)

Mismanagement at Lonmin's Marikana operation was legion, in spite of IFC marketing propaganda. The church-founded Bench Marks Foundation reported in 2007 (just as the IFC was getting involved) and 2012 (after the main IFC work had been completed) about the ways Lonmin had demonstrably failed in the main areas of corporate social responsibility: job creation and subcontracting (including labor broking); migrant labor, living conditions, and the living-out allowance; ineffectual community social investments, lack of meaningful community engagement and participation; and environmental discharges and irresponsible water use, especially in relation to local farming (Bench Marks Foundation 2007, 2012). Considering the broader gender oppression, Samantha Hargreaves (2013) reaches back into the migrant labor system itself:

> The Marikana story is about much more than a strike for higher wages, it is also a story about a crisis in social reproduction. State neglect and corporate greed have fomented household crises stretching from the mines back to the sources of migrant labour in far-flung regions and neighbouring countries. Narrow male-dominated trade union and worker interests mean that hope for a radical resolution lies in the struggles of women in places like Wonderkop. The challenge is linking these with (mainly male) worker struggles and environmentalist solidarity to challenge the extractivist model of development, the social, economic and environmental costs of which are principally borne by working-class and peasant women.

Linking these issues is something the Center for International Environmental Law (CIEL) argued the World Bank had done—in a negative manner—in a report immediately after the massacre:

The mine has had a troubled history with the communities and its workers. A stakeholder perception survey commissioned by Lonmin in 2005 shortly after it acquired the mine and before IFC's investment showed that most respondents regarded the mine with "negativity combined with mistrust, suspicion and in some cases hatred." In fact, the conflict between the unions, which is thought to have sparked the violence this week, was visible even seven years ago. The survey reported a history of mistrust between all three unions. Participants reported union favoritism and discrimination at the mine and urged Lonmin to "treat people equally, regardless of race, job level or union affiliation." Despite criticism from communities and NGOs that industrial mining projects often result in serious human rights violations and little economic development, the IFC continues to justify its investments as a "key source of jobs, economic opportunities, investments, revenues to government, energy and other benefits for local economies." In documents disclosed on the Lonmin deal, IFC asserted that: "This investment is expected to have beneficial results for the workforce and surrounding communities." Indeed, IFC documents state that Lonmin "supports the protection of human life and dignity within their sphere of influence by subscribing to the principles laid down in the United Nation's Declaration of Human Rights." And yet despite attesting to a close working relationship with the South African police force on matters of security, a statement made yesterday [i.e. 16 August 2012] by Lonmin chairman Roger Phillimore characterized the violence as "clearly a public order rather than a labour relations associated matter". . . . In addition to seeking a full investigation into the violence and what led to it, CIEL has called on World Bank President, Jim Yong Kim, to revisit the Bank's investment in this project in light of recent events, specifically, and its approach to lending in the extractive industries more generally.

(CIEL 2012)

Exactly 2 weeks after the massacre, Kim went to nearby Pretoria and Johannesburg for a visit. Tellingly, he neglected to check on his Lonmin investment in Marikana and instead gave a high-profile endorsement to an IFC deal with a small junk-mail printing/posting firm that was prospering from state tenders (Bond 2012).

The *mismanagement* of mining at Marikana can be addressed from macro to micro scales, from economic to political to social to ecological. Doing so allows a strong political and financial reality check on the discourses of managerial harmony and prosperity that the IFC and Lonmin long maintained about the huge platinum operation in Marikana, which was long the main source of Lonmin's profits and its status as the world's third-largest platinum miner. The reality is that thanks to Lonmin's exploitative practices—especially paying just U.S. $500/month for extremely dangerous rock-drilling until the 2012 strike forced a 22 percent wage increase—and its cooptation of the National Union of Mineworkers (NUM), added to the African National Congress (ANC) government's willingness to send in police to defend capital against labor, communities, and environment, 34 mineworkers were killed and 78 injured within a 20 minute barrage of fire on August 16, 2012. The prior week, 10 other mineworkers, two policemen, and two security guards were killed, and in the subsequent year, more than a dozen more mineworkers and Marikana Massacre survivors lost their lives due to residual tensions at the mine, including several cases of homicide and suicide directly related to the massacre's aftermath. A government body, the Farlam Commission, set up to investigate dragged on, creating yet more conflict given police reluctance to admit often grotesque errors. As one example, several of the bodies of empty-handed dead mineworkers were photographed by police shortly after the massacre, but soon crude weapons were placed in the corpses' hands for new photographs, but by accident *both sets were submitted to the Farlam Commission.* Wide-ranging mismanagement of public order policing at Marikana is frankly conceded by police professionals.

The case of Lonmin's and the IFC's mismanagement of the Marikana mine is critical not only for South Africa but as an example of the more general "Resource Curse." When a ruling party in any African country sinks to the depths of allowing its police force to serve white-dominated multinational capital by killing dozens of black workers so as to end a brief strike, it represents an inflection point. Beyond just the obvious human-rights and labor-relations travesties, the incident offered the potential for a deep political rethink, unveiling extreme depths of ruling-class desperation represented by the fusion of ANC Deputy President Cyril Ramaphosa's black capitalism, the London mining house Lonmin's collaboration (through Ramaphosa) with the mining and police ministers, the brutality of state prosecutors who charged the victims with the crime, the alleged "sweetheart unionism" of the increasingly unpopular NUM, and the fragility of a Congress of South African Trade Union (Cosatu) split between Zuma/Ramaphosa loyalists and those with worker interests at heart. The split became untenable in August 2013, the very day of the Marikana Massacre anniversary, when the left-leaning Cosatu leader Zwelinzima Vavi declared war against the Cosatu president after he was forcibly suspended following an office sex scandal. But it was thanks to Marikana that positions hardened and those culpable became defensive. Only a few in the society—including several former ANC leaders who began openly questioning tactics of the dominant political class—confronted the chilling lessons about the moral degeneration of a liberation movement that the world had supported for decades. The first set of lessons regards the broader economic context.

A CONTEXT OF MACROECONOMIC MISMANAGEMENT

Lonmin "has had a hugely beneficial impact on South Africa's economy," according to a promotional film about the mining house produced by the IFC in 2011 (IFC 2011). The context for this inaccurate statement is macroeconomic management by Trevor Manuel, a political appointee who chaired the World Bank Board of Governors in 2000 and whose 1996–2009 reign as South Africa's finance minister was mainly celebrated by conservative and neoliberal economic commentators. Yet the policies Manuel imposed did not work, and 4 months before he left office to become Planning Minister, *The Economist* (2009) gave Manuel the highest mark for instability and risk amongst emerging market peer countries. Aside from a high exposure to potential bad lending and a high foreign debt, the main reason South Africa rated so poorly was the outflow of profits, dividends, and interest, which soared in 2007–08, creating a huge current account deficit (i.e., the combined huge payments outflow and a smaller trade deficit). Lonmin is directly implicated in this outflow, given that the vast majority of its shares are held in London.

With such a massive outflow of capital, hard currency was required so as to permit the multinational corporations (including Lonmin) to pay their shareholders. As a result, there was a rise in South African's foreign debt from U.S. $25 billion in 1994 to U.S. $135 billion in 2013. What makes the very high global and local debt load much worse is the interest rate; among the largest trading partners, only Greece's has been higher, according to the Department of Trade and Industry (2011). One reason why interest rates have been so high in relative terms is to guard against the capital flight that periodically crashes the currency. South Africa's liberalized exchange control system initially compelled a massive interest rate increase in 1995–96 to guard against the flight of capital that accompanied the exchange control deregulation of March 1995. But this policy change—overwhelmingly beneficial to rich white South Africans, including Lonmin managers—generated a sustained high real interest rate that shifted flows of capital away from potential productive capital investment into the financial sector.

All of these processes correspond with international trends and beg the question: Should the post-apartheid government have so enthusiastically endorsed globalization? The past 40 years have witnessed much lower growth rates in South Africa, in comparison to the 40 years before (1943–83). The period of globalization, in other words, was a far more difficult environment for an increasingly uncompetitive South Africa than the earlier epoch (1931–46 especially) of "deglobalization," which as a result of the Great Depression and World War II compelled the economy to be more self-reliant. As a result of lower foreign direct investment, loans, and trade, South Africa had birthed its secondary manufacturing industry (beyond the mining equipment sector) and become much better balanced in the process. With labor demand higher, the rate of growth of the black wage share rose more than 50 percent (from 11 percent to 17 percent; but the black share of wages only hit 21 percent in 1970). The overall GDP growth rate (8 percent) from 1931–46 was fastest recorded in modern South African history.

Finally, the combination of slower growth, higher interest rates, and a declining share of wages to profits meant that, like much of the world, the

South African working class soon became overly indebted at the household scale. As a political-economic phenomenon, this was actually not unusual, for the move to liberalized economic relations across the world shifted many power systems from direct coercion in the spheres of labor control (in South Africa especially migrancy from Bantustans under apartheid-allied dictators) and socio-political power, to indirect coercion by finance and law. The formalized migrancy system and evolution of labor relations on South Africa's mines did not improve the socio-economic conditions of workers, given the rising debt burden. By 2012, this combination of adverse economic dynamics left "anywhere between 10–15 percent of SA's workforce with a garnishee order issued" to compel repayment, according to Malcolm Rees of *Moneyweb* (Rees 2012). Wages as a share of the social surplus had fallen from 55.9 percent in 1994 to 50.6 percent by 2010, which in absolute terms translated to U.S. $17 billion (Forslund 2012). In addition, much greater inequality in wage income was also a factor, contributing to a rapid rise in the Gini coefficient over the same period. One reaction by the working class was to turn to rising consumer debt in order to cover rising household consumption expenditures. Having risen rapidly to U.S. $4.96 billion in late 2007, the outstanding unsecured credit load registered with the national credit regulator had then escalated to U.S. $13.75 billion by March 2012 (Steyn 2012). From 2005 to 2008, the average repayment of household debt doubled, from 6 to 12 percent of disposable income. This was actually a huge load when distributed across the spectrum of workers in a context of severe inequality, for according to Rees (2012), "*Moneyweb* reports indicate that at least 40 percent of the monthly income of SA workers is being directed to the repayment of debt."

In this macroeconomic and microeconomic context of mismanagement, the implications for a labor dispute were sharp, as we see in the detailed study of the massacre.

THE MARIKANA MASSACRE

The site of the immediate conflict was the platinum belt. South Africa's share of world platinum reserves is more than 80 percent. The belt stretches in a distinct arc around the west side of the Johannesburg-Pretoria megalopolis of 10 million people, and up towards the Zimbabwe border. The area also has vast gold and coal deposits, and the nine main mining firms operating in this region recorded U.S. $4.5 billion in 2011 profits from their South African operations.

There are six basic factual considerations about what happened at Marikana, 100 km northwest of Johannesburg, beginning around 4 pm on August 16, 2012:

- The provincial police department, backed by national special commando reinforcements, ordered several thousand striking platinum mineworkers—rock drill operators—off a hill where they had gathered as usual over the prior 4 days, surrounding the workers with barbed wire and firing teargas.

- The hill was more than a kilometer away from Lonmin property, the mineworkers were not blocking mining operations or any other facility, and, although they were on an "unprotected" wildcat strike, they had a constitutional right to gather.
- As they left the hill, 34 workers were killed and 78 others suffered bullet-wound injuries, all at the hands of police weapons, leaving some crippled for life, with 16 shot dead while moving through a small gap in the fencing and the other 18 murdered in a field and on a smaller hill nearby as they fled.
- No police were hurt in the operation—although it appears that a sole miner with a pistol fired as he entered the gap—and some of the police attempted a clumsy cover-up by placing crude weapons next to the bodies of several men after their deaths.
- Two hundred and seventy mine workers were arrested that day, followed by a weekend during which state prosecutors charged the men with the "murder" of their colleagues (under an obscure apartheid-era "common purpose" doctrine of collective responsibility), followed by an embarrassed climb down by the national prosecutor after the society registered utter disgust.
- There was no apparent effort by police to discipline errant troops in subsequent months, except when massacre-scene photographs showed that weapons were planted on dead mineworker bodies, and indeed the police moved into Marikana shack settlements again and again to intimidate activists in the wake of the massacre, including fatally shooting—with rubber bullets one Saturday morning—a popular local councilwoman (from the ruling party) who sided with the protesting mineworkers and communities.

The details about how the massacre unfolded were not initially obvious, for mainstream media embedded behind police lines (unaware at the time of the "killing kopje") and official police statements together generated a "fog of war," as former Intelligence Minister Ronnie Kasrils remarked (Kasrils 2012). The effect was to stigmatize the mineworkers. It was only a few days later that observers—the September Imbizo Commission, University of Johannesburg researcher Peter Alexander and his research team, and *Daily Maverick* reporter Greg Marinovich—uncovered the other shootings (Alexander, Lekgowa, Mmope, Sinwell, and Xezwi 2012). Most journalists relied on official sources, especially the police and National Prosecuting Authority, even when they were discredited by persistent fibbery.

Such media bias allowed the impression to emerge in conventional wisdom that police were "under violent attack" by irrational, drugged, and potentially murderous men from rural areas in the Eastern Cape's Pondoland, as well as from Lesotho and Mozambique, who used *muti* (traditional medicine) to ward off bullets. Plenty of press reports and even the South African Communist Party's (SACP's) official statement refer to the workers' spiritual sensibilities—"a sangoma is today still able to convince sections of the working class that bullets turn into water if you have used 'intelezi'" (Nzimande 2012a)—to try to explain why they might have charged towards the police, through the 5-meter gap in the barbed wire, with their primitive spears and wooden sticks. *Business Day's* editor opined that the strikers "were convinced by a *sangoma* [traditional healer] a few days earlier that if they let him smear some black powder into cuts on their foreheads they would become invincible. This is not necessarily a demanding audience" (Bruce 2012).

Although the facts will always remain clouded, it seems far more likely that as the first few dozen mineworkers came running through the gap and saw the police line-up, they then began edging alongside the fence rather than moving directly at the heavily armed police—although it is apparent that one of the workers fired with a (sole) handgun. The police claim six handguns were recovered from dead, wounded, and arrested mineworkers, but this was thrown into question by evidence of systematic post-massacre tampering at the scene of the crime—police troops placed weapons next to bodies at some point after the massacre—because, by mistake, they surrendered photographs taken both before and after the deed to the Farlam Commission that Zuma mandated to investigate the massacre.

Another layer of complexity related to prior murders of six workers, two security guards, and two policemen close by, starting when a march on August 11 by striking workers against the NUM—accused of selling out the workers—was met with gunfire, allegedly from NUM officials. Tension in the area mounted quickly, and when the security guards and police were killed, apparently by some of the Marikana mineworkers, this generated a sensibility of vindication; gruesome footage of the murdered cops had circulated amongst the police who were on duty on August 16. Later, the assassination of NUM shop stewards increased in pace as well. But it must be recalled that this was not brand new conflict, for strike-related violence over the prior year at Lonmin and the other major platinum mining operations left scores of other workers dead, with 50 murders just six months earlier when 17,000 mineworkers were temporarily fired nearby at the world's second-largest platinum firm, Implats, before gaining wage concessions.

South Africa learned a great deal about labor's desperation in subsequent days, because explaining the intensity of the Lonmin workers' militancy required understanding their conditions of production and reproduction. The typical rock-drill operator's take-home pay was said to be in the range of U.S. $511 per month, with an additional U.S. $204/month as a "living out allowance" to spare Lonmin and other employers the cost of maintaining migrant-labor hostels. Most workers were from the Eastern Cape's

Pondoland, Lesotho, and Mozambique; many therefore maintained two households, having families to support in both urban and rural settings. At the same time, structural changes in the mines were blurring the distinction between shop steward and foreman, hence drawing NUM local leaders into a cozy corporatist arrangement with the mining houses. But controlling the workers would be another matter, and NUM found itself challenged by a new union that had come from its own dissident ranks, the Association of Mining and Construction Union (AMCU).

Indeed, the tens of thousands of workers who subsequently went on wild-cat strikes in the Northwest, Limpopo, Free State, Mpumalanga, Northern Cape, and Gauteng Provinces did not do so out of the blue. They began leaving NUM in droves from late 2011 because of its worsening reputation as a sweetheart union, mostly moving to AMCU. The workers had participated in various forms of labor and community-based protests over the prior few years, as the 350 percent price increase for the metal during the 2002–08 boom left the main companies—AngloPlats, Implats, and Lonmin—extremely prosperous, without evidence of trickle-down to the semi-proletarianized workforce. So it was that 3,000 Lonmin rock-drill operators demanded a raise to U.S. $1420/month as a basic gross "package" amount; they struck for over a month (3 weeks beyond the massacre) and ultimately received what was reported as a 22 percent wage package increase, which in turn catalyzed prairie-fire wildcat strikes across the immediate mining region and then other parts of the country in September to November. Similar militancy was soon evident in trucking, the auto sector, municipal labor, and other sectors.

But as with a vast proportion of ordinary South Africans, this was a time of extreme household indebtedness. It soon became clear that the Marikana workers were victims not only of exploitation at the point of production, but also of super-exploitative debt relations, in which, as Milford Bateman (2012) remarked: "We have perhaps just witnessed one of the most appalling microcredit-related disasters of all in South Africa." Financial desperation was compounded by legal abuse, carried out by the same race/gender/ class power bloc—white male Afrikaners—who had, in their earlier years and in the same geographical settings, been apartheid beneficiaries. Microfinance short-term loans that carry exceptionally high interest rates were offered to mineworkers by institutions ranging from established banks—one (Ubank) even co-owned by NUM and another (Capitec) replete with powerful ANC patrons—down to fly-by-night loan sharks (whose local nickname is "mashonisa"). The extremely high interest rates charged, especially once arrears mount, were one of the central pressures requiring workers to demand higher wages.

Still, none of this labor-capital conflict—implicating mining houses and financiers—would have flared into such an explosive situation at Marikana, many believe, were it not for the mismanaged relationships between state, ruling party, and trade union elites that developed over the prior two decades with the major mining houses. These cozy relations, even relegitimizing companies with very low morals that regularly engaged in labor-broking, apparently incensed the ordinary workers, raising their staying power to such high levels.

CORPORATE-STATE-LABOR MANAGEMENT

Tiny Rowland died in 1998, after losing control of the company 5 years earlier due to his ties to Libyan dictator Muammar Gaddafi. Lonmin then rebranded—its "Integrity, Honesty & Trust" slogan adorns billboards at Marikana—and by 2007 must have been confident that with the World Bank backing its community investment strategy, it could mainly ignore the nearby Nkaneng shack-settlement's degradation. The lack of clean running water, sanitation, storm-water drainage, electricity, schools, clinics, or any other amenities make Nkaneng as inhospitable a residential site to reproduce labor power as any other in South Africa, yet Lonmin's approach to the community's troubles was insignificant. Instead of building decent company housing for migrant workers, for example, it relied on the inadequate living out allowance, much of which was just added to wages targeted for remittance to the home region, leaving Nkaneng nearly uninhabitable. Mineworkers had continued migrancy relations but the rise in dependents per mineworker was apparently noticeable, from 8 to 15, according to labor expert Gavin Hartford (2012).

Lonmin's successful public relations onslaught probably gave its executives confidence that long-standing abuse of low-paid migrant labor could continue, with NUM itself having become so coopted that shop stewards were reportedly paid three times more than ordinary workers. NUM general secretary Frans Baleni earned U.S. $160,000 per year at that stage and gained notoriety when he had advised Lonmin to fire 9,000 of the same Marikana mineworkers at its Karee mine in late 2011 because they went on a wildcat strike. As Baleni's former deputy, Archie Palane, put it:

> It's absolutely shocking—completely unheard of—that a union advises an employer to fire workers. No matter what your differences or what they did, this should simply not happen. It gives the impression that you just don't care. How can you ever expect those workers to trust you to represent them in any negotiations? (De Lange 2013)

Of the 9,000 workers, 7,000 were rehired but they quit NUM and joined the rival AMCU. One result, at nearby Implats, was that of the 28,000 workers, 70 percent had been NUM members in late 2011, but by September 2012 the ratio was down to 13 percent (de Lange 2012).

On the ecological front, the entire platinum belt contributes to the toxicity and overall pollution so that South Africa's *Environmental Performance*

Index slipped to 5th worst of 133 countries surveyed by Columbia and Yale University researchers in early 2012 (Environmental Performance Index). The Mineral Energy Complex's prolific contribution to pollution is mainly to blame, including its coal mining that generates coal-fired power used in electricity-intensive mining and smelting operations. In this context, Lonmin might have considered its ongoing destruction of the platinum belt's water, air, agricultural, and other eco-systems to be of little importance—within a setting in which pollution was ubiquitous.

Moreover, the North West provincial and Rustenburg municipal governments were apparently rife with corruption. Emblematic was the 2009 assassination of a well-known ANC whistleblower, Moss Phakoe, which a judge found was arranged by Rustenburg mayor Matthew Wolmarans. Again, in this context, Lonmin and the other big mining houses in the platinum belt might have considered South Africa just one more Third World site worthy of the designation "Resource Cursed"—a phrase usually applied to sites where dictatorial and familial patronage relations allow multinational capital in the extractive industries to, literally, get away with murder. Around two dozens of anti-corruption whistleblowers like Phakoe were killed in the first few years of Zuma's rule.

And, of course, family enterprise suited the Zumas, who had a reported 220 businesses. It was not surprising to learn, for example, that along with the Gupta family—generous sponsors of Zuma's patronage system—son Duduzane was co-owner of JIC Mining Services, the platinum belt region's largest firm specializing in short-term labor outsourcing (sometimes called "labor broking," though JIC denies this, and NUM has a recognition agreement with the firm). Nor was it a secret that the president's nephew Khulubuse Zuma played a destructive role in nearby gold-mining territory as Aurora co-owner, along with Nelson Mandela's grandson and Zuma's lawyer. Indeed, that particular mining house had perhaps the single most extreme record of ecological destructiveness and labor conflict in the post-apartheid era, reflecting how white-owned mining houses gave used-up mines with vast Acid Mine Drainage liabilities to new black owners who were ill equipped to deal with the inevitable crises (Mangcu 2012).

This in turn was all part of the much-proclaimed deracialization of apartheid capitalism. As *Business Day* editor Peter Bruce wrote in 2003: "The government is utterly seduced by big business, and cannot see beyond its immediate interests" (Bruce 2003). Those interests were to facilitate capital accumulation—"we must strive to create and strengthen a black capitalist class," said Thabo Mbeki, upon taking over from Mandela in 1999—specifically within the ANC's leading political power blocs, as well as to underwrite sufficient power of patronage to ensure the ANC could gain voting majorities into the indefinite future (Mbeki 1999). Here, a critical factor was the ANC's investment arm, Chancellor House.[1]

COSATU, MALEMA, RAMAPHOSA, AND
A FRACTURED RULING PARTY

The stage was set, immediately after Marikana, for renewed debates over whether the Tripartite Alliance was a progressive or now regressive political arrangement, especially between the center-left unionists and communists who are close to official power and thus defensive of the political *status quo*, on the one hand; and on the other, critical, independent progressives convinced that South African politics could become more acutely polarized. Overlaying the crisis and these debates was the internal ANC split between pro- and anti-Zuma forces, which spilled over into Cosatu prior to its September 2012 congress before, at the Mangaung electoral conference of the ruling party, Zuma squashed his opponent and then deputy president Kgalema Motlanthe with three quarters of the vote. It was this political battle that initially paralyzed labor leadership, given the danger Cosatu would unleash centrifugal forces that its popular leader Vavi could not control. There was even talk of NUM opening up a leadership challenge to Vavi, on grounds that the 300,000-member union (Cosatu's largest single member) was strongly pro-Zuma and insisted on the official Cosatu support that Vavi had initially resisted (Munusamy 2012).

Such political maneuvering left Cosatu mostly silenced about Marikana, as NUM's weight and the parallel subversion of other union leaders made it too difficult for the federation to visibly back the upstart platinum, gold, and other mineworkers. In any case, what these wildcat strikers were doing might, more conservative unionists believed, even throw the institutions of centralized bargaining into chaos. The demand for higher wages was both extreme, and thus opposed by NUM, and ultimately successful in the case of Marikana's courageous workers. The 22 percent raise—at a time inflation was around 6 percent—that the workers won after a month of striking was remarkable. It inspired the country's labor force to look at their particular pay packets askance.

But by failing to issue immediate statements about Marikana, many fewer workers mobilized in solidarity against the joint onslaught of multinational capital and the state, so that Cosatu was simply unable in late 2012 to intervene when so many cried out for a shift from the proverbial "War of Position" to a "War of Movement." Cosatu's longing gaze to Zuma for a genuine relationship reminded many of its support for him during the darkest 2005–07 days of corruption and rape charges. Yet it was now, in the Marikana moment, even more apparent that Cosatu's conservatism was the principal barrier to social progress in the country. Its weakness was tangible at two levels.

First, and in sharp contrast to Cosatu's posture, there was a partially filling of the void by Julius Malema, the ANC's former youth leader. Malema himself had been somewhat discredited by his alleged implication in corrupt "tenderpreneurship" (insider deals for state contracts) in the neighboring province of Limpopo. Yet he managed to gather 15,000 angry people at Marikana 2 days after the massacre and voiced powerful critiques of Zuma, Lonmin, and their associated black capitalist allies, such as Lonmin part-owner Ramaphosa.

Meanwhile, the second way in which Cosatu's weakness was manifested was in the subsequent rise of Ramaphosa to renewed power within the ANC. Any such rebirth of Ramaphosa had seemed virtually inconceivable immediately after the start of the Farlam Commission. At this occasion, a startling series of revelations emerged about Ramaphosa's "smoking-gun" emails sent to other Lonmin executives and government ministers exactly 24 hours before the massacre (Smith 2012).[2] To further contextualize this information, one has to remember that Ramaphosa's company Shanduka was the majority shareholder of the Lonmin black empowerment subsidiary, which gave him 9 percent ownership in Lonmin and a seat on the board. Shanduka was in 2012 being paid U.S. $360,000/year by Lonmin for providing "empowerment" consulting, not to mention Ramaphosa's board salary and dividend returns on Lonmin share ownership.

This was not a bad arrangement for the mining house, for one of Ramaphosa's emails on August 15 reflected the power relations that Lonmin gained in its association with the former mineworker leader: "The terrible events that have unfolded cannot be described as a labour dispute. They are plainly dastardly criminal and must be characterized as such. There needs to be concomitant action to address this situation." Ramaphosa wrote to Lonmin's Albert Jamieson: "You are absolutely correct in insisting that the Minister, and indeed all government officials, need to understand that we are essentially dealing with a criminal act. I have said as much to the Minister of Safety and Security. I will stress that Minister [Susan] Shabangu should have a discussion with Roger [Phillimore, Lonmin chairman]." Revealing these emails, the lawyer for the 270 arrested mineworkers, Dali Mpofu, explained:

> It's a long line of emails under, in the same vein, effectively encouraging so-called concomitant action to deal with these criminals, whose only crime was that they were seeking a wage increase. . . . At the heart of this was the toxic collusion between the SA Police Services and Lonmin at a direct level. At a much broader level, it can be called a collusion between State and capital, this phenomenon is at the center of what has occurred here. . . .
>
> This collusion between State and capital has happened in many instances in this country. In 1920, African miners went on strike and the government of Jan Smuts dealt with them with violence, and harshly, and one of the results of that was that they reduced the gap between what white mineworkers were getting and what black mineworkers were getting and the pact that had been signed in 1918 of introducing the color bar in the mines was abandoned. That abandonment precipitated a massive strike by the white mineworkers in 1922 and that

strike was dealt with by the Smuts government by bringing in the air force—the air force and about 200 people were killed. This is one of the most important happenings in the history of this country, and in 1946 under the leadership of the African Mineworkers Union, the African workers, 70,000 African workers also went on a massive strike and the government sent 16,000 policemen and arrested, like they did to our, the people we represent, some of the miners under an act called the War Measures Act.

So this has happened, this collusion between capital and the State has happened in systematic patterns in the history of, sordid history of the mining industry in this country. Part of that history included the collaboration of so-called tribal chiefs who were corrupt and were used by those oppressive governments to turn the self-sufficient black African farmers into slave labour workers. Today, we have a situation where those chiefs have been replaced by so-called BEE partners of these mines and carrying on that torch of collusion.

(Mpofu 2012)

The BEE billionaire Ramaphosa's collaboration with white elites was also reflected in his attempt a few months earlier to purchase a prize buffalo at a game auction for U.S. \$2.3 million (City Press 2012a), an event underscored by Malema as indicative of the gulf between the new South Africa's 1 percent and the workers. Not surprisingly, Malema was quickly rewarded with overwhelming support from Marikana miners on two occasions—including a memorial ceremony he arranged, at which he kicked out several of Zuma's cabinet ministers who had come to pay respects. But, on his third visit, police denied him his constitutional rights to address another huge crowd. Even while contesting fraud charges in his home base (where facilitating provincial tenders had made him rich), Malema thus became, briefly, an unstoppable force across the mining belt in North West and Limpopo Provinces, and even Zimbabwe, calling for radical redistribution. At one point 3 weeks after the massacre, the South African National Defense Force was declared on "high alert" simply because Malema addressed a group of disgruntled soldiers (van Wyk 2012).

Yet money still talks in South Africa. By December 2012, Malema's own apparent power had ebbed. And Ramaphosa had won the ruling party's deputy presidency against Malema's two main allies—with more than three quarters of the vote. Cosatu was also very clearly in retreat with Vavi nervously appealing to Ramaphosa not to act like a capitalist. And Malema himself was completely out of the national political equation, humiliating himself with a co-authored letter to the ANC leadership just before the Mangaung conference began, begging that he be allowed back into the organization: "We remain loyal supporters and members of the ANC, willing to be corrected and guided under its principles" (City Press 2012b). This request was simply rebuffed by Zuma's team.

In addition to expressing relief at Malema's fate, business openly celebrated Ramaphosa's defeat of anti-Zuma candidates Tokyo Sexwale and Matthews Phosa. With Ramaphosa as the new deputy president, ANC Secretary-General Mantashe could brag: "He will open up avenues for the ANC to interact with business, and maybe reduce the suspicion on the part of business about an ANC that is supposedly hostile to business—although it is not" (Mkokeli and Paton 2012). There remained some questions as to whether Ramaphosa would himself simply be swallowed up by the Zuma team's own corrupt practices. Indeed, this was precisely the equation posed by *Business Day's* Bruce (2012a): "He [Ramaphosa] will provide Zuma with the sort of credibility cover only the likes of Trevor Manuel still have to offer. . . . Of course, as much as Ramaphosa can save Zuma, so can Zuma defile Ramaphosa if he is unable to wean himself off what appears to be a staple diet of financial dependency on friends of one kind or another, or business 'associates' who see in the president an easy mark." Time alone will tell I would say.

For the moment, however, the vociferous endorsements of Ramaphosa by big business at the end of 2012 meant the ANC's economic talk-left-so-as-to-walk-right strategy was well understood. In the words of commentator Adam Habib: "The ANC says it's committed to the notion of economic transformation. If that is true, how do you elect a billionaire as your deputy president? He has an admirable political record, but his track record on economic transformation is abysmal" (de Waal 2012). The potential for Ramaphosa to act in the interests of South Africa's untransformed business-in-general coincided perfectly with his own personal portfolio's tentacles, spread right across the South African economy, as Mandy de Waal pointed out:

> Ramaphosa has interests in resources, energy, financial services, food and beverages, and property. Shanduka has investments in some of the most influential and powerful businesses in South Africa (and in some cases globally). These include Macsteel, Scaw Metals SA, Lonmin (through Incwala Resources), Kangra Coal, McDonald's SA, Mondi Plc, Lace Diamonds, Pan African Resources Plc, Coca-Cola, Seacom, MTN, Bidvest, Standard Bank, Alexander Forbes, Investment Solutions, and Liberty Group. Besides the executive role he has at Shanduka, he is the joint Non-Executive Chairman of Mondi Group, and the non-executive chair of MTN, and a number of other companies Shanduka has interests in like Standard Bank and Bidvest. He is also on the board of SABMiller.
> (Dixon 2012)

REBUILDING FROM MICROPOLITICS

With Zuma reelected ANC president at Mangaung and with Ramaphosa as his deputy and presumed replacement in 2019 after Zuma's second term would end, the ruling party's political turmoil appeared to stabilize, and the stage shifted again to the issue of civil society versus state and capital. An early 2013 call for a national strike from the most militant of mineworkers reflected ongoing frustrations. By the end of 2012, the forces for genuine change had not been well gathered from below. Prospects for labor and community activists unifying at the base needed more attention. To exist in Marikana and similar mining towns meant to face incessant police repression bordering on unqualified brutality.

Nonetheless, the brief emergence of a women's mutual-aid movement amongst mineworker wives and girlfriends, as well as other women from the impoverished Marikana community was one reflection of a new bottom-up politics. At least one martyr emerged from their ranks: Paulina Masuhlo, an unusually sympathetic ANC municipal councilor in Marikana who sided with the workers, was shot in the abdomen and leg with rubber bullets during a police and army invasion of Nkaneng on September 15. She died of the wounds on September 19. Yet for the subsequent week and a half, police and malevolently bureaucratic municipal officials refused the women's attempts to memorialize Masuhlo with a long protest march from Nkaneng to the Marikana police station. Persistence and legal support prevailed, so 800 demanded justice in a women's-only trek from Nkaneng to Marikana police station on September 29, dignified and without casualties.

But the political opportunities that might fuse worker, community, and women's interests in improving conditions for the reproduction of labor power—perhaps one day to be joined by environmentalists—were fragile and easy to lose. Male migrant workers typically maintained two households and hence channeled resources back to the Eastern Cape, Lesotho, Mozambique, and other home bases. This process of mixing short-term residents with long-term Tswana-speaking inhabitants was fraught with potential xenophobia and ethnicism, not to mention gendered power relations. Migrancy has also facilitated syndicates of illicit drugs, transactional sex (even forced sexual labor), traditional patriarchy, dysfunctional spiritual suspicions (e.g., the use of traditional medicine *muti* against bullets that allegedly wears off quickly in the presence of women), widespread labor-broking, and other highly exploitative relations.

As a result, as discussed earlier, it was extremely expensive to swim within this sea of poverty, with desperation microfinance leading to even more extreme exploitation. It remains to be seen whether this fusion of mining and financial exploitation will generate strategic responses. New versions of a debt moratorium or organized debtor's cartel—such as the "bond boycott" strategies that were so common in the early 1990s, in which borrowers banded together to gain strength for collective defaults—would be a logical progression for a micropolitics of resistance in Marikana and many other similar situations. The bank staff responsible for credit control (and repossessions, hence "repo man") tended to resort to threats and practices of violence so that this is not a decision to be taken lightly. In Mexico in early 1995, it took a jump in interest rates from 14 to 120 percent to catalyze the *Moviemiento El Barzon Agrupación Civil*—"*El Barzon*," meaning the yoke-ring on an oxen—movement, which gathered 1 million members to renegotiate debts on the basis of the financial reality: "*Debo, no niego, pago lo justo*" (I owe, I can't deny it, I will pay what is just) (Greider 1997).

The South African precedent was the earliest recorded bond boycott, in Port Elizabeth's Uitenhage township in 1988 in which a Volkswagen autoworkers strike led to Standard Bank attempting to repossess workers' newly-built houses, because of loans that they were having trouble servicing as a result of the strike. Labor and community activists successfully turned the tables on that alliance of a multinational car corporation and domestic financial capital by engaging in a collective refusal to repay. The strategy and tactic changed power relations sufficiently so that instead of Volkswagen compelling Standard to pressure workers to go back to the assembly line, the workers and communities compelled Standard to request Volkswagen to settle the strike. With many dozens of such local bond boycotts and a semi-successful national bond boycott campaign by the South African National Civic Organization (Sanco) in 1992,[3] there was some sense by the mid-1990s that, from below, society could and should unify against financial power.

In mid-1996, a "Campaign against the Bank Rate Increase" began, fusing "Cosatu and its affiliate unions, the ANC, ANC Youth League, SACP, Sanco, SA Students' Congress (Sasco), Congress of SA Students (Cosas), Muslim Youth Movement, Young Christian Students, and the Call of Islam," as *The Shopsteward* reported:

> The campaign's immediate demand was for the reversal of the one percent increase. But there was agreement that, even if the big four drop their one percent hike [of May 1996], interest rates are still too high, particularly when compared to other countries. This has a detrimental effect on economic growth, housing, job creation and the budget deficit, to mention but a few. Many coalition organizations want to take the campaign a step further to review monetary and interest rate policies and there are moves afoot to look at measures, including legislation, to regulate banks' behavior. . . .
>
> The coalition is the first of its kind since the 1994 general elections, involving a broad alliance of organizations, unseen since the days of the anti-VAT campaign in 1991. The campaign has also pleased alliance activists concerned that the ANC has neglected grassroots campaigns in favor of exclusively parliamentary politics. There is a view that parliamentary avenues should complement campaigns at a mass level and that the ANC should continue to act in concert with civil society organizations in transforming the country.
>
> (The Shopsteward 1996)

That brief 1996 campaign did launch several mass actions, but suddenly, in mid-June, momentum was reversed when the ANC acted against civil society by unilaterally imposing the *Growth, Employment, and Redistribution* homegrown structural adjustment policy. Nonetheless, in spite of its truncated nature, the bank campaign was, in concept, one of the ways the "small-a alliance" vision found an early manifestation. Later the SACP too attempted several banking reforms but without substantial benefits, as the balance of forces continually grew more adverse under Mbeki's rule. But this was not unusual during the early 2000s; the country with one of the world's fastest growth rates, India, also suffered a quarter of a million suicides by small farmers, invariably because of over-indebtedness. Bankers did rule the world, as was obvious when the bailout funding of 2008–09 went entirely to creditors and not to the debtors. However, even in countries such as the United States, impressive attempts to generate social pressure against banks suddenly emerged soon after, with Occupy Wall Street only the most visible.

South Africa missed out on the first phase of the complaining against the "one percent," one reason being that the traditions of South African progressive politics always paralleled classical socialist reasoning. As a result capitalist malevolence—Marikana being only one example—invariably called forth the simple demand that the means of production be nationalized. In late 2012, Zuma, Shabangu, and their pro-business allies succeeded rather easily in ridding the ANC of such chatter, not least because Malema's own troubles rose to crisis proportions, thus temporarily neutralizing his more populist voice. Indeed, the expulsion of the ANC Youth League faux radicals left virtually no major figures aside from the general secretary of the National Union of Metalworkers of South Africa, Irvin Jim, to demand nationalization of strategic resources.

Nationalizing Lonmin and other platinum corporations would have been a smart move as South Africa controls more than 80 percent of world platinum reserves. The price spike occasioned by the Lonmin, Implats, and Angoplats strikes—30 percent over 6 weeks—suggested great potential for a platinum cartel similar to OPEC's oil cartel. The main buyer of platinum in 2012 was the European auto industry, but while the EU economic crisis continued, demand was intrinsically soft. Major platinum mines could thus make plausible threats arguing that if workers did not return, they would simply close shafts. The same week that Lonmin conceded the big wage increase to several thousand Marikana rock-drill operators, the company found it could cancel even more precarious short-term contracts of another 1,200 workers.

REVOLUTION, REVULSION, AND REARGUARD DEFENSE

Because of this convoluted political conjuncture, the most hopeful outcome of Marikana was to be an "economistic" one, namely the wage increase won by the striking workers. This in itself was no mean feat, as Peter Alexander argues:

In other settings, events of this kind have led to the defeat of a move-ment, or at least its abeyance. But that is not what happened here. On the contrary, the strike got stronger. Workers faced trauma, the tribu-lations of burying their dead in far-away places, threatened sackings, lack of money for food, and attacks from unions and politicians. But, by 7 September the company was reporting that attendance at work was down to two per cent, and after that it gave up providing statistics. There was an undeclared state of emergency and a community leader was killed, but still the workers fought on, until, on 18 September, they agreed to a settlement that secured them victory. Had the strike col-lapsed, people across the country fighting poverty and injustice would have been cowed. The opposite happened and, from the perspective of the state and the bosses, the killings were an appalling miscalculation, an enormous setback. Somehow, despite 34 colleagues being killed and with many more injured or detained, workers found the strength to pull themselves together and determine that the strike would continue. This was one of the most remarkable acts of courage in labour history, anywhere and at any time.

(Alexander et al. 2012)

But if the acts of courage were, Alexander reminds us, forged from frustra-tion and anger, they also lacked a sufficiently strong and clear political agenda. And such agenda was necessary to mobilize the tens of millions of disgruntled South Africans into a force capable of breaking sweetheart relations between state, ruling party, labor aristocrats, parasitical capital, and the London/Melbourne mining houses. For some, Marikana was potentially the break-through event that independent progressives long sought, one that could reveal more graphically the intrinsic anti-social tendencies associated with the ANC-Alliance's elite transition from revolutionaries to willing partners of some of the world's most wicked corporations. And such a narrative was indeed the one promoted by the otherwise extremely fractured South African left.

Some factions associated with the relatively broad-based (though labor-less) Democratic Left Front and the Marikana Support Campaign, did sponsor regular political meetings from Johannesburg and Cape Town and also solidaristic activities in the platinum belt. Nonetheless, the first of such meetings at the University of Johannesburg a week after the Marikana Mas-sacre provisionally included a leading NUM representative on the program (he was shouted down and chased from the hall),[4] another left faction led by Johannesburg's Khanya College broke away to found the "We are all Marikana" campaign.[5] Resolutely opposed to any legitimation of Cosatu's Alliance unionism, this network also gathered ordinary workers for educa-tional events (although momentum appeared to slow within a month after the massacre). In contrast, one other small revolutionary party in Mari-kana engaged in much higher profile recruiting and consciousness-raising: the Democratic Socialist Movement (associated with the Committee for a

Workers' International). However, its limitations were also obvious, for in December 2012, as its representative conceded: "The modest founding of the Workers and Socialist Party with just 20 delegates present has made concrete the idea of an alternative based on a socialist program committed to nationalization of the commanding heights of the economy of which the mining industry remains a key component" (Democratic Socialist Movement [DSM] 2012).[6]

The fact remains that even though it may often have seemed that a "pre-revolutionary" situation existed in a South Africa that had one of the highest protest rates in the world, the lack of connection between those with grievances remained the most crippling problem. And this "disconnect" continued amongst traditional critics of ANC neoliberalism in late 2012. One critical example was the lack of any real attempt to coordinate international solidarity. Here, in fact, was a huge void in Marikana-related political work, an opportunity lost by South Africans despite the willingness of NGOs to call on the World Bank in order to divest from Lonmin just one day after the massacre (CIEL 2012) and the fact that at least a dozen spontaneous protests broke out at South African embassies and consulate offices across the world in subsequent days.

There was, though, the hope that, as another example, the women of Marikana, organizing across the divides of labor and community, could set an example so desperately needed by the broader left. Their organizing efforts ranged beyond Marikana itself, as they briefly helped to connect the dots elsewhere in the society, including in nearby terrains ranging from mining dorpies to land struggles in North West, Limpopo, and Gauteng provinces. Yet South African women are as diverse and ethnically divided as the broader society: wives, girlfriends, mothers, daughters, sisters, health-workers, educators, sex-workers, cooks, cleaners, and salespersons. These women had the additional burdens of handling trauma counseling for victims of violence and providing mutual aid to those who were suffering enormously, directly and indirectly, as a result of the wildcat strike wave's reduction of immediate cash in communities. As in other societal sectors, much political work was needed in order to create a coherent oppositional voice amongst women.

The same could be said of "progressives" who had long been associated with the ANC because of the century-old party's best instincts. After 1994, many of them continued their determined work of liberation from within civil society. In this political space, organizations could be found that jumped into the Marikana political breech with much needed support activities. These included, for example, the Socio-Economic Rights Institute, Sonke Gender Justice, Studies in Poverty and Inequality, Students for Law and Social Justice, the Treatment Action Campaign, and Section 27 (which is named with reference to the country's Bill of Rights). Yet where was the organizational and ideological coherence that could render this trend a cumulative and defining force?

As for the official "left" nothing worth salvaging appeared. As *Business Day's* Peter Bruce (2012b) wrote 4 days after the massacre: "What's scary about Marikana is that, for the first time, for me, the fact that the ANC and its government do not have the handle they once did on the African majority has come home. The party is already losing the middle classes. If they are now also losing the marginal and the dispossessed, what is left? Ah yes, Cosatu and the communists—Zuma's creditors." It was almost surreal to find Cosatu and communist leaders anxiety-ridden at the prospect of widening worker revolt. It was no wonder that controversy-seeking liberal journalist R.W. Johnson could easily find an SACP ideologue to serve as his "useful idiot" in making this bizarre case:

> *This time the Left was in favor of the massacre* [emphasis added]. Dominic Tweedie of the Communist University, Johannesburg, commented, "this was no massacre, this was a battle. The police used their weapons in exactly the way they were supposed to. That's what they have them for. The people they shot didn't look like workers to me. We should be happy. The police were admirable." The Communist Party's North West section demanded the arrest of AMCU's Joseph Mathunjwa and his deputy, James Kholelile.
>
> (Johnson 2012)

Yet in a context where social protest in the townships had reached very high levels in mid-2012 with no hope of relief, the panic of bosses and their spokespeople—neoliberals such as Peter Bruce—was easy to discern. Some commentators feared the potentially uncontrollable contagion of disrespect. Thus Frans Cronje of the South African Institute of Race Relations immediately rose to the ANC's defense, declaring in mid-September that "a myth has taken hold in South Africa that service delivery was a failure" (Hedley 2012). Cronje's defense of state provision of water, electricity, and housing reverberated well with *Business Day* editorialists as well as SACP leader Blade Nzimande (2012b), who warmly endorsed the "research." Yet when Cronje was asked whether he had determined what percentage of post-1994 communal water taps were still working among those given to more than 15 million people, he conceded that he had no clue (Cronje 2012). The last serious audit—a decade earlier by researcher David Hemson, at the request of the then water minister, Ronnie Kasrils—put the share at less than half, using even the most generous definition of what is "working," and the sector's management has degenerated since then (Hemson 2003).

Plenty to be frightened about, one would say. It's a small wonder that someone in the camp of the apparently frightened, like *Business Day* columnist Steven Friedman (2012), could, in the wake of Marikana, appeal for a return to a "social partnership" strategy because such an approach "has not failed us—it has not been tried." Meanwhile, the corporatist elites did meet in mid-October 2012, issuing what were soon seen as meaningless statements against wildcat strikes and worker violence against scabs. However, the big business representatives at that gabfest were apparently loathed to even name themselves publicly (Cohen 2012).

CONCLUSION

The strike wave continued rising through late 2012, no matter narratives about social "leadership." Truck drivers received an above-inflation settlement in October 2012 after resorting to sometimes intensely violent methods to disrupt scab drivers, in the process creating shortages of petrol and retail goods in various parts of the country. While Durban's Toyota workers, municipal offices, and the farm workers of the Western Cape also engaged in wildcat strikes, no one was taking the signals from Pretoria seriously. By March 2013, with vineyards having been burnt to the ground by angry workers, the state and most large farmers agreed to a 52 percent increase in the daily wage (to U.S. $12). This militancy was not new, of course, for in September 2012, the World Economic Forum's *Global Competitiveness Report* placed South Africa in the world's number one position for adverse employee-employer relations (in a survey done prior to Marikana) (World Economic Forum 2012).

Partly as a result of labor militancy, major rating agencies began downgrading the country's bond rating, for example, to BBB level by Standard & Poor's. The resulting higher interest rates to be paid on the country's prolific foreign borrowings—about six times higher by 2014 in absolute terms than inherited from apartheid in 1994—created yet more fiscal pressures as well as household and corporate repayment stress. Given Europe's crisis, a potential hard landing in China, and South Africa's vulnerability to the world economy, much lower GDP growth rates in 2013 and beyond were anticipated. And instead of countering that prospect with an interest rate cut by the South African Reserve Bank, as was projected, the country's shaky financial standing put countervailing upward pressure on rates.

In the period after Marikana, the situation remained fluid. In spite of the shift in bargaining power away from NUM, it was impossible to assess which forces would emerge from the chaos given ongoing labor contestation. The strategies of crisis management deployed by Lonmin, the ANC and NUM, the South African Police Service and the Farlam Commission, all proved inadequate to restore legitimacy. Even if Lonmin's share price rose 23 percent in the year from August 16, 2012, following the 30 percent crash in the week immediately after the massacre, the sector is in trouble. The largest producer, AngloPlats, lost half of its output in 2013 and threatened to lay off several thousand workers, and the second largest, Impala, lost more than a fifth of share value in the first half of 2013. Lonmin had raised U.S. $817 million in a share rights issue in December 2012 and repaid its vast debt. Its profits increased marginally, and after replacing its sickly CEO Ian

Farmer with Zimbabwean Ben Magara, finally in July 2013, Lonmin moved to recognize AMCU—with 70 percent worker support—as majority trade union negotiator (in turn causing extreme tension with NUM and several more deaths) (Peters 2013).

However, AMCU's National Treasurer, Jimmy Gama, remained dissatisfied that in August 2013: "There have not been any significant changes in the last 12 months regarding the issues that labour was protesting for, before they were killed in Marikana. . . . Workers are still living in shacks, in the hostels but, it is incumbent on all stakeholders—labour, government and the companies—to deal with those issues." He expressed hope that Magara would "take discussions to another level" but his NUM opponent, union spokesperson Lesiba Seshoka, was even more pessimistic: "I would say that things have remained the same, and worse, actually because of a number of things. Before the big massacre on the sixteenth, the situation in Rustenburg was very tense, people were dying, they were attacked, and killed and the situation remains like that. This is why, we think the ground is getting fertile for another Marikana, because nothing much has changed threats and intimidation remain the order of the day, people are dying." A mining industry executive, Neil Froneman, remarked: "Unfortunately very little has changed from a visible point of view. I think what has changed and it's not that visible is that stakeholders have recognised and have accepted that there's a need to do things differently" (Candy 2013).

The Farlam Commission contributed to *status quo* retention and, along with the Department of Justice, lost credibility for not using its substantive budget to fund the lawyers of the massacre victims and their families' presence at the Commission hearings. One of the public interest lawyers for the mineworker victims, Jackie Dugard (2013) of the Socio-Economic Research Institute, identified these problems in September 2013:

> [I]t is clear that the overly bureaucratic and insensitive way in which the commission began had set the tone for an inquiry that has been continually hampered by problems. The most recent setback is the issue of the lack of funding for the legal team representing the 270 mineworkers who were injured (but not killed). This has been sharpened by the government's announcement last month that it would not provide funding for the injured mineworkers' legal team. . . . If the process so far has taught us anything, it is that we need to place victims at the centre of such inquiries. We also need to spend enough time planning and establishing appropriate procedures, ensuring funding arrangements (including possibly excluding lawyers), clarifying the role of evidence leaders and meticulously managing the evidence and testimony. If justice is to be served effectively and sensitively, we cannot afford to repeat these mistakes.

In addition to the Farlam Commission, public relations problems also haunted Ramaphosa as well as Manuel, both in major speeches at the

University of the Witwatersrand in Johannesburg. On August 29, 2013, Manuel delivered the Ruth First Lecture (in honor of a revolutionary assassinated by the apartheid regime 31 years earlier). It was a creditable account of the multiple kinds of damage done by the Minerals-Energy Complex to South Africa. But he refused to take questions, leading to a protest by a dozen Marikana mineworkers and community activists who were kicked out by security guards while holding posters saying: "Trevor Manuel, was your Cabinet behind the decision to fire on Marikana with live ammunition?" (Montsho 2013).

On September 9 at the same university, Ramaphosa gave a lecture on the government's National Development Plan (NDP), the commission about which he was co-chairing (under Manuel's chair). As a newspaper report recorded:

> Several members of the audience used the question and answer sessions to level criticisms at Ramaphosa and the NDP. One man criticised Ramaphosa, saying that the election of one of the richest people in the country as deputy president of the ANC was worrying. "The NDP is old wine in new bottles, and that's what we are asking for," he said sarcastically. "We are asking for more Marikanas, more shooting, more inequality, more brutality and less service delivery." Earlier, Marikana Support Campaign members sang and danced in the hall. The group sang against capitalism and held up posters saying: "Don't let the politicians get away with murder" (Areff 2013).

Would they, indeed, "get away" with Marikana, or would the massacre's stain forever spread? The public relations battle will remain critical for many years, insofar as ANC leaders must try to win back many hearts and minds lost at Marikana, initially for the 2014 national election, in which Malema's new Economic Freedom Fighters were the "left" force in the May 2014 elections, achieving a respectable 6% of the vote. But the PR flops a year after the massacre were more revealing.

What was definitive, by then, was the waning of any remaining illusions that the forces of "liberation" led by the ANC would take South Africa to genuine freedom and a new society. Marikana had these consequences and Ramaphosa's December 2012 election could do nothing to restore faith in the ruling party. Just the opposite, as Malema's Fighters arose to become the main left challenger to the ANC with vast support amongst Marikana mineworkers (notwithstanding Malema's dubious past). In the coming years, if protesters keep dodging police bullets and moving the socio-economic and political-ecological questions to center stage, and if the crony corporatist arrangements between the ruling party and firms like Lonmin do not change, the ANC's neoliberal nationalism could either arrange a properly fascist backlash or, more likely under Zuma's ongoing misrule, continue shrinking in confusion with regular doses of necessary humility.

NOTES

1. To illustrate, one notorious deal included buying a quarter share of the local subsidiary of Hitachi, which in a suspicious deal, won a tender for the supply of U.S. $5 billion worth of boilers to the vast coal-fired power plant now under construction not far from Marikana, at Medupi, and its successor Kusile. The World Bank made its largest ever project loan to support that deal. With then Eskom chair Valli Moosa also a member of the ANC Finance Committee at the time, the South African Public Protector labeled his conflict of interest "improper." But reflecting the balance of political power and financial facilitation by Robert Zoellick's World Bank, the deal went through and two subsequent years of delays could be blamed, perhaps not surprisingly, on faulty boilers. (The day that Jim Kim arrived in Johannesburg, several hundred Medupi construction workers embarked on a strike that included burning some of the facilities, resulting in the evacuation of 17,000 workers, a problem that did not attract his attention while in the country or in his blog upon returning.)
2. For more on his battered credibility, see Mkokeli (2012).
3. As a result of the resistance, township housing foreclosures that could not be consummated due to refusal of the defaulting borrowers (supported by the community) to vacate their houses, and the leading financier's U.S. $700 million black housing bond exposure in September 1992, was the reason that its holding company (Nedcor) lost 20 percent of its Johannesburg Stock Exchange share value (in excess of U.S. $150 million lost) in a single week. Locally, if a bank did bring in a sheriff to foreclose and evict defaulters, it was not uncommon for a street committee of activists to burn the house down before the new owners completed the purchase and moved in. Such power, in turn, allowed both the national and local civic associations to negotiate concessions from the banks. The practice is reviewed in Mayekiso (1996) and Bond (2000).
4. The most evocative description of that meeting is probably by Athi Mongezeleli Joja (2012). To illustrate the divisions that quickly emerged, although an impressive revival of the Black Consciousness (BC) tradition had risen since the early 2000s through the *New Frank Talk* series, the sole public intervention on Marikana by the September National Imbizo was to visit 2 days after the massacre in order to begin the reconstruction of events, but without subsequent commentary or activism. A month after the massacre, BC adherents along with an unusually subdued left-autonomist network conjoined in an intellectual conference at Johannesburg's Wits University, in an event known as the "Tribe of Moles," led by an emerging black intelligentsia suspicious of classical socialist formulations and friendly to insurgent opportunities. But surprisingly, in a whole day of debating race, representation, and radical politics, the word Marikana was not mentioned once from the stage or floor. When asked during a break about the evolving situation, including Marikana women's organizing, the country's most prominent BC proponent, Andile Mngxitama, called the cross-racial/class/geographical gender organizing underway (including middle-class women from NGOs) a distraction, for after all the corpses were "black bodies"—and hence he gave impetus to the frequent claim that contemporary South African BC argumentation soon degenerates into race essentialism.
5. http://www.facebook.com/KhanyaCollegeMovementHouse/posts/139762889503120.
6. http://www.socialistsouthafrica.co.za/ and see Workers and Socialist Party (WASP) founding statement online at http://www.politicsweb.co.za/politicsweb/view/politicsweb/en/page71654?oid=347787&sn=Detail&pid=71616.

REFERENCES

Alexander, Peter, Thapelo Lekgowa, Botsang Mmope, Luke Sinwell, and Bongani Xezwi (2012) *Marikana: A View from the Mountain and a Case to Answer.* Johannesburg: Jakana.

Areff, Ahmed (2013) "Ramaphosa Booed by Angry Crowd," *The Star*, September 11. Online at http://www.iol.co.za/news/politics/ramaphosa-booed-by-angry-crowd-1.1575813, accessed on September 12, 2013.

Bateman, Milford (2012) "Microcredit and Marikana: How they are linked," *The Star*, September 18.

Bench Marks Foundation (2007) "The Policy Gap—A Review of the Corporate Social Responsibility Programmes of the Platinum Industry in the North West Province," Johannesburg. Online at http://www.bench-marks.org.za, accessed on August 24, 2013.

Bench Marks Foundation (2012) *A Review of Platinum Mining in the Bojanela District of the North West Province.* Johannesburg: Author.

Bond, Patrick (2000) *Cities of Gold, Townships of Coals.* Trenton, NJ: Africa World Press.

Bond, Patrick (2012) "Jim Yong Kim's Trip to South Africa was just a PR Exercise for the World Bank," *The Guardian Poverty Matters Blog*, September. Online at http://www.guardian.co.uk/global-development/poverty-matters/2012/sep/12/jim-yong-kim-world-bank-south-africa, accessed on September 12, 2013.

Bruce, Peter (2003) "SA needs a Market Economy," *Business Day*, June 4.

Bruce, Peter (2012a) "Man of Action Ramaphosa Good for Zuma," *Business Day*, December 19.

Bruce, Peter (2012b) "The Thick End of the Wedge," *Business Day*, August 20.

Burger, Alex and Benedicta Sepora (2009) "A Mine of Their Own: The Women of Lonmin," *World Bank.* Online at http://siteresources.worldbank.org/INTGENDER/Resources/NewsletterPage6.pdf?cid=PREM_GAPNewsEN_A_E, accessed on September 12, 2013.

Candy, Geoff (2013) "A Year After Marikana: Has Anything Changed?" *Moneyweb*, August 16.

Center for International Environmental Law (CIEL) (2012) *CIEL calls on World Bank to revisit investment in Lonmin.* Washington, DC: Author. Online at http://ciel.org/Law_Communities/Lonmin_17Aug2012.html, accessed on September 12, 2013.

City Press (2012a) "Buffalo Soldier Cyril loses out," April 4.

City Press (2012b) "Please take me back, I'll be good—Malema," December 17. Online at http://www.citypress.co.za/news/buffalo-soldier-cyril-loses-out-20120414/, accessed on September 12, 2013.

Cloughly, Brian (2008) "A Repulsive Farce: The Unacceptable Face of Capitalism," *Counterpunch*, October 3. Online at http://www.counterpunch.org/2008/10/03/the-unacceptable-face-of-capitalism/, accessed on September 12, 2013.

Cohen, Tim (2012) "Time for a Bold New Idea of What it Means to be SA," *Business Day*, October 15. Online at http://www.bdlive.co.za/opinion/columnists/2012/10/15/time-for-a-bold-new-idea-of-what-it-means-to-be-sa, accessed on September 12, 2013.

Cronje, Frans (2012) Personal correspondence with author, 22 September.

Daily Business News (2008) "Finance: Lonmin-IFC Partnership wins Nedbank Green Mining Award," Online at http://www.gbn.co.za/articles/dailynews/139.html, accessed on September 12, 2013.

de Lange, Jan (2012) "Archie Palane Points Finger at NUM failings," *MiningMX*, October 10.

de Lange, Jan (2013), "Archie Palane points finger at NUM failings," Miningmx, 28 April. Online at http://www.miningmx.com/page/news/markets/1388854-Archie-Palane-points-finger-at-NUM-failings#.U172GVeTJmo, accessed on September 12, 2013.

Democratic Socialist Movement (2012) "DSM and Mineworkers found WASP," 18 December PoliticsWeb. Online at http://www.politicsweb.co.za/politicsweb/view/politicsweb/en/page71654?oid=347787&sn=Detail&pid=71616, accessed on September 12, 2013.

Department of Trade and Industry (2011) Industrial Policy Action Plan, Pretoria. Online at http://www.tralac.org/files/2012/12/IPAP-2-Industrial-Policy-Action-Plan-2011.pdf, accessed on September 12, 2013.

de Waal, Mandy (2012) "Cyril Ramaphosa: ANC deputy, captain of industry," *Daily Maverick*, December 20.

Dixon, Robyn (2012) "South African President Jacob Zuma Retains ANC leadership," *Los Angeles Times*, December 18. Online at http://articles.latimes.com/2012/dec/18/world/la-fg-south-africa-zuma-20121219, accessed on September 12, 2013.

Dugard, Jackie (2013) "Marikana Inquiry's Mistakes Call for a Rethink," *Business Day*, September 11.

Forslund, Dick (2012) "Wages, Profits and Labour Productivity in South Africa," *Amandla!*, January 24.

Friedman, Steven (2012) "We must Stop Blaming and Start Compromising," *Business Day*, September 19.

Greider, William (1997) *One World, Ready or Not: The Manic Logic of Global Capitalism*. New York: Simon and Schuster.

Hargreaves, Samantha (2013) "More Misery in Marikana," *Third World Resurgence*, 271/272 (March/April): 35–37.

Hartford, Gavin (2012) "The Mining Industry Strike Wave," Amandla! Colloquium, 26–27 Sept., Magaliesburg, South Africa.

Hedley, Nick (2012) "Service Delivery: Presidency Blames Apartheid," *Business Day*, September 12.

Hemson, David (2003) *Water Delivery to the Poor Improving but Still Some Way to Go*. Pretoria: Human Sciences Research Council.

International Finance Corporation (IFC) (2006) *Lonmin: Summary of Proposed Investment*. Washington, DC: The World Bank Group.

International Finance Corporation (IFC) (2011) *IFC and Lonmin: Digging Deep for Development*. Washington, DC: The World Bank Group.

Johnson, R. W. (2012) "Marikana Massacre," *Politicsweb*, August 19.

Joja, Athi Mongezeleli (2012) "White Tears Cheapening Black Suffering," Online at http://www.comentarium.com/en_blog-post.jsp?blogPostID=2077693, accessed on May 2, 2014.

Kasrils, Ronnie (2012) "The Slayings Grow More Sinister," *Amandla!*, September.

Lonmin (2012) *Sustainable Development Report for the Year Ending 30 September 2012*. London: Lonmin.

Mangcu, Xolela (2012) "Far Cry from Biko's Political Approach," *The Sowetan*, September 25.

Mayekiso, Mzwanele (1996) *Township Politics*. New York: Monthly Review Press.

Mbeki, Thabo (1999) "Speech of the President of South Africa, Thabo Mbeki, at the Annual National Conference of the Black Management Forum." Annual National Conference of the Black Management Forum. Johannesburg.

Mkokeli, Sam (2012) "Ramaphosa Email a Gift to his Detractors," *Business Day*, October 25.

Mkokeli, Sam and Carol Paton (2012) "Ramaphosa SA's Prime Minister," *Business Day*, December 20.

Montsho, Molaolo (2013) "Miners Disrupt Trevor Manuel's Ruth First lecture," *Mail & Guardian*, August 30.

Mpofu, Dali (2012) "Transcription of the Commission of Inquiry: Marikana—Days 1 to 7, 1 to 31 October 2012," October. Online at http://www.seri-sa.org/images/stories/marikana_consolidatedtranscript_days1-7.pdf, accessed on September 12, 2013.

Munusamy, Ranjeni (2012) "Move to Dislodge Vavi May Fire Back at Zuma," *Daily Maverick*, August 13.

Nzimande, Blade (2012a) "Our Condolences and Sympathies to the Marikana and Pomeroy Victims," PoliticsWeb, 23 August. Online at http://www.politicsweb.co.za/politicsweb/view/politicsweb/en/page71656?oid=321457&sn=Detail&pid=71656, accessed on June 24, 2014.

Nzimande, Blade (2012b) "Transforming University and Society," *Politicsweb*, October 2.

Peters, Fifi (2013) "Lonmin Recuperates after Marikana Tragedy," *Business Day*, August 19.

Rees, Malcolm (2012) "Financially Illiterate Miners Debt Shocker," *Moneyweb*, October 1.

Smith, David (2012) "Ramaphosa has Blood on his Hands, Say Miners," *The Guardian*, October 25.

Steyn, Lisa (2012) "Marikana Miners in Debt Sinkhole," *Mail & Guardian*, September 7.

The Shopsteward (1996) "The Banks Buckle Under Public Pressure," *The Shopsteward* 5 (3) June–July. Online at http://www.cosatu.org.za/show.php?ID=2080, accessed on September 12, 2013.

van Wyk, Andrea (2012) "Take a Chill Pill and Sit Down, Malema tells Defence minister," *Eyewitness News*, September 12.

World Economic Forum (2012) *Global Competitiveness Report 2012–2013*. Davos: World Economic Forum.

11 Keeping Neoliberal Economic Principles at a Distance

The Case of "Radical" Independent Presses in France

Sophie Noël

This chapter discusses the development of small independent presses that have been created in France in the last 20 years in the field of social sciences and social critique. These presses represent pockets of resistance to the growing economic pressures that have emerged in the cultural industries, in the name of the "autonomy" of symbolic spheres. At a time when the book industry is subjected to increasing rationalization and globalization processes, they exemplify the possibility of alternative ways of doing business in the cultural field. Although extremely precarious, these small presses play an important role in the publishing field because they promote a normative and idealized view of culture rooted in the subordination of economic values, or, to use Pierre Bourdieu's terminology, in an "economic world reversed" (Bourdieu 1996).

We shall focus on a group of 33 independent—both economically and politically—French presses publishing in the sector of social sciences at large, which present themselves as "politically engaged" (on the left or extreme left wing politically).[1] They were created between 1985 and 2005, in the wake of anti-globalization and anti-capitalist movements. Situated at the crossroads of different publishing sectors (academic, mainstream, political, and avant-garde), they occupy a small niche characterized by a combination of political and intellectual commitment. These presses are extremely diverse (see Table 11.1): Some are very small businesses run by one or two people, with an output of fewer than five titles a year; others are established businesses with a small staff on a full or part-time basis, publishing 20 to 50 books a year; one out of four is a not-for-profit organization, while the rest act as private businesses eager to become more professional. Their productions range from specialized academic texts to essays addressing a wider readership and annual turnover goes from 15,000 to 50,000 €. A handful of these presses have achieved recognition—*Raisons d'agir*, *Amsterdam*, *La Fabrique*, *Les Prairies ordinaires*—but most of them are little known and occupy a rather marginal position in the publishing field.

Their resistance strategies to economic normalization are obvious at two levels: in the production of these presses, whose books explore the field of social sciences (political and social theory, history, economics, but also

Table 11.1 List of Publishers

Publisher	Creation date	Legal	Staff	Number of books
L'Éclat	1985	Ltd	2	10–25
Climats (bought up by Flammarion in 2005)	1988	Ltd	1	10–25
Syllepse	1989	Association	1	> 25
Encyclopédie des nuisances	1993	Ltd	0	< 10
Ivrea	1992	Ltd	0	< 10
L'Insomniaque	1993	Association	0	< 10
Dagorno	1992	Ltd	0	< 10
Le Temps des cerises	1994	Ltd	3	> 25
Textuel (Actes Sud took a stake in its capital in 2009)	1994	Ltd	10	< 10
Sens&Tonka	1995	Ltd	2	10–25
Sulliver	1995	SA	0	10–25
Raisons d'agir	1996	Association	1	< 10
La Dispute	1996	Ltd	3	10–25
Agone	1997	Association	6	10–25
Les Arènes	1997	Ltd	6	10–25
Le Passant ordinaire	1997	Association	3	< 10
Exils	1997	Ltd	0	< 10
Golias	1997	Ltd	3	10–25
Les Nuits rouges	1997	Association	0	< 10
La Fabrique	1998	Ltd	1	< 10
Nautilus	2000	Ltd	1	< 10
Parangon	2000	Ltd	0	10–25
Aden	2000	Ltd	2	10–25
Les Éditions libertaires	2001	Association	0	10–25
Danger public (bought up by La Martinière in 2005)	2002	Ltd	0	3
Le Croquant	2003	Cooperative	0	10–25
Homnisphères	2003	Ltd	1	< 10
Amsterdam	2003	Ltd	0	10–25
Lignes	2003	Ltd	2	10–25
L'Échappée	2004	Association	0	< 10
Sextant	2004	Ltd	0	< 10
Delga	2004	Ltd	0	< 10
Les Prairies ordinaires	2005	Ltd	0	< 10

philosophy) in order to oppose the excesses of neoliberalism and to question the "rules of the game," and in their organizational structures as they aim at functioning in a different manner from publishing conglomerates, i.e., to put ideas before profit. How do they engage with the market without endangering their symbolic legitimacy? How do they put their political principles into practice? The first section of this chapter will examine the necessary conditions for the existence of anti-institutional or heterodox structures such as "radical" presses in the French publishing field. The second section will look into these publishers' rhetoric and into the staging out of their identity in the public arena; the third section will turn to their actual organizational practices, whether professional or amateur, in order to try and understand how economic principles can be bypassed, or at least kept at a distance.

BOOKS AS COMMODITIES WITH A DIFFERENCE?

Publishing, like most cultural industries, is a dual activity, both commercial (books, whether in printed or digital format, are material products that are put on the market to be sold) and symbolic (the intellectual content embedded in the books). Echoing this, Pierre Bourdieu talked about the "double identity" of cultural intermediaries such as art gallery owners and publishers, who are simultaneously on the side of art and money, stressing the necessity for them to "reconcile what is irreconcilable" (Bourdieu 1996). The tension between these two aspects is not new, as historians of the book have illustrated (Martin and Febvre 1958, Mollier 1988), but it has become more acute over the past 30 years, with the growing trends of globalization and consolidation within book publishing all over the world (Rouet 2007, Thompson 2010). Many voices have made themselves heard to resist this trend and to bemoan the excessive drift towards mercantile practices, the most famous being André Schiffrin, ex-director of Pantheon in New York and founder of The New Press, a not-for-profit house in 1989 (Schiffrin 2000, 2010).

Politically committed publishers[2] typically have the following vision. Situated at the pole of restricted production,[3] they emphasize that symbolic values should prevail over economic considerations in publishing in order to resist the pressures of the main players and, more generally, of the global market, asserting the specific value of books as singularities (Karpik 2010), not random commodities. To do so, they rely on the historical tradition of political commitment in the publishing field in France, with role models like Jérôme Lindon (*Editions de Minuit*) and François Maspero (*Editions Maspero*)[4] who still exercise a strong influence today (Simonin 1994, Hage 2005). As the founder of *Aden*, a radical press, puts it: "Maspero is an absolute master" (interviewed on October 25, 2006). Following this tradition, being a "great publisher" is associated with taking risks and surviving in dire financial conditions in order to make it possible for alternative voices to be heard. Far from being mere "gatekeepers" (Coser et al. 1982), they act as engaged intellectuals imbued with social prestige. A profile of André Schiffrin in the newspaper *Le Monde* provides an example of the romanticized vision of publishers, which owes very little to business flair:

> André Schiffrin is, more than anything else, a *Résistant,* someone who will not surrender to intellectual mediocrity, nor resign himself to the "treason of the intellectuals"[5], to the excesses of the market and to the "suicidal" concentration movements which, in his view, are destroying the publishing sector and the media.
>
> (F. Noiville, on May 11, 2007, my translation)

In order to fully understand the situation of politically committed publishers, it is necessary to give a brief account of the structure of the publishing sector in France. The French book market is dominated, as in most Western countries, by a small number of big corporations, the main one being Hachette, which accounts for 30 percent of the market, followed by Editis (owned by Planeta) with 10.4 percent.[6] Both groups own a variety of imprints that have been gradually integrated into their orbit while maintaining a certain degree of independence in their editorial choices (for instance, *Fayard* and *Grasset* are owned by Hachette, *Plon* by Editis, etc.) The sector is increasingly concentrated as the first 10 groups account for 74.2 percent of the global turnover. The recent purchase of *Flammarion* by *Gallimard,* now occupying the third position on the French national market, has only reinforced this trend while numerous small and very small firms (sometimes a single person) work on what is usually referred to as the fringes of the field (Reynaud 1982). These micro-structures account, according to the unique available study, for 25 percent of the editorial output and 1 percent of the global turnover.[7] However, small structures cannot be dismissed due to their weak economic weight given that some of the most prestigious publishing structures today such as *Actes Sud, Vivianne Hamy,* or *Anne-Marie Métailié* began on very modest scales 20 or 30 years ago. Economic and symbolic capital, to use Bourdieu's categories (1996), is not always correlated in the field of symbolic goods. However, the general trend is that the publishing sector is increasingly polarized between, on the one hand, ever larger media groups that have an in-house distribution service ensuring them a *de facto* control of the access to the market, not to mention their privileged access to national media, and, on the other hand, very small businesses that struggle to keep their heads above water and find it difficult to make their books visible and accessible to the public.

A particular element of the French book market is the high level of state intervention since the beginning of the Fifth Republic (1959) due to complex historical and cultural reasons that will not be addressed here (Dubois 1999).[8] This public policy is justified by the specific economic properties of cultural goods such as books that are experience goods, characterized by a short period of profitability and highly uncertain demand, what Richard Caves calls the "nobody knows property" (Caves 2000). Another justification is of a political and cultural nature, as published texts participate in the creation of cultural and national identities (Canoy et al. 2006). The cornerstone of state intervention is the 1981 law setting a fixed price for books passed at the demand of small and medium-size publishers. The main objective of this law was to protect diversity within the marketplace, enabling the least powerful firms to compete with the dominant ones and, more importantly, to allow a dense network of independent bookshops to stay in business as book chains such as the *Fnac* and supermarkets (and today virtual bookshops like Amazon) entered the game. In this sense, the law has been an undeniable success: Independent bookshops in France account for 29.5 percent of the retail market,[9] as compared with less than 10 percent in the UK, where the Net Book Agreement, establishing a minimum price for books since 1900, was abandoned in 1995.[10]

Independent bookshops play a crucial role in the "ecology" of the book industry and are instrumental in the existence of a large variety of publishers in all sectors. Occupying a similar position as independent publishers in the publishing field, they have a vested interest in supporting their catalogues. They often display and recommend the books of lesser known presses (organizing for example "special events" when new titles come out), hence trying to counterbalance the commercial strength of more established publishing firms. The owner of a bookshop in the North-East of Paris:

> I tend to hide the books that I don't like, I don't put them on the tables. I do my own little boycott, it's a defensive strategy. I focus on books that help us reflect on the world we live in, and readers follow me. People know what to expect when they come to my bookshop.
>
> (Interview on January 30, 2013)

Independent booksellers also believe that books should be given more than a few weeks to reach their readership on the basis that upmarket titles need more time than commercial titles to achieve recognition. Independent publishers therefore strongly emphasize the importance of "quality" bookshops in their struggle to survive in a very competitive market where the "window of opportunity" for books is dangerously shrinking (Thompson 2010: 238), and where bestsellers tend to crowd out other books. Eric Hazan, founder of *La Fabrique*, which first published André Schiffrin's books, makes it quite clear:

> Booksellers appreciate us, and this is something important, really important. It is priceless because they more or less sell what they want. This is why I'm not really in favor of direct sales.
>
> (Interview on July 10, 2006)

Considering that up to 80 percent of most of these publishers' turnover originates from two dozen independent retailers in the major French cities, one can understand their ambivalent feeling about selling books directly on the Internet, even when the latter has proved to be an efficient channel to reach readers for niche publishers (Anderson 2006).

All in all, independent publishers in France can rely on public subsidies at different national and local levels that were put in place in the 1970s (Surel 1997). The French Ministry for Culture has set up a specialized body, *le Centre National du Livre* (National Book Centre, CNL), to distribute subsidies to a wide array of publishers (irrespective of their size) based on the quality of their projects. Its role is to "contribute to the development of slow-selling quality books,"[11] i.e., small-scale upmarket production that no publisher can afford to publish without some public help (for example translations in the social sciences) because their potential readership is too limited. To give just an example, *Les Editions de L'Éclat*, a small avant-garde publisher, developed a series (*Tiré à part*) dedicated to the transla-tion of major authors in analytical philosophy (Hilary Putman, John Searle, etc.). It also publishes books translated from Italian to French (Giogio Colli, Paulo Virno), and from rare languages such as Hebrew or Persian. Most of these translations were made possible by subsidies from the CNL, which covers up to 60 percent of translation costs. Michel Valensi, founder of the press, asserts that:

> If the CNL did not exist there would be much fewer translations in France. . . . We cannot do without it. Or books would be priced around 40 € and no one could afford to buy them.
>
> (Interview on March 23, 2010)

In the sphere of restricted production, books cannot be expected to pro-vide an immediate return on investment: Print runs rarely exceed 2,000 cop-ies, and only a limited number of bestsellers sell more than 10,000 copies. Pierre Bourdieu's *On Television,* published by his own publishing house, *Raisons d'agir,* in 1996, sold more than 100,000 copies in one year.[12] This is a very unusual figure in a sector where average sales revolve around 1,450 copies (SNE 2011). The role of the state in the book industry is thus to counterbalance the law of supply and demand that makes it difficult for some sectors of cultural production to survive without a certain level of pro-tection.[13] This specific institutional context makes it possible for small firms to exist alongside the bigger companies and groups and to compete with them in small niches like social critique that has been a dynamic subsector in the French book market (Noël 2012).

THE RHETORIC OF THE INDEPENDENT PRESS

Having outlined the general context, we can now examine the different types of arguments put forth by politically committed presses on their web-sites, catalogues, and articles published in the national press, in order to stage their "radical" identity. The opposition between the market sphere and that of culture is an ancient topic in literature, linked to the idea of the "prostitution of art." Voltaire believed that authors who wrote for a living had a social status below that of prostitutes (Darnton 1982). At the end of the 19th century, avant-garde literature thought of itself as the embodiment of intellectual values against the corruption brought about by money (Charle 1990). In the field of the social sciences, the antinomy between culture and commerce goes back to Marx and Simmel who theorized the conflict between singular or incommensurate goods—i.e., goods whose value cannot be determined by a price—and the market that extends calculability to all spheres of life (Karpik 2010).

The main argument used by the more radical of these presses is the one related to the commodification of culture. They share a pessimistic and defensive view of publishing as an industry increasingly dominated by market values. They lament the growing commodification and standardization of culture in general and particularly of books produced by conglomerates only interested in their bottom line, irrespective of the quality of the content. Such a vision is steeped in the critique of mass culture pioneered by Benjamin (1968) with the theme of the alienation of the *work of art in the age of mechanical reproduction*, and pursued by Adorno and Horkheimer (1972). It is structured by a series of oppositions: standard versus originality, reproduction versus innovation, industrial versus craftwork, dross versus quality, light versus serious. These presses share an idealized and elitist vision of culture that can be illustrated by *L'Echappée*'s presentation on its website:

> We are independent from conglomerates that are slowly killing publishing by transforming knowledge and books into commodities. We publish books providing food for thought in a society dominated by leisure and permanent entertainment.[14]

Such themes are laced with the "artistic critique" of capitalism (Boltanski and Chiapello 2006) that reflects on the "disenchantment" and "alienation" of modern existence. The commodification of culture is criticized inasmuch as it leads to the publication of "ready to think texts that are chain-produced by an industry" as one editor put it (Interview on January 27, 2007). The rise of media groups is considered to be the main cause for this loss of meaning and "authenticity" in line with the situationist theories, specifically with Guy Debord's radical critique of the society of the spectacle (1995). However, historians have nuanced this view, showing that the "massification" of the book market goes back to the 18th century, and that financial principles were already in place by the end of the 19th century (Mollier 1988).

A less radical line of arguments is concerned with the defense of cultural diversity that was taken up by anti-globalization movements in the 1990s. The notion gained international repute with its recognition by UNESCO in 2001 that asserted the need to preserve the diversity of "cultural ecosystems" (First World Declaration on Cultural Diversity), including linguistic diversity. Publishers of the Spanish-speaking world coined the term "bibliodiversity" at the end of the 1990s in order to adapt the notion to the publishing industry (Pinhas 2011). It has since been widely circulated by the International Alliance of Independent Publishers, a non-profit association that coordinates a support network composed of 85 publishing houses from 45 different countries.[15] Homnisphères, an independent press founded in 2003 argues on its website in the following way:

> The movement of consolidation in the cultural sectors has gained momentum all over the world, and in France in particular, in recent years. This logic is a threat to the diversity of expression and independent cultural production. The diffusion of intellectual works follows a uniform market logic dominated by standardized products and obsession with short-term profitability.[16]

Politically committed publishers hereby stress the fact that they make publishing possible for alternative authors and ideas that would not find their place in conglomerates that expect high sales and mainly focus on bestsellers that are quickly sold and quickly forgotten. Such an assertion is obviously controversial as associating "easy" books with large companies and serious ones with independent publishers is an oversimplified statement. The publishing field is much more complex as large companies tend to reproduce within their own structure the hierarchy between upmarket and commercial books and as independent publishers also sell commercial titles (Sapiro 2010). Conglomerates own publishers specializing in serious literary work for instance, which are necessary for their acquisition of symbolic capital (Thompson 2010: 139–140). Moreover, the concept of diversity is ambiguous as most cultural sectors have experienced an increase in the volume of goods produced (the total book production in France reached a record of 86,295 titles in 2012[17]); a fact that doesn't imply a greater choice for customers in so much as an increasing number of substitutable books put on the market (Benhamou and Pelletier 2006).

Finally, there is a political dimension linked to these cultural arguments. Politically committed publishers believe that books are intrinsically subversive inasmuch as they fuel public discussion in democratic societies and provide intellectual resources to resist the doxa of neoliberalism. As such, these publishers share a rationalist faith in the emancipatory power of the written word. As Eric Hazan declared during a debate organized by a Parisian bookshop in May 2010, "books are the most subversive arms."[18] Many of the authors published by these presses—Noam Chomsky, Slavoj Žižek, Alain Badiou, or Pierre Bourdieu, to name just a few, but also the "revolutionary classics" such as Rosa Luxemburg and the libertarians from the 19th century—have developed a coherent critique of the "neoliberal" order. Their writings are used as resources to foster intellectual renewal and to put into question the "economicization" of all social spheres. *Agone* has for instance published Bourdieu's political writings (Bourdieu 2008). In these collected essays, the French sociologist strongly challenged the "neoliberal counter revolution" at work in previously autonomous spheres such as the arts and scientific research. In the same vein, *Les Prairies ordinaires*, a small avant-garde press created in 2005, has made accessible to the French public authors such as Mike Davis, Wendy Brown, and David Harvey whose radical political slant is highlighted.

ATTEMPTS TO BYPASS ECONOMIC CONSTRAINTS

Although diverse, the values promoted by politically committed publishers are always emphasized as they contribute to the staging of their "radical" identity. One can therefore wonder how they manage to operate in a manner that doesn't betray the values promoted in their books. After all, they run a business that consists in selling books, and as such they have to make enough money to be able to continue and to make a living out of it. Only a small percentage manages to do this after the first couple of years as the market has become tough for small players, even within a relatively protected framework. However, some of these presses have been active for 15 or even 20 years, effectively relying on alternative ways of doing business on a modest scale. Reconciling business with political engagement can take various forms, from rejection to conditional acceptance, that we will now examine.

Intellectual and artistic professions like publishers or filmmakers have a tendency to put forward their "disinterestedness" in economic matters (Bourdieu 1996) and to define themselves by their interest in art and the world of ideas as opposed to the world of commerce and the triviality of everyday life.[19] Politically committed publishers are no exception to this way of functioning as they are inclined to value the intellectual and political dimension of their work and to downplay commercial considerations. There are innumerable illustrations of this agenda. To take just one example, when asked which of his books had sold best, the owner of an avant-garde press with alternative sources of income replied ironically: "I don't know. I'm a very bad publisher, I hardly know how to count" (Interviewed on March 24, 2009). In his view, being a good publisher means to disregard such trivial things as money in order to focus on more prestigious matters. Being a "bean counter" is generally evoked as something to avoid at all costs. In the intellectual field, this kind of discourse is associated with symbolic gratifications: a reputation for being uncompromising and reaching for excellence echoed by critics, booksellers, and commentators.

An exemplary illustration of the "economic world reversed" (Bourdieu 1996) is given by a publisher's narrative of the conditions under which he created his press in 1997 after quitting a senior position with a mainstream trade publisher belonging to *Hachette*. Economic principles are turned upside down as he gives the impression of an improvised endeavor devoid of rational calculation: "Everything happened in a rush, in July 1997, haphazardly. . . . I found the name for the publishing house on my street sign."[20] The lack of financial resources is a central element of valorization that enables him to situate his publishing house on the side of small businesses inspired by challenging the lack of audacity of the bigger groups: "The adventure began in a very small room, with less than €8,000 in my pocket, with no partner or bank backing me." The fact that he launched his company in order to publish an investigation about the Clearstream scandal (Denis Robert and Ernest Backes 2001) that had been turned down by several mainstream presses reinforced the moral nature of the enterprise.

"Commercial Success Is Secondary"

Following the logic of "art for art's sake" (Cassagne 1997) according to which the value of a work of art is irreducible to its commercial worth, modest sales can paradoxically be perceived as a sign of intellectual quality. Economic and political successes are therefore often presented as mutually exclusive, although there are many exceptions. Politically committed presses do publish authors combining symbolic and economic gains such as Noam Chomsky, whose political writings are instant bestsellers, carrying few risks for the publisher. If the commercial dimension tends to be played down by publishers situated at the pole of restricted production, it is nevertheless present, as Anne Simonin has demonstrated in her research on *Les Editions de Minuit* (Simonin 2004). Minuit, an uncompromising publisher with a prestigious list in fiction and non-fiction, launched authors such as the *Nouveau Roman* writers Alain Robbe-Grillet and Nathalie Sarraute in the 1970s while developing more commercially oriented series in order to balance the book list.

The opposition between the two spheres nevertheless needs to be reactivated in order to perpetuate a shared belief. The accusation of aiming for a wide readership instead of publishing "serious books" is a rhetorical weapon often used by politically committed presses in order to mark their difference from potential competitors. They need to differentiate themselves from mainstream trade publishers that compete with them on their own turf by developing "radical" series and poaching their most successful authors thanks to higher advances and better commercial conditions. For instance, Chomsky and Žižek were first translated into French in the 1990s by marginal presses like *Nautilus*, *Les Arènes*, and *Climats* before being taken on by large publishers: *Fayard* (Hachette Group), *Le Seuil*, and *Flammarion*. What is at stake is the legitimate definition of political publishing that is in France inseparable from intellectual commitment. Thus, it is crucial for independent presses to demonstrate that profit is not an end in itself and that intellectual and political motives always take precedence. *Agone*, a political press that employs six people in the South of France for a yearly output of 20 titles and a backlist of more than 100 titles, including Orwell, Chomsky, and Zinn, provides a good illustration of this hierarchy:

> Our aim is never to publish a book because it would be profitable, never to commission a book because of its author's reputation, and never to choose a topic because it is debated in the media.
>
> (Kalinowski and Vincent 2003: 1, my translation)

Agone's founder has developed a blistering critique of "pseudo-independent" presses such as *Gallimard* or *Actes Sud* that use the rhetoric of independence while resorting to the same methods as media conglomerates, i.e., aiming for the highest possible profit margins (Discepolo 2011). Radical thinkers should in his view choose to sign up with presses sharing the same ideals as the ones expressed in their books in order to be consistent with their ideas.

Publishing on a Shoestring

However, economic principles cannot be denied in daily practice. Due to the small size of these operations, there can be no labor division between the artistic/intellectual principle and the commercial one as is usually the case in the cultural sector business (Chiapello 1998). Political publishers have internalized this double bind in order to survive and are thus very fastidious on expenses, managing their operations like small entrepreneurs. The founder of an independent press bought up in 2009 by a larger structure highlights:

> If I were permanently in the red, I would have to stop. I'm an independent publisher; I cannot afford to lose money. I have no personal fortune, no patron. I have to make a living.
>
> (Interview on November 15, 2006)

Publishing is an unregulated sector with very low entry costs due to the development of cheap desktop publishing software. As a result, people working out of their apartments, with limited financial resources, can easily set up a publishing business in their spare time while maintaining a salary on the side. Costs are minimal as they tend to keep every aspect of the work in-house: edition (book commissioning, copy-editing, proofreading), design, but also promotion and sometimes sales representation although the majority depends upon third-party arrangements that are extremely costly. The most professional presses can afford to outsource some of these tasks, but many of these publishers depend on relatives and friends. As Thompson puts it, they benefit from an "economy of favours" (Thompson 2010: 155). But in their daily practices, most of them live from hand to mouth: Cash flow is a continuous problem as they are structurally undercapitalized.

If only a minority of publishers makes enough profit to pay themselves and potentially one or two employees, this kind of ascetic behavior makes it possible to break even if it is in itself an achievement. But the drawback is that they remain very vulnerable financially. Since 2005, 3 out of the 33 presses that were taken into consideration in this case study have been bought by larger firms (*Climats, Danger public, Textuel*), while three others had to close down (*Dagorno, Le Passant ordinaire, Exils*). Business life expectancy has globally deteriorated over the past 30 years in the publishing industry: 50 percent of new presses in all sectors have a life expectancy of less than 5 years (Legendre and Abensour 2007: 28).

Despite these difficult conditions, independent publishing is a world in which passion and commitment play a crucial role. The activity is a kind of calling, a powerful vocation reminiscent of Max Weber's notion of *Beruf*. Central to this vocation is the fact that it is perceived even more positively if it is disconnected from material incentives (Freidson 1986). As a result, self-exploitation is perceived as normal for people who are highly devoted to their work. Professional activity is situated in an enchanted sphere where leisure and work are harmoniously combined. Involvement in this work has no limits since it is associated with intellectual curiosity and a general attitude in life reminiscent of the 19th century *bohème* (Seigel 1986). This attitude goes hand in hand with the dismissal of a traditional bourgeois lifestyle and routine work as opposed to the preferred artistic lifestyle. Being a publisher is therefore more an artistic project than a commercial venture. Eric Hazan, who founded *La Fabrique* when his former company was bought up by Hachette, evoked the "exceptional atmosphere" that characterized his press before it was taken over: People "came to work even when they were sick," and although there were no fixed working hours, everyone stayed in late or came in the office on Saturdays to work, out of sheer motivation (Hazan 2005: 32–33). This scenario illustrates the extension of artistic values to the business world and more specifically to the intellectual spheres. Values such as flexibility, autonomy, responsibility, and the internalization of artistic norms exemplify the new ideal of qualified work for the intellectual middle class (Menger 2002).

However, not all of them manage to maintain this ideal and joining forces with a larger firm can provide a minimum amount of security, seen as an acceptable compromise when one cannot make ends meet. The founder of an independent press that he later sold to a group argued in this way:

> After a while, it is very difficult not to pay the people who work for you. I don't know how the others can do it, but I cannot have people work for free for a "cause." I feel guilty about it.
>
> (Interview on February 5, 2008)

It is worth recalling that to devote oneself to the world of ideas regardless of economic necessity is only possible with a middle- or upper-class social background (Bourdieu 1991) where people can afford to "work for free" for a number of years thanks to family support. Not surprisingly, 60 percent of the founders of politically engaged publishing houses come from such backgrounds. Most of them have to hold a second job in order to make a living (usually in graphic design, teaching, or translating), and only a minority manages to make a living out of their editorial activity. As a result, retired people and individuals with unemployment benefits are quite common.

Professionalization at Stake

This brings us to the question of development. Two different models of organization are possible for these structures: a professional model and an amateur's one. The first option consists in asserting that an uncompromising editorial project is compatible with the market economy (with a little help from public subsidies) and can be much more than a simple pastime. It implies a normalization of practices in the medium-term (for instance, abandoning a non-profit status) as publishing companies are, sooner or later, confronted with increasing financial pressures. The second option consists in remaining marginal, either out of choice or lack of choice. The publishing houses that follow this model share a number of characteristics: they are most often not-for-profit, they run their own sales and distribution services, and they have a limited production. According to them, getting bigger leads to a vicious circle as it implies hiring staff, increasing expenses, and relying on credit, which is considered a dangerous compromise. As one editor put it, "being small is the only way to remain free" (Interview on October 28, 2005). Resisting professional development is a way of avoiding routinization and making sure that the artistic ethos will prevail.

However, the line between amateurs and professionals is quite blurred in the fringes of the publishing field. Politically committed presses have to compete on two fronts, trying to distinguish themselves from the plethora of amateurish self-publishing but also from the bigger companies. One way to do so is to focus on their "added value" compared to mainstream publishing. They usually strive to establish a "special" relationship with their authors—a relationship that is not presented as based on economic interest but on intellectual and/or political affinity. They also take pride in carefully editing and designing their books, seeing themselves as craftsmen rather than businessmen. Devoting their time to a limited number of selected titles is a way to differentiate themselves from "extreme publishing" (Thompson 2010: 223–237): "I only publish the books that I love and I take the time to do it well," says the owner of a small press near Lyon (Interview on February 9, 2007).

Let us consider the case of *L'Insomniaque*, a libertarian publishing house founded in 1993 in the outskirts of Paris by a group of activists working on a freelance basis for other employers (translating and teaching) in order to make ends meet. Publishing is a "secondary identity" (Weber and Lamy

1999) providing them with important symbolic resources that compensate for the economically "irrational" investment in the publishing structure. Passion and political engagement are their main motives, and they go as far as giving away some of their books for free to reach as many readers as possible. This kind of detached commitment makes it possible for individuals lacking the will or the disposition to work in mainstream publishing to become part of the game, even if this is done at the fringes, in the same way as anti-globalization activists do politics but "differently" (Poliak 2008). This dilettante way of doing business is presented as a radical alternative to corporate publishing and as the only way to maintain an independent position: There is no division of labor, no hierarchy between the members of the group, work is unpaid, profit and public subsidies alike are rejected, and books are sold at modest prices. The lack of consideration for money matters is a source of pride:

> In principle, our resources cover the cost of the following year's production, but it's not always sufficient, and everyone has to fork out. We don't make any money with this business; we even have to pay for it!
> (Interview on September 19, 2005)

Although extreme, a case such as this influences the more professional operations that are confronted with its model of economic denial. Hence their recurrent glorification of the alternative principles pioneered in the 1970s: equal pay, equal work responsibility, and collaborative work that tend to compensate for a market-oriented practice. In the same vein, these publishers tend to downplay their managerial position, putting forward the equality between them and their staff in order to be consistent with the values promoted by their books. But at the same time, paid work marks a clear line between both models. As the founder of *Agone* explains:

> No one is a volunteer here. If voluntary work was the only way to make this possible, we might as well stop. It is essential for us to prove that we can do this job and be autonomous.[21]

Preoccupied by their will to function "differently" and to defend the autonomy of intellectual and political criteria against the law of the market, politically engaged publishers are struggling to maintain their position in the publishing field at a time when consolidation and rationalization processes have profoundly altered the landscape of the book industry. If the downplaying of commercial considerations is a constant in the rhetoric they use, they have no option but to play by the rules of the market in which they operate or to remain on the fringes of the field. To paraphrase the title of a famous book, one may be tempted to say that they can only maintain "The Temporary Autonomous Zones" (Bey 1991) within the market framework. This study shows that these publishers do not follow a single pattern of behavior in order to overcome the tension between the economic and symbolic dimensions: They adopt different organizational practices depending on their resources and their position in the publishing field. Their discourse, as well as their way of doing business, is saturated with the contradictions of a fragile position as they have to avoid two ills: renouncing their principles or exhausting themselves. There is a very thin line between their need to become more professional in order to exert a greater influence in the public sphere—with the risk of "losing one's soul" and becoming similar to the model they oppose—and the choice of amateur models that inevitably lead to marginality.

NOTES

1. This chapter is based upon a case study carried out for a Ph.D. in 2010 (EHESS, Paris). Sixty-two semi-structured in-depth interviews were carried out between 2006 and 2010 with publishers, booksellers, and sales representatives. These presses are independent in the sense that they are not part of a bigger group (they own 100 percent of their capital when they are business structures) or linked to a political party or labor union.
2. In French, I have used the phrase "*maisons d'édition critiques*" or "*engagées*," which can be translated by "politically engaged" or "radical" although it is fairly difficult to find an accurate expression in English.
3. According to Pierre Bourdieu, the book market is structured around the opposition between the pole of restricted production, where intellectual criteria prevail, and the pole of large-scale production, ruled by commercial success (Bourdieu 1993).
4. The *Editions de Minuit*, founded clandestinely during the German occupation of France, epitomize an uncompromising conception of publishing. Jérôme Lindon, its director after WWII, maintained this spirit by publishing essays against the French government's policy in Algeria during the war of independence. He also played an important role in the passing of the 1981 "Fixed Book Price" law. Another great publisher, François Maspero founded a bookshop and a publishing house under his name in 1959 that became a central place for leftist groups in the 1960s and 1970s. He also took position against French Algeria and was in favor of anti-colonial movements all over the world.
5. The author is here referring to Lucien Benda's famous pamphlet, *La trahison des clercs* (1927), translated into English under the title *The Treason of the Intellectuals* (2006).
6. Fabrice Piault, "Les 200 premiers éditeurs français," *Livres Hebdo*, 925, October 12, 2012.
7. Dilicom, *Questionnaire auprès des petits éditeurs. Résultats, SNE—Ministère de la Culture et de la Communication*, November 30, 2004. The survey took 2,726 publishing structures into account.
8. State intervention in the field of culture is, however, by no means neutral as the development of cultural policy has also contributed to the diffusion of an economic view of culture (Dubois 2001).
9. Syndicat National de l'Edition (2013) *Repères statistiques France 2012–2013*.
10. Books & Consumers, BML/TNS Marketing Ltd/The Bookseller, 2010.
11. Centre National du Livre (CNL). Online at http://www.centrenationaldu livre.fr, accessed on October 20, 2012.

12. Pierre Bourdieu founded *Raisons d'agir*, a non-profit publishing structure specializing in academic essays on topical issues, in 1996. More than 200,000 copies of its first book, *On Television*, were sold over a period of 15 years (Ferrand 1998).
13. The reduced VAT rate of 5.5 percent for cultural goods follows the same logic.
14. Editions de l'Echappée. Online at "http://www.lechappee.org" www.lechappee.org, accessed on October 20, 2012.
15. Alliance des éditeurs indépendants. Online at http://www.alliance-editeurs.org, accessed on October 19, 2012.
16. Editions Homnisphères. Online at http://art-engage.net/@Editions-Homni spheres,40@.html, accessed on October 20, 2012.
17. Syndicat National de l'Edition (2013) Repères statistiques France 2012–2013S.
18. Article 11 (2010) Thierry Discepolo et Eric Hazan : faire des livres subversifs - sinon rien. Online at http://www.article11.info/?Thierry-Discepolo-et-Eric-Hazan, accessed on September 24, 2012.
19. This distinction goes back to Roman law, which opposed *operae liberales*, which couldn't receive pecuniary remuneration and *operae illiberales* (manual work), which could receive payment for services of an inferior kind.
20. Editions Les Arènes, "Qui sommes nous?" (my translation). Online at http://www.arenes.fr/spip.php?article50, accessed on July 10, 2012.
21. Thierry Discepolo, debate organized by the association Acrimed, *Bourse du travail de Paris*, May 27, 2010.

REFERENCES

Adorno, Theodor W. and Max Horkheimer (1972) *Dialectics of Enlightenment.* New York: Herder and Herder.

Anderson, Chris (2006) *The Long Tail: Why the Future of Business Is Selling Less of More.* New York: Hyperion.

Benda, Lucien (2006 [1927]) *The Treason of the Intellectuals* (tr. Richard Aldington). New York: Transaction Publishers.

Benhamou, Françoise and Stéphanie Pelletier (2006) "Une méthode multi-critère d'évaluation de la diversité culturelle: application à l'édition de livres en France," in Xavier Greffe (ed.) *Création et diversité au miroir des industries culturelles*, pp. 313–344. Paris: La Documentation française.

Benjamin, Walter (1968) "The Work of Art in the Age of Mechanical Reproduction" in Hannah Arendt (ed.) *Illuminations*, pp. 217–252. London: Schocken.

Bey, Hakim (1991) *TAZ. The Temporary Autonomous Zone, Ontological Anarchy, Poetic Terrorism.* New York: Autonomedia.

BML/TNS Marketing Ltd/The Bookseller (2010) *Books & Consumers.*

Boltanski, Luc and Eve Chiapello (2006 [1999]) *The New Spirit of Capitalism* (trans. Gregory Elliott). London: Verso.

Bourdieu, Pierre (1991) "Le champ littéraire," *Actes de la recherche en sciences sociales* 89: 3–46.

Bourdieu, Pierre (1993) *The Field of Cultural Production: Essays on Art and Literature.* Cambridge: Polity Press.

Bourdieu, Pierre (1996 [1992]) *The Rules of Art: Genesis and Structure of the Literary Field* (trans. Susan Emanuel). Cambridge: Polity Press.

Bourdieu, Pierre (2008 [2002]) *Political Interventions: Social Science and Political Action* (trans. Gregory Elliott). London: Verso.

236 *Sophie Noël*

Canoy, Marcel, Jan C. van Ours, and Frederick van der Ploeg (2006) "The Economics of Books," in Victor Ginsburgh and David Throsby (eds) *Handbook of the Economics of Art and Culture*, pp. 721–761. Amsterdam: Elsevier.

Cassagne, Albert (1997 [1906]) *La théorie de l'art pour l'art en France chez les derniers romantiques et les premiers réalistes*. Seyssel: Champ Vallon.

Caves, Richard (2000) *Creative Industries: Contracts between Art and Commerce*. Cambridge, MA: Harvard University Press.

Charle, Christophe (1990) *Naissance des intellectuels: 1880–1900*. Paris: Minuit.

Chiapello, Eve (1998) *Artistes versus managers*. Paris: Métailié.

Coser, Lewis, Charles Kadushin, and Walter Powell (1982) *Books: the Culture and Commerce of Publishing*. New York: Basic Books.

Darnton, Robert (1982) *The Literary Underground of the Old Regime*. Cambridge, MA: Harvard University Press.

Debord, Guy (1995 [1970]) *The Society of the Spectacle* (trans. Donald Nicholson-Smith). New York: Zone Books.

Dilicom (2004) "Questionnaire auprès des petits éditeurs." Résultats, SNE-Ministère de la Culture et de la Communication, November 30.

Discepolo, Thierry (2011) *La trahison des éditeurs*. Marseille: Agone.

Dubois, Vincent (1999) *La politique culturelle: genèse d'une catégorie d'intervention publique*. Paris: Belin.

Dubois, Vincent (2001) "La vision économique de la culture: éléments pour une généalogie," *Bulletin des Bibliothèques de France* 46 (2): 31–34.

Ferrand, Christine (1998) "Contestation: petits prix, mais ils vendent le maximum," *Livres Hebdo* 294 (May 22).

Freidson, Eliot (1986) "Les professions artistiques comme défi à l'analyse sociologique," *Revue française de sociologie* 27: 431–443.

Hage, Julien (2005) "François Maspero: éditeur partisan," *Contretemps* 13: 100–108.

Hazan, Eric (2005) *Faire mouvement: entretiens avec Mathieu Potte-Bonneville*. Paris: Les Prairies ordinaire.

Kalinowski, Isabelle and Béatrice Vincent (2003) "Les clameurs de l'indépendance éditoriale," *Gazette des éditions Agone* 2: 1.

Karpik, Lucien (2010 [2007]) *Valuing the Unique: The Economics of Singularities*. Princeton: Princeton University Press.

Legendre, Bertrand and Corinne Abensour (2007) *Regards sur l'édition*, vol. 2, *Les nouveaux éditeurs (1988–2005)*. Paris: La Documentation française.

Martin, Henri-Jean and Lucien Febvre (1958) *L'apparition du livre*. Paris: Albin Michel.

Menger, Pierre-Michel (2002) *Portrait de l'artiste en travailleur*. Paris: Le Seuil.

Mollier, Jean-Yves (1988) *L'argent et les Lettres: histoire du capitalisme d'édition, 1880–1920*. Paris: Fayard.

Noël, Sophie (2012) *L'édition indépendante critique: engagements politiques et intellectuels*. Villeurbanne: Presses de l'ENSSIB.

Noiville, Florence (2007) "Rencontre avec André Schiffrin," *Le Monde* (May 11).

Piault, Fabrice (2012) "Les 200 premiers éditeurs français," *Livres Hebdo* 925 (October 12).

Pinhas, Luc (2011) "Indépendance éditoriale et défense de la bibliodiversité en Amérique latine," *Communication & Langages* 170: 47–62.

Poliak, Claude (2008) "Attac. Aux frontières du champ politique" in Bertrand Geay and Laurent Willemez (eds) *Pour une gauche de gauche*, pp. 75–90. Bellecombe-en-Bauges: Editions du Croquant.

Reynaud, Bénédicte (1982) "La dynamique d'un oligopole avec franges: le cas de la branche d'édition de livres en France," *Revue d'économie industrielle* 22: 61–71.

Robert, Denis and Ernest Backes (2001) *Révélations*. Paris: Les Arènes.

Rouet, François (2007) *Le livre. Mutations d'une industrie culturelle*. Paris: La Documentation française.

Sapiro, Gisèle (2010) "Globalization and Cultural Diversity in the Book Market: The Case of Literary Translations in the US and in France," *Poetics* 38: 419–439.

Schiffrin, André (2000) *The Business of Books: How International Conglomerates Took Over Publishing and Changed the Way We Read*. London: Verso.

Schiffrin, André (2010) *Words and Money*. London: Verso.

Seigel, Jerrold (1986) *Bohemian Paris: Culture, Politics, and the Boundaries of Bourgeois Life, 1830–1930*. New York: Elisabeth Sifton Books/Viking Penguin.

Simonin, Anne (2004) "Le catalogue de l'éditeur, un outil pour l'histoire," *XXᵉ siècle, Revue d'histoire* 81: 119–129.

Surel, Yves (1997) *L'État et le livre: les politiques publiques du livre en France, 1957–1993*. Paris: L'Harmattan.

Syndicat National de l'Edition (SNE) (2012) *Repères statistiques 2012–2013*.

Thompson, John B. (2010) *Merchants of Culture: The Publishing Business in the 21st Century*. Cambridge: Polity Press.

Weber, Florence and Yvon Lamy (1999) "Amateurs et professionnels," *Genèses* 36: 2–5.

Contributors

Nina Bandelj is Sociology associate professor and Graduate Director at the University of California, Irvine. She received a PhD from Princeton University and was awarded the Martin Seymour Lipset Dissertation Award from the Society of Comparative Research. She was a Jean Monnet Fellow at the European University Institute, in Florence, Italy, and a Visiting Scholar at the Max Planck Institute for the Study of Societies, in Cologne, Germany. Her research examines the social and cultural bases of economic phenomena, determinants and consequences of globalization, and social change in post-socialist Europe. Her articles have been published in the *American Sociological Review*, *Social Forces*, *Theory and Society*, and *Socio-Economic Review*, among others. She is the author of *From Communists to Foreign Capitalists: The Social Foundations of Foreign Direct Investment in Postsocialist Europe* (Princeton University Press, 2008), *Economy and State: A Sociological Perspective* (with Elizabeth Sowers, Polity Press, 2010), and editor of *Economic Sociology of Work* (Emerald Publishing, 2009), *The Cultural Wealth of Nations* (with Frederick F. Wherry, Stanford University Press, 2011), and *Socialism Vanquished, Socialism Challenged: Eastern Europe and China, 1989–2009* (with Dorothy J. Solinger, Oxford University Press, 2012). She serves as Editor of *Socio-Economic Review*, is past co-chair of ISA RC09: Social Transformations and Sociology of Development, and chair of the ASA Economic Sociology section for 2013–14. E-mail address: nbandelj@uci.edu.

Patrick Bond is a political economist at the University of KwaZulu-Natal School of Development Studies in Durban, where he has directed the Center for Civil Society since 2004: http://ccs.ukzn.ac.za. Working closely with advocacy organizations, Patrick Bond's research presently covers political ecology (especially climate, energy, and water), economic crisis, social mobilization, public policy, and geopolitics. Among his authored, edited, and co-edited books are: *Uneven Zimbabwe* (Africa World Press, 1998), *Cities of Gold, Townships of Coal* (Africa World Press, 2000), *Unsustainable South Africa* (Merlin Press, 2002), *Against Global Apartheid*

(Zed Books, 2003), *Zimbabwe's Plunge* (Merlin Press, 2003), *Fanon's Warning* (Africa World Press, 2005), *Elite Transition* (Pluto Press, 2005), *Looting Africa* (Zed Books, 2006), *Talk Left, Walk Right* (University of KwaZulu-Natal Press, 2006), *The Accumulation of Capital in Southern Africa* (Rosa Luxemburg Foundation, 2007), *Climate Change, Carbon Trading and Civil Society* (University of KwaZulu-Natal Press, 2009), *Zuma's Own Goal* (Africa World Press, 2010), and *The Politics of Climate Justice* (University of KwaZulu-Natal Press, 2011).

In service to the new South African government from 1994 to 2002, Patrick Bond authored/edited more than a dozen policy papers, including the *Reconstruction and Development Program*. He has lectured at more than 70 universities across the world, with formal academic affiliations in the U.S., Canada, Zimbabwe, Hungary, Korea, Japan, and South Africa. Patrick Bond earned his doctorate in economic geography at Johns Hopkins University in 1993, after studying finance at the University of Pennsylvania's Wharton School and economics at Swarthmore College. E-mail address: bondp@ukzn.ac.za.

Krista Bywater has a doctorate in sociology from the University of California, Santa Barbara. Her dissertation is titled: "Water for Life, Not for Profit: Globalization, Development, and Water Struggles in India." Currently, she is an assistant professor of Sociology at Muhlenberg College in Allentown, Pennsylvania. Her areas of specialization include development, globalization, and environmental sociology. She has published in these areas, and her recent scholarship includes "Anti-privatization Struggles and the Right to Water in India: Engendering Cultures of Opposition" in *The Right to Water* (Farhana Sultana and Alex Loftus eds., London, Earthscan, 2012) and "Dancing on the Edge: Women, Culture, and a Passion for Change" in *On the Edges of Development: Critical Interventions* (Kum-Kum Bhavnani, John Foran, Priya Kurian, and Debashish Munshi eds., New York, Routledge, 2009). E-mail address: kbywater@muhlenberg.edu.

Tristan d'Inguimbert holds a master degree in sociology from the *Ecole des Hautes Etudes en Sciences Sociales* in Paris. He has been involved in several ethnographic research projects based on participant observation. He works as a management consultant.

Caroline Dufy is a lecturer at the Institute of Political Studies in Bordeaux and a research fellow at the Center Emile Durkheim. She graduated in sociology from the *Ecole des Hautes Etudes en Sciences Sociales* (EHESS) in Paris. Her main research interest concerns public policies in the Russian and post-Soviet countries' economies and their impact on actors' practices and representations. Among her latest publications is an article analyzing entrepreneurs' trajectories in the transition period in Russia

(*Revue d'Etudes Comparatives Est-Ouest*, September 2011). She also published a book devoted to methodological issues and field research: *L'ethnographie économique* (Caroline Dufy and Florence Weber, La Découverte, 2007). Besides, she has served for 2 years as the coordinator of the French University College in Saint-Petersburg (CUF). She has been an editor of the collection "*Europes terrains d'enquêtes*" (Petra editions) and a member as well as the former coordinator of the network of economic sociology in the French Association of Sociology. E-mail address: c.dufy@sciencepobordeaux.fr.

Esin Gülsen holds a master of sciences in public administration from Mersin University, Turkey, and a bachelor's degree in sociology from Bosporus University, Turkey. Currently, she is a research assistant at Mersin University and a PhD student in Political Science and Public Administration at the Middle East Technical University, Turkey. She is mainly interested in political sociology, political economy, and labor studies. E-mail address: esin.gulsen@metu.edu.tr.

Antoine Heemeryck holds a PhD in Comparative Development Studies, EHESS, France. Currently, he is a senior lecturer at the Spiru Haret University in Bucharest. His latest book is: *L'importation démocratique en Roumanie. Une perspective anthropologique sur une société post-dictatoriale* (L'Harmattan, 2012). He has also edited *La globalisation en perspective: élites et normes* (ed. with Cristi Pantelimon, Niculescu, 2012). E-mail address: heemeryckantoine@yahoo.com.

Tamara Heran holds a *Licentiate* degree in anthropology from Chile's *Universidad Austral*. She was awarded a master's degree in Social Sciences in Comparative Development Studies from the *Ecole des Hautes Etudes en Sciences Sociales* (EHESS) in Paris. Currently, she is a PhD candidate at the EHESS. She is affiliated with the Maurice Halbwachs Center and with the Population-Environment-Development Laboratory (IRD), where she is preparing an empirical study of globalization, work, and gender based on seasonal agricultural workers in Chile's agro-export sector. Her research has mainly focused on topics such as development, globalization, social change, gender, and work. She has presented and published papers on invisible work, gender relations, work flexibility, and the new social mobility of seasonal agribusiness workers in Chile: "Work Flexibility and New Mobilities in Arid Zones: Mobilizing and Mobilized of the Export Agro-industry in Limarí (Chile)" (*Revue Sécheresse*, 2011), and "From Male to Female: Conversion and Gender Relations in Times of Crisis—A Study of Seasonal Workers of Agribusiness in Chile" (in Ulrike Schuerkens, ed., *Socioeconomic Outcomes of The Global Financial Crisis*, Routledge, 2012). E-mail address: tamaraheran@gmail.com.

Julieta Longo holds a graduate degree in Sociology from the *Universidad Nacional de La Plata* in Argentina. Her research interests cover topics such as precarious employment and workplace conflict. Currently, she is a scholarship holder at the *Consejo Nacional de Investigaciones* (CONICET). She is finishing her PhD in Social Sciences at the *Universidad de Buenos Aires*, Argentina. Her thesis entitled "The Labor-Capital Conflict in Precarious Workplaces. A Study in Argentina's Retail Enterprises (2003–2011)" analyzes the relationship between precariousness and workplace conflict. She is a researcher at the *Centro de Estudios e Investigacioned Laborales* (CEIL/CONICET) in Buenos Aires. Her latest articles in reviews are: "The Borders of Precariousness: Perceptions and Meanings of Work for Young Precarious Workers of Hypermarkets" (*Trabajo y Sociedad*, 2012) and "Precariousness and Conflict in Argentina: An Analysis from a Quantitative Basis (2006–2010)" (*Gestión de las Personas y la Tecnología*, 2011). E-mail address: julieta_longo@yahoo.com.ar.

Sophie Noël has a PhD in Sociology from the *Ecole des Hautes Etudes en Sciences Sociales* (EHESS), Paris, and an M. Phil. in Social and Political Sciences from Cambridge University. She is currently lecturer at the University Paris XIII and has obtained a research fellowship permitting her to do research on cultural industries. She has published on political engagement, cultural exchanges, and publishing: *L'édition indépendante critique. Engagements politiques et intellectuels* (Presses de l'ENSSIB, 2012), "L'engagement par la traduction. Le rôle des petits éditeurs indépendants dans l'importation des ouvrages de sciences humaines" in Gisèle Sapiro (ed.), *Traduire la littérature et les sciences humaines. Conditions et obstacles* (La Documentation française, 2012), and "La petite édition indépendante face à la globalisation du marché du livre : le cas des éditeurs d'essais critiques" in Gisèle Sapiro (ed.) *Les contradictions de la globalisation éditoriale* (Nouveau monde Editions, 2009). E-mail address: nolsophie@yahoo.fr.

Ulrike Schuerkens has doctorates in both sociology and social anthropology and ethnology from the *École des Hautes Études en Sciences Sociales* in Paris. She received the diploma *Habilitation à diriger des recherches* from the University Paris V—René Descartes. Currently, she is senior lecturer at the *École des Hautes Études en Sciences Sociales*, Paris, France. She has published extensively on globalization, development, social change, migration, multiculturalism, and colonialism. Her latest monographs are *The Socio-economic Outcomes of the Global Financial Crisis* (ed., Routledge, 2012), *Globalization and Transformations of Social Inequality* (ed., Routledge, 2010), *Globalization and Transformations of Local Socio-Economic Practices* (ed., Routledge, 2008), *Transnational Migrations and Social Transformations* (ed., *Current Sociology*, 53, 4, 2, 2005), *Global Forces and Local Life-Worlds: Social Transformations* (ed., Sage,

2004), *Changement social sous régime colonial: Du Togo allemand aux Togo et Ghana indépendants* (L'Harmattan, 2001), and *Transformationsprozesse in der Elfenbeinkueste und in Ghana* (Lit, 2001). E-mail address: Ulrike.Schuerkens@ehess.fr.

Michel Villette holds a PhD in Sociology from the University of Paris-Sorbonne (1977). He has been manager with the Danone group (1974); assistant professor at the University of Tehran, Iran (1975–1976); management consultant with Eurequip Group (1978–1982); researcher, Center for Advanced Technologies (1982–1987); research director, Institute for Human Resources Management (Paris); professor of management accounting, ESCP-UAP (1990–1992). He has been professor of Sociology at AgroParisTech since 1992 and a researcher at the Maurice Halbwachs Center of the *Ecole Normale Supérieure* since 2005. M. Villette was visiting scholar at the University of California, Berkeley and San Diego (1977), the Helsinki School of Economics (1995), the Wharton Business School (2006), *Universitade Federal de Sào Carlos*, Brazil (2007), and the University of Warsaw, Poland (2008–2011). He has been a consultant for a wide range of global corporations, such as Danone, Saint-Gobain, Lafarge, Matra, Exxon, Eastman Kodak, and Wafabank. His research applies ethnographic and further interpretive methods to managerial situations. He has published more than 30 articles in journals of sociology and management and the prize-winning book *L'Homme qui croyait au management* (Seuil, 1988, 1989). His other books include: *L'Art du stage en entreprise* (La Découverte, 1994, 3rd ed. 2003), *Le Manager jetable* (La Découverte, 1996), *Sociologie du conseil en management* (La Découverte, 2003), and, with Catherine Vuillermot, *Portrait de l'homme d'affaires en prédateur* (La Découverte, 2006, 2007), published in English as *From Predators to Icons: Exposing the Myth of the Business Hero* (Cornell University Press, 2009) and in Chinese by Wealth Press (2011). E-mail address: michel.villette@agroparistech.fr.

Index

For Product Safety Concerns and Information please contact our EU
representative GPSR@taylorandfrancis.com
Taylor & Francis Verlag GmbH, Kaufingerstraße 24, 80331 München, Germany

www.ingramcontent.com/pod-product-compliance
Lightning Source LLC
Chambersburg PA
CBHW070356270326
41926CB00014B/2573